Additional Praise for *Religion, Terror, and Error: U.S. Foreign Policy and the Challenge of Spiritual Engagement*

Douglas Johnston was much ahead of his time in anticipating the explosive revival of religious conflict (*Religion, the Missing Dimension of Statecraft,* 1994). With this book he is leading the way once again, this time to the mitigation of religious conflict.

—**Edward Luttwak,**
Strategic analyst and scholar;
Author of *The Grand Strategy of the Byzantine Empire*
and *Strategy: The Logic of War and Peace*

George Bernard Shaw once said, "The reasonable man adapts himself to the world; the unreasonable one persists in trying to adapt the world to himself. Therefore, all progress depends on the unreasonable man." As this book aptly demonstrates, Doug Johnston is one of those unreasonable men. My experience as the State Department official in charge of influencing foreign publics in the George W. Bush administration taught me that success in the struggle against terror depends on mobilizing the softer arts, while adhering to principle. As head of the International Center for Religion & Diplomacy, Johnston, a graduate of the U.S. Naval Academy, is doing precisely that by deploying religious faith as a force for good around the world through a process of "organic suasion." I urge everyone to read this shibboleth-shattering and important book.

—**James K. Glassman,**
Former Under Secretary of State for Public Diplomacy and Public Affairs;
Former President of *The Atlantic Monthly*

A stimulating and informative insight into a subject that is of critical relevance in today's world. The book offers an incisive and objective analysis of the contemporary debates and perspectives in the world of Islam. With his extensive exposure to the realities on the ground and past scholarship, Dr. Johnston is eminently qualified to project a refreshing and innovative approach that seeks a paradigm shift towards exploring realistic solutions.

—**General Ehsan Ul Haq (Retired),**
Former Chairman Joint Chiefs of Staff, Pakistan

Douglas Johnston was extraordinarily prescient in seeing the role religious energies and identities would play in the post-Cold War world. He is both a visionary and a distinctively skilled practitioner of how an informed and pragmatic understanding of religion in human lives and cultures must be integrated into a 21st Century version of Realpolitik. This book is an engrossing introduction to what he has been doing and learning just below the cultural radar for decades. It is a great gift to policymakers and citizens alike.

—**Krista Tippett,**
Public radio host;
Author, *Einstein's God*

Douglas Johnston's book is essentially a call for a dialogue of life between Westerners and Muslims that expands the scope of interaction beyond the confines of scholarly exchanges, so that behind the plurality of their respective beliefs, a sense of their common humanity can be inferred and felt. I can't think of a better avenue to peace.

—**Anwar Ibrahim,**
Opposition leader of Malaysian Parliament;
Former Deputy Prime Minister of Malaysia

The "rational actor" model for predicting the behavior of nations misses the essentially spiritual questions: what do we hope for, what are we afraid of, who is a friend, who is an enemy, and what is the meaning of our lives? Doug Johnston has had success on the ground practicing faith-conscious approaches to diplomacy. This book is wise and if it is read and discussed by the right people in the right places, it will produce a healthy humility that could be the beginning of a smarter engagement with the Muslim world.

—**David McAllister-Wilson**,
President, Wesley Theological Seminary

The name Doug Johnston is synonymous with thoughtful, courageous and honest peace building in many parts of the world. He has given so much of his life to the quest for peace and harmony among nations and ethnic groups. His key is the careful blend of religious beliefs and shared ethical values. The importance of this book is that it presents a blueprint for action based on his years of experience. It is a must for those who work to end conflicts, great and small, in our society.

—**Cardinal Theodore E. McCarrick**,
Archbishop Emeritus of Washington

Using his extensive experience and deep knowledge of religion and diplomacy, Douglas Johnston has provided an outstanding book that offers a unique approach to today's problems of war, humanitarian concerns, and international relations. His prescriptions reflect our own national religious heritage as well as an understanding of other faiths around the globe. It should be read by those responsible for making or implementing foreign policy, as well as by anyone interested in promoting peace and understanding in a troubled world.

—**Edwin Meese III**,
Former Attorney General of the United States

Religion, Terror, and Error

U.S. Foreign Policy and the Challenge of Spiritual Engagement

DOUGLAS M. JOHNSTON, JR.

Foreword by
General Anthony Zinni, USMC (Ret)

Praeger Security International

PRAEGER

AN IMPRINT OF ABC-CLIO, LLC
Santa Barbara, California • Denver, Colorado • Oxford, England

Library of Congress Cataloging-in-Publication Data

Johnston, Douglas M.
  Religion, terror, and error : U.S. foreign policy and the challenge of spiritual engagement / Douglas M. Johnston, Jr. ; foreword by Anthony Zinni.
      p. cm. — (Praeger security international)
  Includes bibliographical references and index.
  ISBN 978-0-313-39145-3 (hard copy : alk. paper) — ISBN 978-0-313-39146-0 (ebook)   1. United States—Foreign relations—Islamic countries.   2. Islamic countries—Foreign relations—United States.   3. Religion and international relations.   4. Islam and international relations.   5. Intercultural communication—Religious aspects.   6. Islam and world politics.   I. Title.
  DS35.74.U6J64   2011
  327.73017'67—dc22   2010040868

ISBN: 978-0-313-39145-3
EISBN: 978-0-313-39146-0

15   14   13   12   11   1   2   3   4   5

This book is also available on the World Wide Web as an eBook.
Visit www.abc-clio.com for details.

Praeger
An imprint of ABC-CLIO, LLC

ABC-CLIO, LLC
130 Cremona Drive, P.O. Box 1911
Santa Barbara, California 93116-1911

This book is printed on acid-free paper ∞

Manufactured in the United States of America

To Lance and Keith
The Noblest Knights of All

Contents

Foreword

With the collapse of the Soviet Union toward the end of the last century, the era of military and economic power as the principal determinants of superpower status ended. The "hard power" of military might, in particular, has proven insufficient to influence and control events as it once did. Thus, the buzz around Washington these days is about "smart power," a combination of the "hard" melded with the "soft" power of diplomacy and development—in other words, a "whole-of-government" approach to engaging with other societies in resolving national and international security problems. Ironically, it is the military and the Defense Department more generally that are the greatest proponents of this broader approach. They clearly recognize the limitations of military power. As one general put it, "You can't shoot your way to victory."

Expanding our engagement beyond the economic and security dimensions reflects a new awareness that interactions with other societies and cultures have to be more than situational, short-term initiatives designed solely to meet our own immediate security needs. This whole-of-government approach, however, is not without its own set of problems. The cost of expanding government agency mandates and changing departmental cultures that aren't geared to planning for expansive challenges like nation-building are just a few of the concerns confronting those who subscribe to this broader way of engaging a far more complicated and interdependent world.

Another concern is the fact that those whom we seek to engage are often wary of engaging with us. History has conditioned most societies to be distrustful of the motives of mighty empires that suddenly take an interest in their affairs. All too often, such motives have related to dominance, exploitation, or crass opportunism designed to meet short-term needs. Rarely, if ever, have dominant powers engaged in a way that seeks mutual benefit and that demonstrates an appreciation for the local culture. The assumed superiority of the more powerful has left the mess of too many artificial borders, inappropriate systems of governance, depleted resources, and broken cultures. As a result, we should not be surprised that our well-intentioned efforts to engage are often viewed with suspicion.

President Obama's Cairo speech included all the right words as he reached out to the Muslim world in a sincere attempt to convince it that we are changing our approach, that we will respect their culture, and that we will act in ways that are mutually beneficial. Their reaction was, "Great speech, but we will wait to see the actions that follow". While the whole-of-government approach is a good beginning, it will have its own problems, as already mentioned, and will ultimately prove inadequate.

We have other effective ways for engaging with others that can be far more productive and trusted. Among these are our educational institutions, our business sector, non-governmental organizations and other components of our society that have much to offer in connecting to other societies and cultures in ways that are free of government policy objectives or other self-centered motives. The efforts from these kinds of independent connections are transparent and more clearly designed for tangible mutual benefit. Among them, the most creative approach in non-governmental engagement that I have encountered is the subject of this book, religion.

This may seem counter-intuitive since we have tended to see religious differences as monumental obstacles that will, in the minds of some, inevitably lead to Huntington's "clash of civilizations." Religious differences have always been perceived as the irreconcilable components of decision making, components that can only be dealt with by (1) avoiding certain issues altogether, (2) seeking resolution outside of religion, or (3) simply compelling the other side to submit. The intriguing approach offered in the following pages by Doug Johnston is to take on religion, not as an obstacle, but as a positive means of connection. This approach is not meant to be a means of forcing political agendas on others, but rather a way of connecting, communicating, and finding common ground through the moral values of our respective belief systems that have far more in common than not.

We are engaged with societies where religion plays a far more significant role in one's every-day life than in our own, and in which concepts such as separation of church and state are simply inconceivable. In many of these societies, however, religious education has been co-opted by extremists who attempt to corrupt the messages. Rather than ignore, work around, or attack these kinds of conditions, we should, as Dr. Johnston proposes, work through these realities to build trust, find common ground, and structure constructive inter-society communications that can lead to a resolution of differences.

This is a visionary approach that goes beyond the whole-of-government effort and which expands the current definition of smart power. From my two decades of experience in the Islamic world, I am convinced that the vast majority of Muslims would embrace this approach as a means of clearly expressing their beliefs and enabling them to understand ours. The common elements of the three great Abrahamic religions have yet to be tapped as a means of reconnecting societies that have gone off-track in their relationships and which need means to connect that go beyond the security, economic, and political approaches that have failed to resolve the pressing issues that divide us.

General Anthony Zinni, USMC (Ret)

Former Commander-in-Chief
U.S. Central Command

Former U.S. Special Envoy to the Middle East

Preface

My professional life began as an officer in the U.S. Navy, studying and practicing the art of warfare. During this time, I also learned a great deal about the principles of sound leadership and the importance of maintaining respectful relationships, especially during extended intervals of patrolling the oceans' depths in a submarine. Some years later, however, I came to believe that if humankind is to have any hope of realizing its full potential, it will need to develop better ways to resolve its differences. I began to devote time and energy to this theme. As a Christian inspired by the challenge to be a "peacemaker" (Matthew 5:9), I became convinced that although religious principles and matters of faith are all too often co-opted by power politics to aid and abet conflict, these same principles, if properly applied, could actually play a key role in its prevention and resolution.

I then set out to develop the intellectual basis for this new form of engagement in a book titled *Religion, the Missing Dimension of Statecraft*, which was published by Oxford University Press in 1994. During the seven years that it took to produce the book, the Berlin Wall came down; and identity-based antagonisms previously suppressed by the cold war reemerged in the form of ethnic disputes, tribal warfare, or religious hostilities. Because these kinds of conflict typically escape the grasp of traditional diplomacy, the proposed integration of religious reconciliation with official or unofficial diplomacy set forth in the book was seen to offer greater potential for dealing with them.

The book quickly gained global attention as reflected in more than 60 favorable reviews in leading journals and publications, including the *New York Times*, *Foreign Affairs*, the *Washington Post*, the London *Financial*

Times—in addition to multiple printings of the book itself. Five years later, *Sapio* (Japan's equivalent to *Time* magazine) cited it as one of the ten most important books to read in preparing for the 21st century. (I can speak immodestly about this book because it includes the contributions of a number of world-class scholars and foreign policy practitioners.) That same year, I felt inspired to walk the talk by establishing the International Center for Religion and Diplomacy (ICRD).

The purpose of the Center is to enlist the common values and moral teachings of different religious faiths in the service of peace, especially those within the Abrahamic traditions. In practical terms, this means focusing on the positive role that religious leaders, institutions, and dogmas can play in building trust and overcoming differences. It also means making a concerted effort to promote greater understanding, tolerance, and reconciliation in trouble spots where conflict threatens or may have already broken out.

After 10 years of applying religious peacemaking principles to foreign policy, my colleagues and I have found that in certain situations, particularly those involving identity-based conflicts, faith-based diplomacy can break down walls of hostility that are otherwise impervious to the efforts of traditional diplomacy. Faith-based diplomacy, simply put, is diplomacy that engages religious values in bridging differences between adversaries. We discovered that when applied in a collegial manner, this form of engagement can yield surprising results.

One of the early projects that the Center tackled with courageous indigenous partners was an initiative to help reform the madrasas (religious schools) in Pakistan, including those credited with advancing extremist thinking. At one point in this effort (August 2006), two ICRD board members—Harold Jacobi and John Sandoz—and I traveled to Pakistan to visit several madrasas that had been identified with terrorism in one way or another. The first of these was a major madrasa outside of Karachi that was known to have spawned the two most lethal anti-Shiite terrorist groups and was thought to be the chief supplier of fighters for Kashmir and Chechnya. This was our center's first exposure to this madrasa, which would have been out-of-bounds had it not been for the strong credibility that we enjoyed as a result of the highly successful efforts of our Pakistan project director, Azhar (Azi) Hussain, in working with other madrasas in the surrounding area.

As we entered a room packed with madrasa leaders and administrators and seasoned Islamic scholars, it became immediately apparent that there was a great deal of rage in the audience, rage over U.S. foreign policy in general and rage over the conflict that was then taking place in Lebanon between Israel and Hezbollah. To work past the anger, we attempted to provide a balanced view of U.S. involvements around the world, including the Middle East and then said, "But that's not why we are here today. We are here to discuss religious values that we share in common." Then

I quoted several passages from the Qur'an that I had committed to memory, a consolidated paraphrase of which would go as follows, "Oh mankind, God could have made you one had He willed, but He did not. Instead, He made you into separate nations and tribes so that you may know one another, cooperate with one another, and compete with one another in good works." I then said,

My two colleagues and I are here to open the competition in good works. The three of us happen to be followers of Jesus, and we know that you can't be good Muslims without believing some pretty wonderful things about Jesus. So let's ask ourselves, if He were here in our midst today, how would He want us to behave toward one another?

By the time the ensuing discussion played out over the course of the next hour and segued into a social exchange, the earlier rage had been converted to a genuine feeling of acceptance, bordering on fellowship.

We then went to Lahore, where we visited the madrasa that had been linked in the public media to the London bombers. There, we went through the same scenario, with exactly the same results. Several times since then, Azi has run into the leader of that particular madrasa, a widely revered, and somewhat feared individual, who has mentioned on each of these encounters the question posed about Jesus. He indicated that it has caused him to ask himself on a daily basis, "What would the Prophet have me do?" In response to that question, his madrasa has been conducting seminars on peacemaking and conflict resolution.

Following these visits, Azi mentioned that in both madrasas he had heard a collective sigh of relief from the audience when they heard me quote the passages from the Qur'an. That simple gesture of respect was apparently instrumental in defusing the hostility that was present when we entered.

Another interesting episode took place the following year when I had occasion to meet with a number of Taliban commanders in the mountains of Pakistan. The genesis of this meeting was an earlier ICRD workshop for madrasa leaders in which a senior-level Taliban commander participated. In private conversations with Azi, he expressed his view that the Taliban didn't know what America wants. He said that coming after them with guns had left them little recourse but to respond in kind. He had lost two sons in the fighting and seemed sincere in wanting to facilitate some kind of helpful dialogue. This exchange ultimately led to an invitation for me to meet with the Taliban's senior leadership to address that question, which I did two months later.

The meeting, which took place in the Malakand Agency of Pakistan and lasted several hours, involved 57 Taliban commanders and several tribal and religious leaders from Afghanistan and the Malakand region. I made clear from the outset that I was by no means authorized to speak for the

U.S. government, and that, in fact, it was highly likely that my government would be opposed to the idea of even holding such a meeting.

I told them that the purpose of the meeting was to see if we could build on our commonly held religious values to develop a confidence-building measure that could point the way toward peace. For them to be able to participate in such an effort, however, they needed to understand how the West views the situation. I then attempted to convey the western perspective and gave them my impression of what it was that the United States/ NATO wanted, which was for them to lay down their arms, distance themselves from al Qaeda, and reconcile with the Karzai government. Over the course of the spirited two-hour discussion that followed, I responded to a number of penetrating questions that emerged as angry Taliban commanders lamented the plight of their people, expressed a visceral hatred for the warlords, and showed total disdain for President Karzai for having failed in his promise to control the warlords. One such question was why the United States was attacking Afghanistan, in response to which I replied:

Putting it in terms that you hold sacred—hospitality, loyalty, and revenge— before we recognized certain members of al Qaeda as a threat, we welcomed them into our country and gave them hospitality. Then on 9/11, without warning, they struck. We wanted revenge, and we asked the Taliban government to turn over al Qaeda's leadership, so we could bring them to justice. They refused, so we attacked. But we did so with a heavy heart, because most Americans have great admiration and respect for the Afghan people, stemming from our common struggle against the former Soviet Union. Furthermore, it's important for you to recognize that some of your own tribal leaders are now banding together against al Qaeda because they have violated your hospitality as well.

At one point during the discussion, a particularly tough-looking gentleman stood up and, pointing at me, said, "I can't talk to you unless you become a Muslim." After thinking for a moment, I responded by saying, "No problem. 'Muslim' means submission to God. We all submit to God, therefore we're all Muslims." Everyone laughed and we went on with the discussion. It wasn't until sometime later that I learned that both Azi and our *Ahle Hadith* (Wahhabi) partner (who arranged the meeting and spent the better part of a month rounding up the participants) grew nervous when this encounter took place because the way that particular scenario often plays out, you convert or you die. Having been totally oblivious to this, my immediate thought was, "The Lord *really does* look out for fools and incompetents."

Afterward, we broke for prayer and then reassembled in a smaller group to work out the confidence-building measure. Although the plan that we developed ultimately failed, several months later we were able to build on the networking from this encounter to help secure the release of 21 Korean missionaries whom the Taliban had taken hostage in southern Afghanistan (see chapter 13). Preceding their release, our intervention on religious grounds inspired an internal debate among the captors over their respective interpretations of what the Qur'an required them to do.

These and other examples illustrate the kinds of interactions that can take place between adversaries if one is able to bring to bear shared moral values stemming from religious faith. While there is no risk-free way to address the problem of religious extremism, one's chances of doing so safely are greatly improved by bringing the faith dimension to bear in a sincere and respectful manner. Despite the risks and whatever discomfort one may feel in navigating the relatively uncharted waters of spiritual engagement, the stakes are simply too high not to give it our best effort. In Pakistan, those stakes relate to the risk of undemocratic regime change in a nuclear-capable state.

A parting caveat: many of the issues addressed in this book are in an ongoing state of flux, such as the developments in Iraq and Afghanistan and in our strained relationship with Iran. Accordingly, some of the proposed recommendations could be rendered moot by unanticipated events prior to the book's publication. Either way, the reader is invited to focus on the generic principles that underlie these recommendations, since they are integral to the paradigm shift that will be required to enhance global security in the years ahead.

Acknowledgments

One of America's many strengths is its historic openness to new ideas and fresh approaches. This book represents an attempt to capitalize on that openness by suggesting a change in course that can help carry us through the uncertain waters that lie ahead. The book itself is unique in the extent to which there are so many contributors to acknowledge for bringing it to fruition. To put a slightly different twist on Churchill, never have so many owed so much to so many.

Compliments are first due the Henry Luce Foundation, both for the support it provided to make this book possible and for the unrivaled leadership it has taken in infusing academia with the resources needed to establish religion and foreign policy programs within their international relations curriculums. I have had the pleasure of participating in a number of these Luce-funded initiatives, including two which it sponsored with public policy research institutes: the Center for Strategic and International Studies in Washington and the Chicago Council on Global Affairs. I am grateful to both for including me in their deliberations as they developed policy-relevant recommendations for the government. The rich dialogue associated with each of these efforts has certainly influenced my own thinking.

I am especially thankful to John Kiser for his important, thoughtful, and often original contributions, which are reflected across the first two chapters and several toward the end dealing with organic suasion, the new paradigm, and spiritual engagement. The book particularly benefited from John's uncanny aptitude for linking the spiritual and the mundane and for connecting dots that might prove elusive to others. Finally, his familiarity with Robert Coram's biography of John Boyd led to a framework that accommodated both the practical and more philosophical components of the contents. John's substantive and literary contributions to this effort were significant indeed.

Also valuable were the efforts of the working groups formed at the outset to help establish a sound framework for moving ahead. The chairs of these working groups, which constituted the book's Steering Committee, included Jim Wootton, John Sandoz, Joe Montville, Steve Hayes, Abubaker al-Shingieti, and John Kiser. This Committee was also a source of good ideas. The ability to sharpen these ideas through friendly, but spirited, debate was worth its weight in gold.

On the back-end of the book's development, we were exceedingly fortunate to enlist Gen. Anthony Zinni to write the foreword and a gifted "Red Team" to review the book's initial draft, consisting of Dr. Jamal Barzinji, Vice President of the International Institute for Islamic Thought; retired KGB Col. Valentin Aksilenko; Judge William Webster, former head of the CIA and the FBI; and Rev. David McAllister-Wilson, President of Wesley Seminary. A later, penultimate draft underwent a final scrutiny by several world-class scholars and journalists, including Edward Luttwak, Stanton Burnett, Richard Ruffin, and Carl Oglesby.

Other scholars, researchers, and practitioners who provided important input along the way included Gordon Adams, Karen Anderson, Mahveen Azam, Victoria Barrett, Andrea Bartoli, Rick Barton, Michael Braeuninger, John Brinsfield, Bob Bruno, Duke Burbridge, Pia Chaudhari, Sati Clark, Alastair Colin-Jones, Michael Cooper, Nick Danforth, Brooke Davis, Michael Doran, Naz Durakoglu, Will Fleeson, Anthony Gao, Alison Gaske, Agatha Glowacki, Shannon Hayden, Rachel Herbers, James Hoobler, Azhar Hussain, Andrea Jackson, Walid Abdul Jawad, Lance Johnston, Corrine Kalota, Aejaz Karim, Lorelei Kelly, Obrad Kesic, Sophia Khan, Margaret Kibben, Miles Kimber, Jacob Kohn, Peter Kovach, Ramah Kudaimi, Chet Lanious, Lynne Novak, David Newman, Mallory MacDonald, Magsud Mammadov, Stacy Maruskin, Trey Miller, Pauletta Otis, Maria Presley, Khaled Proudi, Yasir Qadhi, Joe Reeder, Benjamin Rogers, Michael Schoenleber, Peter Schwartz, David Sexton, Craig Tichelkamp, Tommy Tomiyama, Aurelian Tudorache, Mike Van Hall, Matt Woodbery, and Shan Zrik.

My sincere apologies to anyone I may have overlooked.

Special thanks are also due Laura Kallenborn and Rose Marshall for their important role as utility infielders. And last, but far from least, are the herculean contributions of Patrick Moore, who spent countless hours researching various topics, tracking down endless footnotes, producing copious drafts, and jumping through multiple hoops to ensure everything was in order for publication. His great spirit throughout was an inspiration to all.

The final tribute is to John Boyd, the U.S. Air Force Colonel whose cutting-edge thinking, while originally inspired by the need to achieve aerial supremacy in air-to-air combat, has shown us a way to move beyond the rational actor model of decision making that continues to limit our horizons in the practice of international politics. Unless I miss my guess, Colonel Boyd's thinking will be inspiring breakthroughs in new areas for years to come.

I

Observation

CHAPTER 1

Beyond the Rational Actor

If you know others and know yourself, you will not be imperiled in a hundred battles; if you do not know others but know yourself, you win one and lose one; if you do not know others and do not know yourself, you will be imperiled in every single battle.

—Sun Tzu, *The Art of War*

SETTING THE STAGE

The air was pregnant with possibilities. In the aftermath of the Persian Gulf War and the cold war before it, the United States was without peer in all of the categories by which one customarily measures international influence: military power, political ideals, economic strength, and cultural resonance. The world was seemingly ours to shape, and geopolitical discussion was dominated by constant reference to a "new world order."

In the blink of a decade, how far the mighty have fallen. Our military power is in the eyes of many stretched to the breaking point, our economy has been seriously weakened, our political ideals have been tarnished by Abu Ghraib and the resort to rendition, and our government is vilified in many parts of the world as never before. Clearly, a golden opportunity has been squandered and the republic is in urgent need of a major course correction, hence the high hopes accompanying Barack Obama's ascendancy to the presidency. In applying the needed rudder to get us back on track, though, it will be important for him and everyone else to understand how it is that we strayed so far off course.

LOSING OUR WAY

On the threshold of the new millennium, America was adrift with no clear strategy to guide its foreign policy. A simplistic ideology was no substitute for a serious strategy. Our leaders were finding it increasingly difficult to keep track of how things fit together. Even while the international community was searching for a new systemic equilibrium based on an evolving multipolarity, U.S. leaders were making countless ad hoc, unilateral decisions as they dealt with a growing assortment of vexing situations that defied conceptual integration. Neither isolationism nor containment—the country's two longest-running and most successful grand strategies—provided much guidance, nor did engagement or expansion of democracy, as practiced up to that point by the Bush 41 and Clinton administrations.

To be sure, the evolution to superpower dominance carried with it several U.S. assumptions about international politics: (1) that de facto American hegemony was preferable to a bipolar or multipolar balance of power; (2) that liberal democracy, coupled with a free-market economy, represented the ultimate form of good governance (the "end of history," so to speak); and (3) that military force would be of declining utility in world affairs owing to America's overwhelming advantage.

Looking ahead, it seemed clear that U.S. foreign policy needed a new organizing principle commensurate with its interests, capabilities, influence, and imagination—a principle that would give added meaning to the strategy of engagement and provide a better frame of reference for dealing with an increasingly interdependent world.[1] Before this realization could be acted upon, the events of September 11, 2001, intervened; and all else was put on hold as America reacted to the devastating consequences.

A WAKE-UP CALL

With the attacks on the World Trade Center and the Pentagon, the aimless giant was rudely awakened; and any opportunity for further drifting was foreclosed for the foreseeable future. In the aftermath of those attacks, the United States embarked on a dual-track strategy—a track of justice and retribution in Afghanistan and a track of preemption in Iraq. Whatever one may think of the decision to attack Iraq, both tracks were rationalized by the belief that the leading vital interest of every nation-state is protecting the security of its citizens.

The United States also announced a number of defensive measures to protect the homeland: improving security measures for the nation's aviation system; taking action to protect critical infrastructure; increasing the nation's preparedness for a disaster; and enhancing information sharing among federal, state, local, and international partners. Numerous other steps have also been taken to protect the country, especially on the intelligence and counterterrorism fronts; but most of these initiatives have constituted defensive measures in reaction to symptoms rather than actions to address underlying cause. Thus far, the country has been spared a second attack, but the threat persists, as evident from the failed attempts of the Detroit "Christmas bomber" and the May 2010 Times Square car-bomber. Clearly, if we are to deal effectively with the problem of religious extremism, something more will be required.

Despite the widely recognized need to address the challenges of religious extremism, how to do so remains a puzzle for most policymakers. Respectful engagement with other cultures and countries only takes one part of the way, since that has more to do with good manners than with religious faith. America's past inability to understand and deal with religious imperatives has led to uninformed foreign policy decisions in such places as Iran, Lebanon, and, most recently, Iraq. To avoid similar mistakes in the future, we will need to expand our definition of realpolitik to include religion and other cultural factors. Above all, if we are to see the world complete and whole, we will need to make a concerted effort to understand how religion informs the world views and political aspirations of those who do not similarly separate church and state. To reduce this ambitious undertaking to manageable proportions, we will confine our examination in this volume to dealing with the challenge of extremism in the name of Islam.

DEALING WITH CAUSE

American foreign policy must develop a capacity for spiritual engagement on various levels. This will require moving beyond the *rational actor* model of decision making that has long dominated our practice of international relations—a model which assumes that states will behave according to the rational pursuit of their national self-interests, foremost among which is maximizing power.[2] Absent, however, is any room to accommodate the impact of religious imperatives or other supposed irrational factors, hence the need to move beyond. In short, developing a new, more-encompassing framework for analysis will be required if we are to engage effectively the challenges posed by religious extremism.

BEYOND THE RATIONAL ACTOR

Col. John Boyd is not a widely known thinker outside the military. He didn't write books. His ideas were practical, scientific, and against the grain of Air Force doctrine. His most important legacy was his impact on the concept of maneuver warfare (as opposed to attrition warfare),[3] and it can be found in hundreds of meticulously prepared briefings that he gave during 20 years of intellectual insurgency against his own military's bureaucracy. He was also a profane, blunt-speaking truth teller.[4] Orphaned by the U.S. Air Force for bucking the dominant mind-set of "faster, higher, farther," this brilliant fighter pilot of the 1960s became an adopted son of the U.S. Marine Corps. Not well-known outside the Marine Corps today, he had a simple view of war shaped by his reading of a 2,000-year-old strategist, Sun Tzu. Boyd's views were, and still are, at odds with the American love affair with technology.

His mantra for the military's technology idol worshippers: "Machines don't fight wars, terrain doesn't fight wars. Humans fight wars. You must get into the minds of humans. That's where the battles are won."[5] As Boyd dove deeper into the study of ground war, he came to understand war as something that every person experiences in some form. Conflict is embedded in human nature. To prevail, whether in war, business, or personal relations, one must understand what one's adversary believes. To empathize also means to see yourself through your adversary's eyes.

The ability to get inside the mind of the enemy fascinated Boyd. This led him to study conflicts and battles in which numerically inferior forces defeated much larger ones, summed up in his four-hour briefing, "Patterns of Conflict." He saw brute force, head-on collision warfare (a.k.a. "high diddle diddle, go up the middle") as being less and less the paradigm for the future. Speed, ambiguity, deception, getting inside the head of the adversary, and, most important, *doing what is least expected* will be the hallmarks of success for future commanders. And the very best will be those who, in the tradition of Sun Tzu, unravel the enemy before the battle.[6]

This is what Marine Lt. Col. Stanton Coerr, writing in the January 2009 edition of the *Marine Corps Gazette*, thinks Osama bin Laden accomplished. "It's as if bin Laden had read Boyd and foreseen the American overreaction to 9/11." Boyd explains:

Pull the adversary apart by causing him to generate or project mental images that agree neither with the tempo nor transient maneuver patterns he must compete against. Enmesh the adversary in a world of uncertainty, doubt, mistrust, confusion, disorder, fear, panic and chaos.[7]

"America reacted precisely as Bin Laden knew we would," Coerr reflects, "with a huge public, angry, unilateral, *military* lashing out in Muslim lands. In doing so, we allowed bin Laden to become the voice for the Muslim world . . . authentic in the face of First World mechanized overkill."[8] As of this writing, America has lost close to 6,000 lives and one trillion dollars in reaction to an attack that cost the lives of 19 hijackers and well under a million dollars.[9] While America focuses on winning battles, our opponent will be focused on winning wars by striking where we are weakest, remaining in the shadows, promoting instability, and draining our treasury. As bin Laden himself said:

All we have to do is send two mujaheddin to the furthest point east to raise a cloth on which is written al-Qaeda, in order to make the [U.S] generals race there to cause America to suffer human, economic and political losses . . . so we are continuing this policy of bleeding America to the point of bankruptcy.[10]

Boyd's theory helps us understand why this is so.

THE OODA LOOP

Successfully getting inside the enemy's mind is part of a complex, four-part process that became known as the Boyd Cycle or OODA Loop: observation, orientation, decision, and action (see Figure 1.1). William Lind, a leading figure in the U.S. military reform movement of the 1970s, succinctly captured this cycle in his now-famous handbook on maneuver warfare:

Conflict can be seen as time-competitive observation-orientation-decision-action cycles. Each party to a conflict begins by observing. He observes himself, his physical surroundings and his enemy. On the basis of his observation, he orients, that is to say, he makes a mental image or "snapshot" of his situation. On the basis of this orientation, he makes a decision. He puts the decision into effect, i.e., he acts. Then, because he assumes his action has changed the situation, he observes again, and starts the process anew.[11]

The process is a continuous one, involving constant feedback, adaptation, and adjustment to ground truth. This is not simply about peeping over the hill and scoping the physical terrain. This is about climbing cultural mountains. As Marine Col. Thomas Hammes writes in an earlier issue of the *Marine Corps Gazette*, "The OODA loop expands to track not just our enemy's reaction, but how the entire environment is reacting—the people, the host-nation government, our allies, our forces, even our own population."[12] It is as relevant to diplomacy and domestic politics as it is to warfare. Indeed, one might go so far as to label it the empathetic "whole actor" successor to the rational actor model of decision making—a process instead of a model that provides a thoughtful way for dealing with the complexities of the times, many of which defy modeling (in contrast to a time when life was simpler, with its seemingly more straightforward balance-of-power calculations).

Boyd's thinking is a creative mix of ideas from physics, history, and his own experience of warfare both with enemies doing battle and those within the military bureaucracy. The first principle in facing an adversary is also the oldest: know your enemy and know yourself (and how you are perceived by the enemy). This falls within both observation and orientation. These steps also require recognizing the potential for mismatch between an observation and a description of that observation, which arises from the observer's own mental processes. If not self-aware, the observer will naturally describe his observations through the lens of his own internal

Figure 1.1
John Boyd's OODA Loop. (Permission given by author Chet Richards)

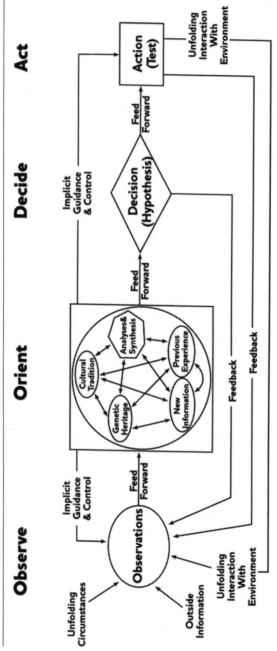

Observe   **Orient**   **Decide**   **Act**

Note how orientation shapes observation, shapes decision, shapes action, and in turn is shaped by the feedback and other phenomena coming into our sensing or observing window.

Also note how the entire "loop" (not just orientation) is an ongoing many-sided implicit cross-referencing process of projection, empathy, correlation, and rejection.

From The Essence of Winning and Losing, John R Boyd. January 1996.

dogmas and preconceived notions, which are prone to be out of synch with an unfolding, constantly changing outside world.[13]

To know the enemy (or a friend) requires knowing one's own prejudices and blind spots. Boyd had studied engineering. From physics, he was familiar with the Heisenberg Uncertainty Principle, which states that the process of observation changes the object being observed. In the world of human activity, and foreign policy in particular, it is a problem that comes from bringing prefabricated truths and Eurocentric biases to our perceptions of other cultures and individual motives. How do we avoid a mismatch between the observation and the description of that which we are observing? Otherwise put, how do we break through our mere perception of a situation to grasp its reality?

Boyd's second principle was learned from fighting bureaucratic wars: always use your enemy's own information. As long as we dismiss our enemies as fanatics, wackos, or cowardly barbarians, we will never know them. These default labels for the unthinking will prevent us from ever making the critical distinctions that can help us "disaggregate" our adversaries.

OBSERVATION AND ORIENTATION

One, possibly very big, part of the observation and orientation problem that American policymakers have with "radical Islam" stems from having too narrow an aperture for viewing unfolding world events. This has produced an unhealthy obsession with "the Islamic threat"—an obsession that enhances the prestige of those we fear, making the "threat" greater and more threatening than it is. As this mismatch between our mental images and objective reality increases, so does confusion, uncertainty, and disorder. The only alternative to this dialectic of misperception is to rebuild one's mental image.[14]

The knowledge that Americans who are engaged with the Muslim world (whether as ally or adversary) need most to acquire is found in the Qur'an. Quite simply, it is the Muslims' guide for living, their constitution for both personal and community behavior in service to God. In essence, the Qur'an is for Muslims a cross between Saint Benedict's Rule and the U.S. Constitution.[15] Like our own Constitution, the Qur'an is subject to different interpretations by scholars of the law. Parts of it are ambiguous. What is the context of the different proclamations and ordinances? Should it be modernized and updated, or should it be interpreted in light of original intent? How does one determine original intent?

The Qur'an is orders of magnitude more difficult than the U.S. Constitution, especially if one is not religious. Arabic and Chinese are not easy languages; nevertheless, U.S. foreign service officers are expected to learn them. Like reading the Bible, understanding the Qur'an requires finding learned, pious, and humble guides. Any text can be trashed or misunderstood with a hostile attitude. Knowing enough of the Qur'an to be able to

follow it wisely will win respect from foe and friend alike. It was in recognition of this fact that Alexis de Tocqueville recommended that translations of the Qur'an be provided to French officials in his report to the
French government on its 10-year-old misadventure in Algeria that began
in 1830.[16]

Equally important is understanding what it means to live sincerely a
life of submission to God's will, as the Lord's Prayer enjoins Christians to
do. Americans who are estranged from religion could benefit by getting
to know their own God-loving communities for whom tight adherence
to scripture is their higher law: the Amish, Mennonites, Trappist monks,
Mormons, Seventh Day Adventists, and other faith traditions that attempt
to live by the Book. Such people can serve as bridges for the secular and
nonreligious in understanding Muslims whose thinking about God is little different from that of committed Christians. For God-fearing believers,
God, not nation-state, is the ultimate Commander-in-Chief. Spiritual engagement is precisely that—engaging not scornfully but empathetically
with those whose "spirit" is different and playing to that spark of the Creator that resides in all His creatures, albeit some more visibly than others.
A fundamental challenge inherent in this changed approach to decision
making is the possible unwelcome effect of dividing the military soul. It is
difficult to be empathetic and fight to kill, hence the tendency over history
to dehumanize one's opponents both on and off the battlefield.

The insights that flow from such inquiries belong to the orientation
phase, which Boyd considered to be the most important link in the chain.
Of particular importance is the "implicit guidance and control" function
of this phase that concurrently feeds back to the observation phase and
ahead to the action phase, based on the observer's ongoing ability to syn-
thesize a number of different variables such as cultural traditions, religious
imperatives, genetic heritage, previous experience, and new information.
It is this guidance and control function that enables the observer to adjust
his or her responses to a constantly changing situation. Although the time-
lines for aerial combat and the conduct of international affairs are vastly
different, the OODA principles remain valid for both. This new frame of
reference should enable us (1) to acquire a more nuanced understanding
of today's circumstances, (2) to reorient our thinking, and (3) to reshape
our strategy accordingly.

CHAPTER 2

A Closer Look at Today's Challenge

We need to worry a lot less about how to communicate our actions and much more about what our actions communicate.

—Adm. Michael Mullen

On September 11, 2001, more than a few airplanes were hijacked; Islam was as well. "We are not at war with Islam," President Obama declared during his spring 2009 tour of the Middle East. Nevertheless, the United States, along with other countries, is in a struggle with a multiplicity of groups committing violent acts in its name. Although these *irhabi* (terrorist) groups represent only a small fraction of the world's Muslims, they have attracted various degrees of sympathy among the faithful. Some are motivated by a global supremacist Islamist ideology, others by local territorial and cultural grievances.

It is important at the outset to be as precise as possible in the lexicon used to describe terrorism and those who practice it. For example, the all-too-common usage of the word *jihad* in the West is highly inappropriate for describing the kind of activity ascribed to Osama bin Laden. Although the term has become synonymous with "holy war" and forcing others to become Muslims, these are not concepts to be found in the Qur'an. In point of fact, jihad is a word that has many meanings and sacred import. There is jihad for knowledge, jihad for justice, jihad for truth, and jihad for the faith. Above all, true jihad is about striving to live righteously in war and peace, and in such a way that mercy and compassion trump hatred and violence.[1]

An inspiring example of true jihad from recent history is that of Emir Abd el-Kader, an Arab freedom fighter who, in resisting the French occupation of Algeria in the 19th century, won global acclaim for his brilliance as a military commander and for the tolerance, humanity, and forbearance that he consistently demonstrated as a champion of his faith both on and off the battlefield.[2] In light of current realities, however, a caution from Mustafa Ceric, the Grand Mufti of Bosnia, is in order:

The word crusade, even though it may mean many good different things for Christians, for the Muslims it means only one thing: the military campaign against Islam. In the same way, the word *jihad* to Muslims may mean many good things, but for the non-Muslim it means only one thing: the violent actions against their faith. Therefore, all of us should be extremely careful in using the words so that no one has need to apologize later that he or she did not mean by crusade what the Muslims mean, and that he or she did not mean by *jihad* what the non-Muslims mean.[3]

Today's false jihadists present a dangerous and virulent mutation of a great world religion, an Abrahamic cousin of Judaism and Christianity that bequeathed a rich spiritual, intellectual, and artistic legacy to European culture. To deprive al Qaeda of the sacred legitimacy of the word *jihad*, Dr. David Kilcullen, an Australian military anthropologist and former senior advisor to Gen. David Petraeus in Iraq, uses the term *takfiri terrorist* to describe followers of Osama bin Laden's ideology. *Takfiris* arrogate to themselves the authority to declare as infidels those Muslims with whom they disagree, and they collectively constitute a heresy within Islam since *takfirism* violates the clear Qur'anic injunction that there be no compulsion in religion.[4]

Beyond the use of *takfir* by Muslims, another appropriate term for terrorism is *irhab*.[5] Using terms like *jihad* (holy war, etc.) and *mujahideen* (holy warriors) only gives bin Laden and his fellow extremists false credibility within the ranks of Islam. Thus, control of the language has an enormous impact on the recruitment of insurgents and the motivation of those recruited.[6]

We will find our greatest success to the extent that we inculcate Marxism as a kind of religion. Religious men and women are easy to convert and win, and will easily accept our thinking if we wrap it up in a kind of religious terminology.

—*Vladimir Lenin*

Using the right language involves more than just understanding Arab terms. For example, the oft-used description of peaceful believers as moderate is a nonstarter in the Muslim world, since Muslims do not consider themselves to be moderate in their beliefs. Like "Turn the other cheek" in Christianity, they know the Hadith "Do not let anger turn you away from justice." Difficult to practice but nevertheless an "immoderate" goal. As expressed by HRH Prince Hussam bin Saud bin Abdulaziz al Saud of Saudi Arabia, "The difference between the 'moderate' and the 'extremist' is often not an issue of belief, but a matter of action. The purpose of dialogue is to restrain violent action, not dilute belief. Muslims share the same beliefs about the most contentious issues facing them; where they differ is in how to deal with them."[7]

To demonize Islam, as some extreme voices in the West do, is to demonize a billion and a half Muslims. If Professor Khaled Abou El Fadl, a prominent American Muslim scholar, is correct in his assessment that more than one billion practitioners of Islam consider compassion, mercy, love, and justice to be the core values of their faith, it would seem that the basis for incompatibility between Islam and other faiths is narrower than most observers might think. El Fadl further notes that the ethical aspiration for most mainstream Muslims is to work in concert with those of other faiths to discover "the potential for beauty and goodness that God has deposited into every human being,"[8] thus the obvious folly of lumping extremists with the mainstream.

Yet Muslims and non-Muslims around the world have a threat to counter, one that has a Muslim face, distorted by hatred, and that uses the Qur'an as a weapon. The virulence of this hatred was captured by a Russian journalist, Alexander Khokhlov, who interviewed al Qaeda and Taliban prisoners following 9/11 and the assassination of Ahmad Shah Massoud, the famed Soviet resistance fighter and chief commander of the anti-Taliban Northern Alliance. One of the prisoners told Khokhlov:

I am from Pakistan. I am 27 years old. I graduated from a madrasa. I had thirty *jihad* warriors under my command. They captured me five years back and kept me in jail, but the jail cannot break my spirit, it cannot make me change my convictions. Our main enemy is America and the rest of the West. Russia is also our enemy because of Chechnya. You, Russians, have many Muslims in your country. Soon, we will come there to liberate them from infidels. We are fighting in Afghanistan, against Muslims, because we need a strong home base here to mount the great offensive on the West. . . . America? America is a happy and therefore cowardly country. The hungry one always wins over the sated. The poor one always wins over the rich one. We have nothing to lose. . . . American bombs can destroy our cannons and tanks, but cannot destroy the idea, which I cherish in my heart. You are doomed. We will burn out Uzbekistan and then we will lead the hungry Uzbeks to fight and die with the name of Allah under the walls of your Moscow. We will kill you, Russians, and we will kill all Jews. In America, we will create the atmosphere of horror. There are many skyscrapers and jets there. There are many awful plagues besides anthrax. You are doomed and no one can save you. Islam will rule the world. . . . There is no mercy for infidels. Dogs will die like dogs.[9]

Another war prisoner shouted at the same journalist:

The time will come for my prayers on the ruins of Tashkent and your pagan Moscow! The world will belong to Muslims! Your women will be our beddings and your children will be our slaves! And all you non-believers are doomed for horrible death! . . . My life has no meaning for me. My life belongs to Allah, and I am ready to kill you now and sacrifice myself so that even one pagan dog like you will be dead![10]

The threat posed by such rage is very real, but what is the proper response when the principal recruiting tool of the *irhabis* is the claim that America and the West are waging war on Islam? That is one of several topics this book will address.

DEFINING THE CHALLENGE

First, a few words about the title of this book. *Religion* is derived from the Latin *religare*. A religious person is one who binds himself or herself to specific theological doctrines and practices, usually among a community of like-minded believers. Karl Marx and subscribers to the Enlightenment predicted that such beliefs would wither away with the passage of time. Science, technology, and human reason would work to promote the welfare of humankind without resort to divine wisdom and accompanying premodern superstitions and fairy tales. Yet, as is abundantly clear today, religion has not withered away, least of all in the science- and technology-obsessed culture of the United States. Nor is it likely to wither away so long as human beings have an urge to look for deeper meaning in their lives other than seeking pleasure and avoiding pain.

Terror is an inherently political term. As the cliché goes, "One man's terrorist is another man's freedom fighter" or "War is the terrorism of the powerful; terrorism is the war of the weak." Because of terrorism's political nature, not even the United Nations has been able to agree on a satisfactory definition for the term. "The willful attacking of innocents" seems to attract the greatest support, but even that reasonably straightforward proposition invites hesitation when recalling the atomic and fire bombings of World War II (events that are often cited in the cyber world by al Qaeda sympathizers advocating total war) and various other attempts over time to break an enemy's will through consciously including civilian casualties. To some extent, the more recent shock and awe strategy used in Iraq could be seen as knocking on this same door, at least by those on the receiving end.

It is a serious error to identify terror with religion. The laudable principles of neighborly concern and the betterment of humanity to which most world religions subscribe do not in any way justify acts of terrorism. In fact, they do quite the opposite. In Islam, the Holy Qur'an makes very clear that the killing of one innocent life "shall be regarded as having killed all mankind."[11] Sadly, all religions have been co-opted by power politics at one time or another to serve as a badge of identity or a mobilizing vehicle for pursuing dubious ends.

Error also creeps in on a systemic basis owing to the limitations of the rational actor model.[12] To be sure, many of the problems between Islam and the West have less to do with religion per se than with political power and the distribution of resources. However, America's inability to deal with religious considerations has led to errors in defining and comprehending a new and unfamiliar kind of enemy, one that uses a combination of religion and total war reasoning; has local and international dimensions; is globalized, networked, and nonhierarchical; and has no fixed territorial base. In addressing these errors, this book will offer detailed prescriptive remedies for dealing with the various aspects of religion, the long-missing dimension of western statecraft.

In 2007, 5.8 billion of the world's 6.8 billion inhabitants identified themselves as members of religious communities.[13] To ignore the motivating influence of religious faith and not to have a sympathetic understanding of those whose identity is strongly bound with the dictates of their faith— Orthodox Jews, Amish, Mennonite communities, monks and priests, Sikhs, Muslims more generally—is to handicap ourselves severely in dealing with much of the rest of the world. Moreover, recent trends suggest that religion's impact is growing stronger over time, as manifested, for example, in the growing influence of religious political parties in democratic governments overseas. Further, changes in religious demography, such as the rapid growth of Christianity in the global South and increased Muslim immigration to western nations, are reshaping public attitudes and government policies. If the ethical dimensions of the religious values that are important to more than 5 billion people can be effectively adopted to solve problems, they will become a powerful force for good that no policymaker can afford to overlook. William Vendley, Secretary General of World Religions for Peace, has noted that

of the 25 million [people] who live in zones of conflict, 23 million could be accessed through their religious communities. Of the 40 million who have HIV/AIDS, up to 35 million could be reached through their religious communities. Of the 3 billion who live on less than two dollars a day, some 2.8 billion could be reached through their religious communities.[14]

This suggests that any effective long-term strategy to counter extremism that involves addressing systemic problems such as those mentioned above should seek to capitalize on religion's extensive reach as well as its ethical values.

One obstacle to moving forward with such a strategy, however, is the fact that those who work in the executive branch of the U.S. government (especially in the national security arena) feel constrained by separation of church and state considerations from engaging with the clerical elements of other societies. As a result, whether by cautious interpretation of policy or by personal inclination, they do not feel comfortable allying with the important religious leadership elements that could help combat a whole range of problems, including extremist ideology.

Those who commit crimes in the name of Islam by turning themselves into human cruise missiles are routinely dismissed in public discourse as being "crazies" or "cowards"— not very useful terms for engendering a healthy respect for one's enemy, one who is very smart and seems to know us much better than we know him. Most suicide bombers are not particularly religious, and almost none are known to have been mentally ill, yet their actions in the name of Islam and accompanying media coverage have significantly contaminated western thinking about all Muslims. Research has shown that nationalism in reaction to foreign occupation is the primary driver of suicide terrorism.[15]

LEADING BY LISTENING

The battle against Islamist extremism cannot be won as America's struggle. That battle has to be waged primarily within the house of Islam. Yet this contest, which is intimately connected with centuries of history marked variously by indifference, conflict, and comity between what were once called the Christian and Muslim worlds, is now unhelpfully and inaccurately reduced to Islam versus the West. In rejecting this bumper sticker description of a complex and dynamic challenge that makes fractal physics look easy, this book starts with a simple premise: for the United States to lead, it must also learn to listen. American policymakers must learn to listen to and weigh the advice of others who have a more intimate knowledge of any given theater of conflict. Americans must share the struggle with people and leaders around the world who often have a better understanding of what actually constitute genuine "enduring threats" and those that may be more accurately characterized as transitory or situational in nature. History counsels one not to lean exclusively on one's own understanding. Can U.S. policymakers and implementers, with strong America-centric perspectives and little or no experience in dealing with Muslims and the Muslim world, possibly have sufficient wisdom to go it alone? Probably not.

There is no point in dialogue if we are not prepared to change our minds, alter our preconceptions and transcend an orthodoxy that we have long ceased to examine critically.

—*Karen Armstrong*

Successful international companies have learned to employ and trust foreign nationals in their highest circles of research and management. The great R&D powers of corporate America—IBM, DuPont, GE, Boeing,

Exxon, and others—have internationalized their research to draw on the best minds throughout the world in solving problems. It is not merely IQ or nationality that is at stake, but different ways of defining problems, looking at those problems, and thinking about solutions. In the military sphere, one man who has appreciated the need for different perspectives and surrounded himself with diverse and highly talented advisors is Gen. David Petraeus, Commander of International Security Forces in Afghanistan. To be effective, government policymakers will need the wisdom of wider perspectives than those provided by their own worldview or of westernized foreigners who speak the same language. Can wise foreign policy even be conducted by a democracy in which lawmakers are so deeply beholden to narrow interest groups driven by domestic political imperatives? America's continued resort to *unilateral* economic sanctions in the face of their proven ineffectiveness gives testimony to the ongoing, often counterproductive influence of domestic political pressures.

Fifty years ago, a Canadian English professor, Marshall McLuhan, foresaw a world shrunken by technology. The global village has indeed arrived—with a vengeance. Television and Internet providers deposit any part of the world they wish into our living rooms on a daily basis. Everybody's problems are now our problems. There is no "over there," and almost all problems worthy of mention today appear to require a global response. Having shrunk distances to the speed of light through the Internet, might not the U.S. government benefit from the habits of mind used by successful international companies operating in diverse world markets—habits that are equally relevant to the war on *irhab* (which is also a global phenomenon)? International businessmen know the folly of going into new markets without the assistance of capable local partners who understand the culture and who are connected to the right people. Should foreign policy be conducted any differently? When McDonalds entered France years ago, it brought with it American puritanism about alcohol: no beer, no wine. Local advice was ignored. After losing millions, it eventually adapted to the French way.

A NEED FOR BALANCE BETWEEN THE TEMPORAL AND THE ETERNAL

A new paradigm for international relations must take into account the growing transnational nature of much that goes on in the world today, the multicultural character of societies in a mobile world, and the slow recalibration of values brought about by the fouling of the world environment. This recalibration is not new; it goes back to Teilhard de Chardin,[16] the 20th-century French Jesuit priest and philosopher who was the first to integrate modern scientific and evolutionary findings with Christian doctrine. The process centers on finding the right balance between individual self-expression and the communal good; between flat, small-scale and large, hierarchical structures; between material and spiritual needs—all subjects in which Islamic voices are as prophetic as non-Islamic. In essence, the great debate that is emerging between cultures and within cultures is over the simple proposition of a Jewish teacher who once said, "Man does not live by bread alone." Muslims are not alone in wondering what has happened to the soul of western culture, which currently finds itself engulfed in self-indulgence, material excess, technological distraction, excessive litigiousness, and consumption beyond one's means. Nor are they alone in thinking it is the exclusion of the transcendent from politics that is the fundamental source of secular disorder. At its deepest level, this is a debate over whether modernization associated with technological progress equates to higher civilization.

Human beings throughout the world have the same basic needs and values. They have physical and material needs. They have emotional and spiritual needs—love, friendship, knowledge, self-expression, and moral development. Different cultures and subcultures mix them in different proportions. In the United States, the Amish, the Marine Corps, and Trappist monks are at one end of a spectrum where community well-being (family) trumps individual self-development and self-expression. Their communally defined rituals and values of modesty, moral integrity, self-restraint, and external dress make them closer to mainstream Islam than to mainstream American secular culture.

In place of the unidimensional rational actor model still in vogue within the national security community, this book proposes the adoption of an empathetic "whole actor" alternative. The whole actor, following nature, is also a multifaceted actor. More often than not, the whole actor has a transcendental sensibility akin to that expressed by the Little Prince in Saint-Exupéry's famous children's story who says, "What is essential is invisible to the eye."[17] Obviously, there is a diversity of opinion in the world on the subject of transcendent reality. Alcoholics Anonymous calls it the Higher Power. Atheists call it nonsense. Others may call it the Big Perhaps.

The human family can be divided very broadly into three groups: (1) *Believers*: Those observant believers in a creator of the universe (of all that is seen and unseen) by some name and who form communities of faith, ritual, and moral precepts. As Rabbi Gamaliel in the book of Acts suggests,[18] genuine religions withstand the test of time. Islam is a genuine religion that has thus far met that test. (2) *Agnostics and Gropers*: Those who do not actively participate in any formal faith community and who may also be against organized religion but who are not necessarily opposed to a belief in God (or spirit). Such people have often been impressed more by the destructive face of religious convictions throughout history than by the charitable and compassionate face. (3) *Materialists*: Those who believe only in phenomena that can be explained by human reason, while recognizing there are still things that humans do not yet understand. For convinced materialists, the grave is the end of the line and speculation about an afterlife is idle prattle.

They may recognize there is intelligence in nature, but they do not attribute it to a benevolent creator.

America was founded by men and women who were clearly *believers*. A cursory look at a map of the United States bears witness to their faith in a Supreme Power, with its Bethlehems, Shilohs, Bethesdas, Hebrons, Jerusalems, and hundreds of other biblical references. The majority of America's Founding Fathers were either Christians or Deists. They freely used such expressions as the Divine Architect, the Supreme Power, and the Divine Will. They found it reasonable to believe there cannot be a creation without a creator. Thomas Jefferson acknowledges such reasoning by making specific reference in the Declaration of Independence to the "Laws of Nature and Nature's God." No matter how much of creation can be explained by physics, chemistry, and mathematics, where did the law of thermodynamics originate? Albert Einstein, when asked if he believed in God, replied that his God was "the laws of physics." If the laws of physics are eternal laws, why can't uncovering those laws be viewed as a form of ongoing revelation in which scientists give witness to the interdependent order, complexity, and finesse of "Nature's God"? Indeed, for many religious people, nature itself is a form of divine revelation.

All things considered, it could actually be more rational to believe in a creator than not, since science doesn't really have much to say about origins. Isaac Newton observes an apple falling from a tree and develops a formula for predicting the rate of speed at which future apples will fall. All of a sudden, we own the phenomenon of apples (and by extrapolation, all objects) falling, when in actuality all we did was describe in mathematical terms what we saw. The following observation by Robert Jastrow, a self-proclaimed agnostic astronomer, sums it up:

Now we see how the astronomical evidence leads to a biblical view of the origin of the world. All the details differ, but the essential element in the astronomical and biblical accounts of Genesis is the same; the chain of events leading to man commenced suddenly and sharply, at a definite moment in time, in a flash of light and energy. . . . The scientist's pursuit of the past ends in the moment of creation. This is an exceedingly strange development, unexpected by all but the theologians. They have always accepted the word of the Bible: *In the beginning God created heaven and earth.* . . . For the scientist who has lived by faith in the power of reason, the story ends like a bad dream. He has scaled the mountains of ignorance; he is about to conquer the highest peak; as he pulls himself over the final rock, he is greeted by a band of theologians who have been sitting there for centuries.[19]

Or, as the renowned sociologist Peter Berger puts it, "The critique of secularity common to all the resurgent [religious] movements is that human existence bereft of transcendence is an impoverished and finally untenable condition."[20]

What different religious actors do with their beliefs is in part the focus of this book. This requires trying to understand why religion can be both a force for so much good and also for so much evil. Christianity has been used to justify the slaughter of Indians, the enslavement of blacks, the persecution of Jews, the killing of abortion doctors, the lynching of Mormons, and the killing and torture of other nonconforming Christians. Today, Christianity is being used by some to demonize Islam and Muslims more generally. Yet Christianity is also being used to embrace Muslims as brothers. The multiple faces of Christianity are no different than the multiple faces of Islam. There are Muslims who ignorantly demonize all Christians and Jews, and there are Muslims who protect Christians because the Qur'an encourages it.[21] The concerns of both non-Muslims and Muslims worried about the future of their faith are legitimate; some of the methods and rhetoric are not, if we wish to live together peacefully on a shrinking planet. A good beginning would be for non-Muslims to understand that most Muslims see themselves as agents of a theological imperative in which politics is considered to be a means rather than an end.

Although nonbelievers are as capable (or as incapable) of leading good, moral, and productive lives as believers, if one starts with the premise that human beings are made in God's image, it then becomes our challenge to emulate the Quakers in finding that spark of God in others, even those who reject the very notion of a spiritual realm. This approach can also be found in the Hindu greeting *Namaste*, which means "I bow to the divine in you." Ali, the son-in-law of the Prophet Muhammad, said much the same thing in the early days of Islam in a letter to his governor in Egypt concerning the governor's attitude toward his subjects, "Be not in the face of them a voracious animal, counting them as easy prey, for they are of two kinds: either they are your brothers in religion or your equals in creation."[22]

The tools that all of us have been given are reason and conscience. Even nonbelievers can usually accept the inherent reasonableness of the Golden Rule—as you want to be treated, so treat others. Like Newton's Third Law of Motion (for every action there is an equal and opposite reaction), human behavior also tends to be reciprocal. Anger begets anger and generosity begets generosity, though not necessarily in equal measure. This sets human nature apart from physical nature.

A nonreligious person, rather than invoking the Golden Rule, might say, "Let's put on their hat and look at the situation from their point of view." The ability to empathize with others, to see the world from their perspective, like brains or good looks, may not be dispersed in equal measure, but most humans are capable of empathizing at least some of the time.

EMPATHETIC ENGAGEMENT

A frequent message Americans hear from Muslims is to let Muslims combat radical Islam. American intervention, unless executed with much greater finesse and nuance than has been the case to date, has tremendous potential to make things worse. As is often said about the role of lawyers in an organization, America should "be on tap, not on top." The seeds of bitterness sown by a well-intended but deadly mixture of ignorance and destruction in the Iraq and Afghanistan interventions will have long-term consequences that can only be imagined. If the much less destructive intervention in Iran in 1953 (when our CIA collaborated with the British in the overthrow of then Iranian President Mohammed Mossadegh) is any clue, with its consequences 26 years later in the overthrow of the Shah and the subsequent seizure of the U.S. Embassy, it is critical that American leadership listen more attentively to what Muslims are saying—and not just westernized Muslims, or so-called moderate Muslims, but those in the opposition.

Why? In order to approach decisions differently, that is to say, empathetically, to ask ourselves some simple questions: How would we react if our sovereignty were violated in the casual manner with which we violate that of other countries? How would we react if some other country was pressing for regime change in America? How would Americans react to a foreign occupation? In his documentary film *The Fog of War*, Robert McNamara ruefully recounts his biggest mistakes with regard to the Vietnam War: failure to empathize with the enemy was number one.

America forgets at its peril its own history of rebellion against Great Britain, its cultural birthmother. Why do we assume that what would be unacceptable to us should be acceptable to others? More recently, a self-described Christian, Timothy McVeigh, showed us what a seeming disregard for American life by American officialdom can produce in our own country—violent hatred.[23] How much broader would be the reach of the Timothy McVeighs if an abusive American officialdom were kowtowing to a foreign power as it killed American citizens? It would be difficult to imagine for most Americans. It is not in our historical experience.

THE PARALLELS OF HISTORY

Islam is at war with itself. This is not a new insight, but it might be helpful to recognize analogous phenomena in our own culture. The so-called bad guys—the different varieties of theocrats or shari'ah-loving Muslims (which is most Muslims) do not bear a large difference from those Calvinists of the 17th century who populated the shores of New England. The attitude of many Muslims today toward their respective governments is similar to those hardy, morally outraged souls whom the Anglican Church collectively called the Dissenters. They were disgusted by the immorality and corruption of an English monarchy that called itself Christian, and they were persecuted for it.[24]

It could be said that the first American colonies in New England were founded by the Christian equivalent of *Salafis* (Muslims who seek to live their lives according to the literal teachings of Islam as manifested in the behavior of the Prophet); in other words, Christian believers who sought to live a life as close to the apostolic example of the followers of Jesus as humanly possible, guided only by holy scripture, to create "a shining city on a hill," bound not by regulations and laws but by "love in the heart." Just as for Muslims today, John Winthrop drew no distinction between church and state. The governance of the Bay Colony was based on divine law. Voters had to be members of the church. These dissenters, mockingly called Puritans by their detractors, soon fell out with each other over moral, theological, and political issues, producing a proliferation of subgroups in the process. Over time, a number of colleges were founded across the country to reflect these differing moral philosophies and denominational preferences.[25]

A similar phenomenon is happening within the Muslim world—division, fractionation that can be, and often is, not only religious in nature, but political and economic as well.[26] As expressed by one Muslim researcher, there are as many Islams as there are varieties of couscous. This produces a complex broth of forces that few can understand who are not from the region in question, and even those who are have great difficulty in doing so. Yet there is an underlying emotional fuel that is very similar to that which impelled American colonists to violence: a sense of injustice and its handmaiden, anger. To many in the Middle East today, America has simply replaced its now aged mother—Perfidious Albion.[27] Justice, not freedom, is the overriding issue.

What is needed is intelligence of mind and spirit together, which in Arabic is encompassed in the term *aql*. This is a word with no precise equivalent in English; but *aql* is necessary to grasp spiritual truths and is a quality that people possess in varying proportions.[28]

Fourth-century Christian monks inhabiting the Egyptian desert summarized the qualities compromising *aql* with a single word: discernment. The discerning monk avoids extremes. Discernment teaches him to walk the royal road, keeping him "from veering to the right, that is, with stupid presumption and excessive fervor beyond the boundary of reasonable restraint. It keeps him from going left to carelessness, sin, and sluggishness of spirit."[29] For Saint Anthony, discernment was ultimately "good sense." It is the "mother, the guardian and guide of all the other virtues." Jesus called it the eye and the lamp of the body. Yet discernment is only possible, Saint Anthony told his young monks, when one is truly humble. It requires openness to a higher wisdom. With this as our challenge, let us proceed to the here and now.

II

Orientation

CHAPTER 3

The Muslim View of the West

Nobody goes to the other side for fun. There must be a pain in your heart.
—Abdul Wahab, Afghan Taliban commander

While many Muslims admire citizen liberties in the West, including free speech and the fairness of our judicial system, they also harbor a number of deep-seated grievances. Foremost among them is the perceived impact on the Muslim world of U.S. foreign policy,[1] which is simultaneously perceived as meddling, imperialist, and colonialist in nature. Several years ago, Kurdish economist and political theorist Ismael Hossein-Zadeh of Drake University summed up these grievances as follows:

Proponents of the theory of "the clash of civilizations" attribute negative reactions in the Muslim world to the suffocating policies of the imperial powers almost exclusively to Muslims' fear of modernization. Yet, such essentially political reactions are prompted mainly by the predatory imperial policies and the unwelcome, onerous, and constant symbols of foreign presence in their lands, their markets, and their daily lives. That presence is imposed in a variety of ways: sometimes via direct military occupation, sometimes through military bases and advisors, sometimes through financial gurus of transnational corporations, sometimes through economic embargoes, and sometimes through aggressive commercialism and shabby cultural products such as violent video games or pornographic movies.[2]

The above concerns are not new and were expressed long before September 11, 2001. Nearly 50 years ago, the Iranian writer Jalal Al-e-Ahmad invented a new word to describe the effect of westernization on his society. His word in Farsi was *gharbzadegi*, which has been variously translated as "occidentosis," "westoxification," or "westernitis." It was introduced in a book clandestinely published in Iran in 1962 and was used to criticize Iran's imitation of western models of politics, culture, education, and economics, a process that Al-e-Ahmad claimed was destroying Iran's cultural identity. Ayatollah Khomeini conveyed the same sentiments in his speeches and writings:[3]

The poisonous culture of imperialism [is] penetrating to the depths of towns and villages throughout the Muslim world, displacing the culture of the Qur'an, recruiting our youth en masse to the service of foreigners and imperialists.[4]

More specifically, there is great concern throughout Islam over what Muslims perceive to be the destructive consequences of modernity and its value-free rationality: the triumph of materialism, the decline of morality, unequal global development, the collapse of family and community, and the erosion of religious belief itself.[5]

The Muslim attitude toward the West, however, was not always this negative. The earliest attitudes were developed at a time of unrivaled political and military success as the scope of early Islamic conquests (during the 100 years following the Prophet Muhammad's death) exceeded those of the Roman Empire at its peak. This success was interpreted as hard evidence of divine favor, and Christians and Jews living under Islamic rule in Moorish Spain were viewed as nonthreatening fellow monotheists whose own mandate to rule had come and gone. Thus for medieval Muslims, Europeans represented a living reminder of Islamic superiority. The first major challenge to this aura of greatness came in the 11th century with the launch of the first of a number of Christian Crusades to evict Muslims from the Holy Land.

Muslims ultimately retained their hold on the Holy Land, but their self-confidence suffered a major blow in the 15th century with the loss of Spain, the last Arab Islamic presence in the West. This, in turn, marked the beginning of Islam's subsequent displacement to the East by a dynamic European state system, a process that gained considerable momentum in the 16th century.[6]

Further influence was lost with the advent of colonialism arising from western exploration and the opening up of the New World. Prior to Marco Polo, Islamic traders had been the middlemen in Europe's highly lucrative trade with the Orient; but when European entrepreneurs realized that the middlemen could be bypassed as they exploited these new opportunities for wealth, the resulting economic stagnation in Islamic lands soon led to infighting and other forms of political-economic dysfunction.

The last vestige of Islamic self-confidence all but totally disappeared with the collapse of the Ottoman Empire and the abolishment of the caliphate in the wake of World War I. Effectively excluded from the shaping of modern history, Muslim resentment toward the subsequent colonialism of intrusive western powers became firmly rooted. As expressed by American scholars Nathan Funk and Abdul Aziz Said:

To this day, the experience of Western imperialism remains the overarching framework within which Muslims reconstruct their memories of the past. A widely shared impression among present-day Muslims is that Islam is struggling to regain its international stature after a prolonged eclipse associated with Western colonial expansion.[7]

The later treatment of Muslim-majority countries as proxies in the cold war, with little to no regard for their own aspirations, further exacerbated this resentment.

It is not stretching the bounds of credulity to conclude that the contemporary reaction of most Muslims to the West is one of defensiveness, a reaction that has been on full display in response to the post-9/11 efforts by the United States to exert its influence in South Asia and the Middle East. Feeling under siege by the West, there is a natural proclivity on the part of many Muslims to do whatever is necessary to protect Islamic values. Most of them reject terrorism and attacks on civilians as aberrations that contradict their religious norms, but they view al Qaeda as an understandable by-product of foreign hegemony and agree with its stated goals of (1) removing all U.S. military forces from Muslim countries, (2) including Islamist participation in the functions of governance, and (3) preserving and affirming Islamic identity. They also feel that western policies are contributing to the appeal of radical ideas. Finally, a majority of Muslims "see U.S. support for democracy in Muslim countries as conditional at best."[8]

The following is an abbreviated catalog of grievances that many Muslims currently harbor against the West, most of which relate in some way to the sentiments expressed above:

1. *The malaise/decline of Muslim societies is the legacy of European colonialism and American neocolonialism (implying that Muslims bear less responsibility than the West for their lack of democracy, poor economies, and the like).*

For several centuries, many Muslims lived under colonial rule. When the European powers divested themselves of their colonies in the middle of the 20th century, the contrived borders and unelected rulers of the new nation-states that resulted were often arbitrarily selected or approved by the Europeans. Later, a number of these same unelected rulers were overthrown by military dictators or juntas. A common Muslim complaint is that Europe and America effectively turned a blind eye to these events and supported whoever assumed power in order to secure their allegiance in the cold war and to ensure uninterrupted access to their oil.[9] (Western publics, however, point to government corruption, lack of education, and Islamic fundamentalism as the greatest obstacles to Muslim prosperity.)

When respondents to a Gallup poll were asked what the United States could do to improve the quality of life for Muslims in their home countries,[10] the most common responses after reducing unemployment and improving the economy were as follows: "Stop interfering in the internal affairs of Arab/Islamic states," "Stop imposing your beliefs and policies," "Respect our political rights and stop controlling us," and "Give us our own freedom."[11]

2. *Islamic extremism and terrorism are merely reactions to western imperialist policies.*

This is the broader concept that produces such claims as "The U.S. brought 9/11 on itself." The implication is that Muslims bear less responsibility than the West for the fact that extremism exists in Islam. As Hossein-Zadeh puts it:

While, for example, the establishment media, eagerly portrays every angry reaction to foreign aggression by every child anywhere in the Muslim world as a manifestation of Islamic fundamentalism, it rarely points out the fact that powerful fundamentalist Christian and Jewish forces support the more destructive military operations of geopolitical policies that trigger such violent reactions in the first place. . . . Western imperial policies in the Muslim world are, therefore, directly responsible for Muslims' resort to religion and the rise of fundamentalism because those policies prop up loyal but dictatorial rulers who suppress the economic and democratic rights of their people in order to safeguard their nefarious interests, along with those of their foreign patrons.[12]

3. *The West is an aggressor that has killed more people and committed more atrocities than Muslims.*

   - Hossein-Zadeh contends that "the atrocities committed in the name of Christianity far surpass those committed in the name of Islam."[13] To prove his point, he lists a page and a half of wars that were fought "in the name of Christianity and civilization."

   - In response to President Bush's 2005 speech to the National Endowment for Democracy, American Muslim activist Mauri' Saalakhan remarked, "When the 'insurgents' deliberately attack and kill innocent people (including Muslims), they demonstrate how far removed from Islam they are. But how many 'innocents' have been cold-bloodedly sacrificed (labeled collateral damage) by western forces, Mr. President?"[14]

   - Dr. Ahmad bin Muhammad, an Algerian professor of religious politics, stated on Al-Jazeera TV:

The guest from America asked how a young man could blow up a bus. If only she had asked how a president could blow up a peaceful nation in Iraq. How does a president help the arch-killer of occupied Palestine? Why doesn't she ask from where Hitler was brought up—Hitler, who murdered 50 million innocent people. Why doesn't she ask where the people who dropped two atom bombs on Japan were educated? Who killed three million innocent Vietnamese? Who annihilated the Indians? Who maintained imperialism to this day? Who waged the Spanish civil war, which exacted a toll of 600,000 in 36 months? Why don't we ask these questions? Who has over 15,000 nuclear warheads—Muslims or the non-Muslims? The Muslims or the Americans? The Muslims or the Europeans? We want an answer. Where was Bush educated—if education is really what makes a person a criminal? . . . Who invented slavery in recent centuries? Who colonized the other—us or them? Did Algeria colonize France, or vice versa? Did Egypt colonize England, or vice versa? We are the victims. [15]

4. *Western society's permissiveness is an assault on Islamic values.*

- When Gallup asked Muslims what they resent most about the West (in an open-ended question), "the most frequent response across all countries among moderates and radicals [was] 'sexual and cultural promiscuity,' followed by 'ethical and moral corruption,' and 'hatred of Muslims.'"[16]
- A 21-year-old Muslim student from Kenya stated in a 2006 survey:

The greatest change in my society has been a large-scale Westernization . . . Americanization of the community. Mostly it affects the young people from the way they think to the way they dress and act. . . . It has become rarer now to find a person as well versed in his own language as he is versed in English. Societal values are being lost as the people race to that which they see as better, with immorality, alcoholism, and such vices on the rise. It is becoming harder to find someone well versed in his religion in a community that once produced great scholars . . . a gradual but sure alienation of people from what is truly theirs.[17]

- When respondents from 10 Muslim countries were asked which attributes they associated with the United States, one of the top picks was "morally decadent" (64%).[18]

5. *The United States is not serious about spreading democracy and props up autocratic regimes.*

According to the Gallup poll referenced above, "Majorities in Jordan, Egypt, Iran, Pakistan, Turkey, and Morocco disagree that the United States is serious about spreading democracy in their region of the world."[19] Fifty-two percent of "moderates" disagree, while 72 percent of the "politically radicalized" disagree.[20]

The principal reason for this attitude is the fact that western rhetoric on freedom and democracy has often been accompanied by support for repressive leaders. A recent and poignant example of this was provided by the Bush 43 administration's vacillating rhetoric with respect to Egyptian democracy. In 2005, then Secretary of State Condoleezza Rice protested presidential opposition candidate Ayman Nour's imprisonment but appeared to backtrack when she returned to Egypt a year later to describe the Egyptian regime as part of "an important strategic relationship" (while failing to make any mention of Nour or the country's lack of democratic progress). Secretary Rice also described Egyptian, Jordanian, and six Gulf State autocrats as "responsible leaders," since they were part of the anti-Iran alliance in the region. Also buttressing this perception was the U.S. decision to sever relations with (and funding to) the Hamas-led Palestinian government despite the fact that it was democratically elected.

Almost two-thirds of the politically radicalized in 10 Muslim countries disagreed that the United States "will allow people in the region to fashion their own political future as they see fit without direct U.S. influence," while 48 percent of the political moderates held this view.[21] As expressed by Pakistani columnist Ayaz Amir:

It's one of the biggest myths of our time that America wants democracy to flourish in the lands of Islam. How can it when democracy doesn't suit its interests? If we have popular governments in Muslim countries the first thing they will demand is an end to American hegemony.

The Americans were happy with the Shah, they can't abide by democratic Iran. They can't abide Hamas which is the elected representative of the Palestinian people. They can't abide Hezbollah which has representative status in Lebanese politics. Democracy in the Muslim world and the interests of American foreign policy just do not mix.[22]

According to Saalakhan, "It appears 'Al Qaeda' has been a catch-all phrase of convenience for repressive [post-9/11] U.S. domestic and foreign policy. It has also provided many of America's allies with a green light to increase repression against legitimate calls for genuine democratization in their respective countries; and all of this is done in the name of another catch-all phrase, 'the war on terrorism.' "[23] Extremism often becomes the only avenue for political expression when these regimes effectively close off peaceful avenues for change.

6. *The War on Terrorism is really a war on Islam and Muslims.*

- Saalakhan states that one of America's five mistakes in the Muslim world is "advancing the notion of a *global Islamic conspiracy against the West.*"[24] He says there is a *"belief among Muslims around the globe that Islam has replaced communism as the new boogeyman on the block."*[25]

- American Islamic scholar Akbar Ahmed observed the following on his 2006 journey through the Muslim world:

I was not surprised therefore to find that the distorted perception of Islam in the West—which includes the attacks on the Prophet—was uppermost in the minds of Muslims when asked what they thought was the most important problem facing Islam. The expected answers—Israel, the plight of the Palestinians, the situation in Iraq—were all overshadowed by the idea that Islam was being maligned in the

West. Those planning a strategy in the capitals of the West to win the hearts and minds of the Muslim world need to keep this reality in mind.[26]

- Among the top responses in the Gallup poll to the question "What do you admire least about the West?" was "hatred or denigration of Islam and Muslims."[27] A major contributor to this perception has been the numerous diatribes against Islam and the Prophet Muhammad by prominent Christian leaders, who have millions of loyal American followers. The absence of a response in kind relates to the deep reverence that Muslims hold for the figures of Jesus and Mary, who are considered by Islamic tradition to be the only two humans since Adam and Eve not to have been touched by Satan at birth.

- "Substantial majorities in a 2007 WorldPublicOpinion.org survey of residents of Morocco, Indonesia, Egypt, and Pakistan said the United States' goal is to 'weaken and divide the Islamic world.' Most of those surveyed see the desire to spread Christianity in the Middle East as one reason behind this goal, and to keep Islam from growing and challenging the Western way of life as another."[28]

- A great deal of Muslim resentment has resulted from U.S. Homeland Security measures that have made it close to impossible for American Muslim charities to transfer donations to worthy causes in Muslim countries.

Among the other incidents since 9/11 that have played into the general perception that the West is waging a "war against Islam" are the Danish cartoons controversy, Pope Benedict's remarks at the University of Regensburg, prisoner abuse at Abu Ghraib and Guantanamo, and the public execution of Saddam Hussein.

No less than 75 percent of the Muslim world associates the word *ruthless* with the United States.[29] As noted by John Esposito, a Georgetown University professor and scholar of Islam, and Dalia Mogahed, Senior Analyst and Executive Director of the Center for Muslim Studies, The Gallup Organization:

One U.S. diplomat who was in Egypt when the Abu Ghraib scandal broke out said she was told by the locals: "We would expect this from our own government but not from you." Ironically, it may be because of America's idealized image as a beacon for democracy that its actions elicit such passionate anger. The perception is: For you, America, to go against your own values and how you would treat your own people and to abuse Muslims in this way means you must *really* despise us and our faith.[30]

Beneath this angst is a pervasive distress borne of a seemingly endless string of defeats on the world stage following the dissolution of the caliphate in the wake of World War I, Pakistan's losses to India, the Arab states to Israel, and Chechnya to Russia, to mention only a few. These reverses represented more than ordinary setbacks. Other religions either promise nothing (Judaism) or rewards in the afterlife. Islam, however, also promises victory on earth. The peaceful appeal of some Sufi orders notwithstanding, Islam grew to a considerable extent because of its initial victories. Defeat thus created serious doubts as to the religion's veracity. As summed up by Pakistani militant Maulana Masood Azhar, "Puritanical Islam faces extinction at the hands of an ascendant secular culture, just as the fledgling religion was challenged by unbelievers in its earliest days."[31]

7. *The United States is incapable of negotiating a fair peace in the Middle East because of its deep-seated favoritism toward Israel.*

In actuality the angst runs deeper than that. Because of the controversy surrounding its origins, the mere existence of the state of Israel is viewed as an affront to many Muslims who fail to understand why the Palestinians should pay the price for Nazi atrocities against the Jews. Indicative of this sentiment are the comments of former Secretary of State Dean Acheson in response to a question by John B. Henry, a Washington businessman who at that time was a Harvard student conducting research for his senior thesis on the Vietnam War. In the words of Henry:

It was the high point in my 2.5 hour interview with Acheson in his office at Covington & Burling in June 1970. David Halberstam, who was a speaker at my Kennedy Institute of Politics seminar, told me that I should ask the great man: "When a society gets bogged down in something irrational, how does it go about the process of extrication?" When I asked Acheson this question, I thought I was throwing him a softball on the Vietnam War. Acheson replied: "Young man, let me take you back to the Middle Ages when a Christian kingdom was founded in the middle of a hostile Islam. It lasted 90 years. There were three near misses. In the end, the sands of Islam blew and there was no more Christendom. Young man, let me tell you what is the biggest mistake in post-war American foreign policy. It isn't the war in Vietnam. It was the Truman Administration's decision to support the creation of the state of Israel. We will rue the day we ever did this. Whereas the crusades were an extension of European power to create a Christian kingdom, America's support for the state of Israel was an extension of American power to create a Jewish kingdom. From an Arab point of view, they are the same thing—a land grab."

THE TERRORIST MIND-SET

The above grievances are widely shared, but one must go deeper to understand the extremist's point of view. In response to the political reverses over time—colonialism chief among them—and the socioeconomic failure of most Muslim regimes, an aggravated siege mentality has taken root among most extremists in which all problems afflicting Muslims are seen to be the result of a carefully crafted conspiracy on the part of the United States, Israel, and various other suspects.

Many in the West have wondered how it is that Osama bin Laden can mount suicidal attacks against innocent civilians and declare a holy war against Christians and Jews when both innocents and People of the Book (Christians and Jews) are protected categories of people in the Qur'an and suicide itself is specifically prohibited. Perhaps a good place to begin is by examining how bin Laden rationalized this in his "Letter to America" published in the November 24, 2002, issue of the Manchester *Guardian*. After listing a number of grievances relating to Palestine, Somalia, Chechnya, Kashmir, Lebanon, and the actions of so-called puppet Arab regimes, he states:

It is commanded by our religion and intellect that the oppressed have a right to return the aggression. . . . Is it in any way rational to expect that after America has attacked us for more than half a century, that we will then leave her in security and peace?[32]

He goes on to say,

You may then dispute that all the above does not justify aggression against civilians, for crimes they did not commit and offenses in which they did not partake.[33]

In answering his own question, he keys to the fact that the American people choose their government through their own free will—a choice that stems from their agreement with its policies—and that they pay the taxes which

fund the planes that bomb us in Afghanistan, the tanks that strike and destroy our homes in Palestine, the armies which occupy our lands in the Arabian Gulf and the fleets which ensure the blockade of Iraq. So the American people are the ones who fund the attacks against us.[34]

And then he repeats,

Allah, the Almighty, legislated the permission and the option to take revenge. Thus if we are attacked, then we have the right to attack back. Whoever has destroyed our villages and towns, then we have the right to destroy their villages and towns. Whoever has stolen our wealth, then we have the right to destroy their economy. And whoever has killed our civilians, then we have the right to kill theirs.[35]

There are also forces internal to Islam to consider. As strategic analyst Michael Vlahos argues in *Terror's Mask: Insurgency Within Islam*, rather than thinking of Islamic militant activities as the work of terrorist groups within a particular political subculture of Islam, one should view their collective efforts as representing a broader insurgency within Sunni Islam. This insurgency is a struggle for the heart and soul of the faith as manifested in a mosaic of intersecting movements, or "brotherhoods," that work together as a single Muslim fraternity.

In its early history, Islam under the caliphate came close to creating a universal empire. Then it splintered and lost its cutting edge as it succumbed to the pleasures of life. Whenever this has happened, as it has periodically, a new leader would sweep in out of the desert to set things right and renew the corrupted *umma* (global community of Muslim believers). Bin Laden and his colleagues made specific reference to this drama of renewal in one of the several videos that were released following the attacks of September 11. To quote his companion in that video, "And the day will come when the symbols of Islam will rise up and it will be similar to the early days . . . of al-Ansar"—referring specifically to the supporters of Muhammad. And that is how a number of Muslims view bin Laden's activities today—as the emergence of a heroic leader to re-create the spiritual experience of the original struggle to establish a universal *umma*. Thus 9/11 is seen to be a transcendental achievement, not merely a passing gesture of martyrdom. The very act of struggle itself is a triumph that joins one to God and puts one on the path to renewal, a struggle that according to early Muslim scholars will last until the end of time.

The secular Sunni states—especially those of Egypt, Syria, and Algeria—also rank high as targets of this struggle. And, while hardly secular, Saudi Arabia is targeted as well, for having permitted the stationing of U.S. military forces on its holy soil. As Bernard Lewis, a widely recognized scholar of Islam, put it more generally:

By abandoning the law of God, the *Shari'a*, and replacing it with imported foreign laws and customs, they ceased to be Muslims. . . . Such rulers and those who carry out their orders are therefore infidels and as such are not entitled to the obedience of the believers. . . . Far from obeying such rulers, it is the duty of the true Muslim to disobey and indeed remove them in order to bring about a restoration of the true Islam through the enforcement of Holy Law.[36]

The vision that bin Laden offers as an imagined alternative to today's uncertainty, however, is that of a restored caliphate from an older, more tranquil world, especially that of the first four "rightly guided" caliphs. Although that period in Muslim history was a time of spectacular successes on the battlefield, the institution of the caliphate itself was marked by violent instability throughout.[37]

Finally, for some there is a strong psychological attraction to the militant pursuit of religious faith as well. Daveed Gartenstein-Ross, an American Jewish convert to Islam, who later became an FBI informant, offers the following observation:

Part of Islam's seduction is its otherness—how different it is from anything else. And it would be a mistake to shortchange how satisfying a life is inside radical

Islam. As I descended into radicalism, I had a greater feeling of certainty than I had known before. I felt that for the first time, I could truly comprehend and follow Allah's will—and I knew that those who disagreed with me were just following their own desires. There was a sense of community that came with this certainty. I was part of an exclusive club composed of those who could see beyond the shallow Western liberal values with which I was raised.[38]

THE WAHHABI DIMENSION

No discussion of terrorism and Islam would be complete without some treatment of Wahhabism, a branch of Islam founded on the ideas of the noted scholar Ibn Taymiyya around the turn of the 13th century. Taymiyya's ideas were revived in the 18th century in northeast Arabia under the leadership of Sheikh Muhammad ibn Abdul Wahhab. His interpretation of the Qur'an and shari'ah (Islamic law) competes with the four classical schools of Muslim thought. Wahhabism in its modern form is the strictest version of Islam; and although it is widely known to be strongly rooted in Saudi Arabia and Qatar, now most Wahhabis are South Asian rather than Arab because of the vast diffusion of the Deobandi movement. The Darul-Uloom madrasa founded in 1867 in the town of Deoband, Uttar Pradesh, India, trains teachers and preachers in a rigid version of Islam explicitly derived from Saudi Wahhabism, specifically to win over South Asian Muslims from the more tolerant traditional forms of Islam. The Darul-Uloom madrasa has given birth to more than 15,000 madrasas in India, Pakistan, the United Kingdom, and around the world that usually bear its name and are dedicated to its method (which uses Urdu as the language of instruction) and to its extreme doctrine. South Asian Muslims, who outnumber Arab Muslims, largely practiced syncretistic forms of Islam before the advent of the Deobandi movement—they used to worship alongside Hindus at the tombs of famous religious figures.

Employing Wahhab's ideas over the centuries, Muslim scholars have established a powerful conservative ideology based on the premise that all existing political regimes lack Islamic legitimacy and that Islam itself has become stale and weak. Wahhabis seek to revitalize both faith and society, hand in hand. The result is a hard-line movement seeking to reestablish Islam as it is perceived to have been in the time of the Prophet but to do so primarily through political activism. This type of religious fundamentalism can be threatening, but it is not inherently violent. Osama bin Laden has nevertheless commandeered a number of Wahhabi precepts in his rationale for violent struggle.

SCRIPTURAL MANIPULATION

It is important to note that bin Laden and his al Qaeda operatives do not stand alone in their use of violence in the name of religion. Other lim groups like Hezbollah, Jewish extremists like Kach, and the so-called Lord's Resistance Army of Uganda all carry out violent acts in the name of God. And that is just among the Abrahamic faiths. How are such terrorists able to manipulate religion so easily for their own violent ends? In looking at organizations identified with acts of terrorism, one sees a definite pattern in their methods. Perhaps the most used means for achieving religious legitimacy for violent behavior lies in the misuse of sacred texts. In his self-appointed role as a religious spokesman, bin Laden cites selected passages from the Qur'an and the Hadith to justify his actions.[39] One Qur'anic verse in particular, verse 29 of sura 9, constitutes a widely used call to violence for bin Laden and his colleagues:

Fight those who believe not In Allah nor the Last Day, nor hold that forbidden which hath been forbidden by Allah and His Messenger nor acknowledge the Religion of Truth, from among the People of the Book, until they pay the Jizya with willing submission and feel themselves subdued.[40]

Taken at face value, it seems clear that it is the duty of Muslims to fight the People of the Book unless they pay a special tax and submit to Muslim rule. But in the historical context to which the Qur'an is intimately tied, this passage refers specifically to the newly organized Muslim community in Mecca defending itself against its opponents, in this case, the Jews of Medina. This tax, or *jizyah*, is often cited as an example of Islam's fundamental bias against other religions. This is not supported, however, by the definition provided in the Qur'an. Indeed, it suggests quite the opposite.

As in any secular state, citizens of a Muslim state must contribute to the functioning of its government. This includes mandatory military service to defend the state or, at times, to expand Islam. However, the Qur'an holds that a non-Muslim cannot be compelled to fight for Islam. Hence, non-Muslims are given the choice of either fighting or paying a tax in support of the government's defense efforts. It is a tax without any of the religious precepts that accompany *zakat*, the mandatory tax paid solely by Muslims to help the poor. Thus, the *jizyah* is an accommodation to other religions that is intended to provide a fair sense of burden sharing in defending the state. To justify treating Christians and Jews as enemies of Islam, Osama bin Laden consistently highlights this verse without any reference to historical context. It is this kind of selectivity, or isolation of scripture, that is used to justify intolerance (and which perverts the true meaning of what was originally intended).

Another al Qaeda favorite is sura 4, verse 89: "Slay the enemy wherever you find them." Again, in isolation, this verse seemingly promotes an aggressive spirit of violence. However, if one continues on to verse 90, one finds the opposite to be the case: "If they leave you alone and offer to make peace with you, God does not allow you to harm them." Muslim extremists purposely overlook this verse and thus compromise the Qur'anic intent.

There is no end to the verses that al Qaeda can find to meet its ends, just as the Dutch Reform Church did to justify apartheid and Jewish zealots currently do in the West Bank. None of the Abrahamic faiths are exempt from the kind of selective theological justification that lays the groundwork for violent extremism. For example, one could highlight the unholy actions of King David in isolation from the rest of the Old Testament and come up with a very inaccurate picture of Judaism and Christianity; yet these words and deeds are part of the scriptural basis for both religions. It is easy to see how a priest or rabbi could elevate such aspects to the position of cardinal teachings and thereby create a divine mandate for violence.

Within Islam, there is a historically institutionalized process of independent reasoning called *ijtihad,* which has played an integral role in the intellectual history of the faith. *Ijtihad* allows the believer the freedom to find the true Islam through his or her own studies and thought, giving room to mystic Sufis and militant Islamists alike. Another way of putting it: *ijtihad* is the periodic reexamination of how religious values should inform daily life in light of major changes in the external environment. The doors of *ijtihad* were closed by most Sunni scholars in the 10th century, but individual Muslim scholars nevertheless continue their search. As Professor Abdul Aziz Said of American University has noted, however, "When Muslims were strong in various periods of history, they were open to new ideas. When they are weak, they are afraid of new ideas."[41]

MARTYRDOM AS A WEAPON

Central to the evolution of religious terrorism have been the activities of Hezbollah, the militant Shiite group operating in the Middle East. Under the spiritual leadership of Shaykh Fadlallah, Hezbollah took advantage of the chaos of war-ravaged Lebanon in the early 1980s to resist Israeli occupation.

Inspired and supported by the newly founded Islamic Republic of Iran, Fadlallah established a coalition of Sunni and Shiite Lebanese, as well as Palestinians, in opposition to the "common enemies of Islam," which included France, Israel, the United States, and the Maronite Christians of Lebanon. Fadlallah connected the plight of the Lebanese and Palestinian refugees to self-sacrifice as the only appropriate response for defending Islam. He promoted the righteousness of suicide by stressing martyrdom as a means for bringing back the Messiah, thus fulfilling the vision of the Qur'anic apocalypse. He used the concept of a cosmic war and the imminent approach of the "end times" to justify the use of violence by the faithful in the fight to overcome evil, thus creating a divine suicidal mandate for his followers.

Fadlallah's campaign calling for the unthinkable act of killing one's self in the name of religion, while unprecedented, was seemingly justified and politically well-timed. The disaffected youth in the refugee ranks seized on the concept of martyrdom as their best weapon against the otherwise insurmountable enemy that caused their suffering. Fadlallah's teachings focused on the violent and apocalyptic traditions of Islam and replaced the stagnant Palestinian nationalist movement with a religious one, thus giving a new sense of hope to those Arabs and Muslims who had made the Palestinian cause their own. Searching for a face-saving escape from years of humiliation, many Arabs were willing to accept Fadlallah's call for the creation of an Islamic state. A mass media campaign conveyed this thinking throughout the Arab world, and it was readily accepted on a broader scale. Social services provided by Hezbollah that were not being provided by the Lebanese government, much like those provided more recently by Hamas in Palestine, lent further legitimacy to Fadlallah's words. Political passions and the sense of injustice left by colonialism overwhelmed any concerns about unsound religious foundations and forever changed the Palestinian movement.

Another interesting and important perspective on those who commit suicide is provided by Ed Husain, a former radical British Muslim:

Another point that many of us fail to comprehend [is] that suicide bombers aren't some evil human beings walking in our midst. They're normal, caring individuals and it's that normality and sense of being caring when exploited by others that turns them into being suicide bombers.

And with specific reference to a friend who had recently served as a suicide bomber:

Because he didn't care for his own self and he cared for Palestinians in their repression as he saw them in Syria and also in Palestinian territories . . . it was that selflessness that he could give up his own life in order to serve them.[42]

WHEN RELIGION TRUMPS

Religious scripture, when retrieved selectively and applied situationally in combination with emotions of hatred and rage, becomes a powerful tool for justifying the unjustifiable. This is crucial for the religious terrorist for whom religious legitimacy dwarfs all other considerations. If religious terrorists can point to a "precedent" in sacred scripture or tradition, opponents will find it difficult to dispute the morality of their actions, despite their obvious contradiction with the overarching spirit of the religion. This is true of all major world religions, as illustrated by the recent bitter half-century conflict in Sri Lanka where the peaceful tenets of Buddhism were turned upside down to justify an endless stream of military atrocities.

Far from being any kind of logical extension of traditional Islam, the kind of nihilistic violence and revolution advocated by Osama bin Laden and others is akin to the revolutionary utopianism of Bolshevism and the Russian and Chinese revolutions.

—*HRH Prince Turki-al Feisal, Former Director General of the Saudi General Intelligence Directorate*

To provide a more graphic illustration of the relationship between religion and the terrorist mind-set, one has only to think about the passengers who overwhelmed the hijackers on United Flight 93, which crashed in Pennsylvania during the attacks of 9/11. As expressed by Islamic theologian Farid Esack:

The sure prospect of their own deaths didn't keep them from doing what they had to do to prevent greater harm, essentially to save a larger part of humankind. Difficult as this may be for us to understand, in the twisted minds of these suicide bombers, they too saw themselves as giving their lives so that a larger part of humanity may live. For them, the United States is the enemy, Satan incarnate, who is causing chaos and destruction around the world.[43]

One could quarrel with this analogy simply by noting that the Americans' activities were inspired by their love for life, while the *irhabis* were motivated by their desire for death and martyrdom.

Finally, from the vantage point of al Qaeda's leadership, one might hypothesize the following perspectives:

1. They see our friendship and cooperation with some fraction of the world's 1.5 billion Muslims as the principal obstacle to their quest for global control under a restored caliphate.

2. Their immediate objective is to expel us from the Middle East so they can (1) overthrow the Arab regimes that depend on us and (2) end the corrupting influence of godless secularism on their culture.

3. They see the confrontation as a war of wits, not capabilities. To the extent that they can use asymmetric warfare to inspire us to overreact by killing, incarcerating, or otherwise persecuting Arabs or other Muslims who may not be sympathetic to al Qaeda, it plays directly into their hands by expanding the pool of future terrorists. As retired Ambassador Chas Freeman cogently stated in reference to Abu Ghraib and our resort to rendition, "In the years of struggle between us, al-Qaeda has not been brought to question its core values or change them. Demonstrably, we have."[44]

4. They are playing us like a concert piano, not only by manipulating our reactions, but by capitalizing on our miscues. By invading Iraq, we effectively transformed an intervention in Afghanistan that had the general support of the Muslim world into what to them now looks like a wider war against Islam. And by implicitly or explicitly equating Islam with terrorism through our careless lexicon, we only exacerbate the situation by making it more difficult for our Muslim friends to cooperate with us in opposing the extremism that threatens them as well.

In all probability, bin Laden and his associates look at the economic crisis in the West and conclude that the return on investment of their 9/11 attacks has astronomically exceeded their wildest dreams. Actually, it goes far deeper than that. Because the collapse of the twin towers of the World Trade Center exceeded al Qaeda's expectations, the fact that they did collapse was interpreted as divine endorsement (much like Islam's early successes on the battlefield during its first 100 years). According to al Qaeda, the hijackers didn't bring down the towers—God did.

CHAPTER 4

The Western View of Islam

How do you understand if you can't differentiate?
How can you differentiate if you don't understand?

—Oliver W. Holmes

The act of listing grievances can be a debilitating exercise, but any move to foster improved relations between Islam and the West will have to take into account the full array of concerns on both sides. In some respects, western grievances are no less severe than those of Islam.

Despite a number of lower-level attacks against the West over the final two decades of the 20th century, Islamist extremism did not rank particularly high among the concerns of most westerners. For the United States alone, these attacks ranged from seizure of the U.S. Embassy and its staff in Iran in 1979 to the blowing up of the U.S. Marine barracks in Lebanon in 1983, the 1993 attack on the World Trade Center in New York, the 1996 bombing of the U.S. Air Force Khobar Towers residential complex in Saudi Arabia, the bombing of the U.S. embassies in Kenya and Tanzania in 1998, and the attack in Yemen on the USS *Cole* in 2000.[1] After September 11, 2001, any perceived complacency changed dramatically, and the reverberations are still being felt.

A Pew Global Attitudes Project poll taken five years after 9/11 showed that "many in the West see Muslims as fanatical, violent, and as lacking tolerance."[2] Majorities of Americans and Western Europeans who have heard of the Danish cartoons controversy credit Muslim intolerance to different points of view as being more to blame for the tensions than any western disrespect for Islam.[3] And in a 2007 poll, also by Pew, "twice as many people use negative words as positive to describe their impressions of the Muslim religion (30% vs. 15%)."[4] More recently, an ABC News/*Washington Post* poll on U.S. views of Islam conducted in March 2009 indicated that 48 percent of all Americans held an unfavorable opinion of Islam—its highest unfavorable rating in these polls since 2001.[5]

HISTORICAL CONTEXT

Despite the seemingly situational nature of western angst toward Islam in the wake of 9/11, the roots of western disenchantment actually run much deeper. In contrast to the previously mentioned political success and cultural self-confidence experienced by early Islam vis-à-vis the West, western attitudes toward Islam were characterized by significant insecurity in the face of the major theological challenge posed by Islam's rise in the seventh century and the ensuing Arab conquests of huge swaths of territory, ranging from Spain to the Byzantine and Persian empires, that quickly followed. Although Islam has understandably been referred to as a "religion of the sword," Mahatma Gandhi had a different view:

I became more than ever convinced that it was not the sword that won a place for Islam in those days, in the scheme of life. It was the rigid simplicity; the utter self-effacement of the Prophet; his scrupulous regard for pledges; his intense devotion to his friends and followers; his intrepidity; his fearlessness, his absolute trust in God and in his own mission. These, and not the sword, carried everything before them, and surmounted every obstacle.[6]

Adding further credence to Gandhi's view is an earlier observation by French historian Gustave LeBon regarding the early advance of Islam in his book *La civilization des Arabes*:

It is obvious that persuasion alone could bring the peoples who conquered the Arabs later, like the Turks and the Mongols, to adopt it. In India, where the Arabs only passed through, the Qur'an spread so far that it counts today more than fifty million adherents. . . . The spread of the Qur'an in China was not less considerable . . . though the Arabs never conquered the least piece of the Celestial Empire.[7]

Islam was victorious for the first thousand years in its competition with Christianity. Once Christianity ended its internal wars at Westphalia in 1648, however, it began expanding in earnest; and Islam has been losing ground ever since. Thus, no small part of today's violence can be attributed to a civilizational grievance.

The dominant image in the West over the centuries was that Islam was irrational, prone to violence, and a threat to western ideals and values. The fact that Islam seemingly gives greater credence to the bonds of religious solidarity than it does to principles of nationality deriving from the Peace of Westphalia only added to this negative image.[8]

The problem today is exacerbated by unbalanced reporting in the western media, which provides almost no coverage for the helpful initiatives of mainstream, peaceful Muslims. Among other manifestations, these have included innumerable *fatwas* against terrorism issued by top Islamic religious leaders both in the United States and overseas.[9] This negative conception has remained intact up to the present in one form or another, with western attitudes ranging from indifference during the period of European colonialism to outright hostility in the wake of 9/11. Aside from isolated and intermittent periods of peaceful coexistence and cooperation such as those that periodically existed under Islamic rule in Andalusia, Baghdad, and Constantinople,[10] the western attitude toward Islam has generally been one of nonacceptance.

THE EUROPEAN QUESTION

A number of books published since 9/11 portray the threat of Islamic radicalism in near-apocalyptic terms. By far the most common theme of such books is the idea that Europe constitutes the critical battleground in the struggle against Islamist extremism, which is out to destroy the western world and will one day succeed if urgent action is not taken to counteract it.

For Europe, the secular state has historically equated to a publicly distanced relationship between church and state in which religion is effectively relegated to one's personal life. There is reason to believe, however, that this secularist label masks a still-strong cultural-religious identity in which many Europeans "believe without belonging."[11] In Germany, for example, without significant public discussion or dissent, the government collects church taxes that support the main religious institutions in Germany; religious organizations dispense most of Germany's foreign aid; and religious organizations and their subsidiaries provide many social services. Religion also influences Germany's foreign policy in at least three key areas: peace, the fight against poverty, and protection of the environment. In a recent poll, two-thirds of the respondents stated that they would like to see more involvement from German churches in ethical international questions and in certain domestic questions.[12]

A full 75 percent of Protestants in Germany indicated that one can believe in God without going to a religious service on Sunday, thus broadening the definition of religion to include moral behavior and values without the necessity of institutions.[13] Coupling this reality with the fact that some new members of the European Union (EU), like Poland, bring with them strong religious traditions and that Islam itself has already become a permanent feature of the European cultural landscape, it seems clear that Europe's secular image will only erode over time. Whether it does or does not, most scholars of religion agree that European secularization is the global exception rather than the rule.[14]

Meanwhile, to avoid the widespread discontent among European Muslims that has already manifested itself in the London bombings, French riots, and the like, it is clear that Europe will have to do a better job of creating a pluralist society to which Muslims can feel they belong and in which they have a political stake to protect. In contrast to the inclusive, equal-opportunity environment of the United States,[15] Europe's attempts at integration have fallen short of what is needed largely because of structural hurdles that result in job discrimination, poor education, and substandard living conditions. Inadequate citizenship opportunities also weigh in the balance.[16] Forty percent of Muslim youth in America between the ages of 18 and 29 consider themselves to be "thriving," whereas that number drops to 7 percent in the United Kingdom.[17] Radicalism can become the de facto avenue of choice in the face of such hurdles since it seemingly offers simple answers to complicated global problems and provides a sense of belonging that the surrounding secular society is unable to provide.

In the words of former British Muslim radical Ed Husain,

At home we were exposed to one culture; at school we were exposed to another. So Britishness was never clearly defined for my generation growing up. And the fact that we've got communities up and down the country that live totally separate lives—I mean in the name of multiculturalism, we've created these monocultural ghettos.[18]

Included among the western grievances are the following:

1. *Europeans are chiefly concerned about current demographic trends.*

There must be an average of 2.1 live births per woman for a population to sustain itself (the "replacement rate"), and most of Europe is well below that rate.[19] The collective impact of high Muslim birthrates, coupled with liberal immigration policies, has resulted in a rapid growth of the Muslim populations in these countries at the same time that indigenous European populations are shrinking. In the last 30 years alone, the Muslim population in Europe has effectively tripled, making Islam the fastest growing religion in Europe today.[20] As one political commentator has warned,

Over the next four decades, there will be a vast emptying out of Central and Eastern Europe: Germany's population down 10.3 percent, Poland down 20.5 percent, the Russian Federation down 24.3 percent, Bulgaria down 35.2 percent. And in Western Europe the only population increase will be almost entirely due to the great migration from Africa and Asia. . . . What does it mean for the United States when the other half of the transatlantic alliance enters a demographic death spiral and becomes semi-Muslim in its socio-cultural-political character?[21]

Other scholars, however, have called such predictions into serious question. Jack Goldstone, professor and director of George Mason University's

Center for Global Policy, for example, says that predictions of Muslims soon dominating Europe are "outlandish" and estimates that the 3 to 10 percent of the Muslim population in major European countries will, at most, double by midcentury.

Europe, in its 50 countries and territories, has about 38 million Muslims, which constitutes roughly 5.2 percent of the continent's total population.[22] In France, which houses the highest percentage of Muslims in Western Europe, Muslims comprise 6 percent of the population. In Spain and Italy, Muslims comprise between 1 and 2 percent and less than 1 percent respectively.[23]

Esther Pan, former staff writer for the Council on Foreign Relations, reported for the *New York Times* that about one million Muslims immigrate to Western Europe every year; and by 2050, Muslims will comprise one in five Europeans.[24] By the same token, the Population Reference Bureau has reported a decline in the fertility rates of Muslim immigrants over time, often at a rate higher than those among non-Muslims. In Austria, for example, fertility rates among Muslims fell from 3.1 to 2.3 between 1981 and 2001 but remained higher than that of Roman Catholics, whose rates dropped from 1.7 to 1.3.

The narrowing fertility gap can also be seen in the Netherlands, where in 1990, women from the predominantly Muslim countries of Morocco and Turkey had fertility rates of 4.9 and 3.2 respectively. By 2005 though, these numbers had dropped to 2.9 and 1.9. While these recent rates are still higher than that for Dutch women (1.7), the trend nevertheless runs counter to the alarmist projections. Whatever the actual pace of transformation, the associated rhetorical claims have a sobering ring:

- Colonel Gaddafi: "There are signs that Allah will grant Islam victory in Europe—without swords, without guns, without conquests. The fifty million Muslims of Europe will turn it into a Muslim continent within a few decades."[25]
- Mullah Krekar (Norwegian imam): "Just look at the development within Europe, where the number of Muslims is expanding like mosquitoes. Every western woman in the EU is producing an average of 1.4 children. Every Muslim woman in the same countries is producing 3.5 children. . . . Our way of thinking will prove more powerful than yours."[26]
- A T-shirt popular among young Muslims in Stockholm reads "2030—then we take over."[27]
- As prophetically expressed by Algerian President Boumédienne before the UN General Assembly in 1974, when commenting on south/north immigration, "Victory will come to us from the wombs of our women."[28]

Even if the majority of Muslims in Europe are not violent, there is wide concern that unfavorable demographic trends coupled with the general reluctance of mainstream Muslims to speak out against the violence will provide a soft cushion of support for the extremists. It should thus come as no surprise that a Gallup poll taken in six European countries during 2007 revealed that clear majorities in each felt that greater interaction between Islam and the West would be threatening to their cultural identities.[29] Nor does it strain the imagination to envision growing anti-immigration sentiment ultimately leading to a new European isolationism.

2. *The general European commitment to multiculturalism and tolerance is causing Europeans to make unwarranted concessions to Muslims and to appease them in ways that will ultimately undermine western values and lead to the "Islamification" of Europe.*

   a. Gradually adopting shari'ah law in European countries and Canada, little by little.
      - In February 2008, the Archbishop of Canterbury suggested that elements of shari'ah should be permitted within the confines of Muslim communities in the United Kingdom where English law could contradict Muslim cultural mores and social values.[30]
      - An Ottawa government report recommended legalizing polygamy.[31]
      - Both the British and Ontario governments have confirmed that "thousands of polygamous men in their jurisdictions receive welfare payments for each of their wives,"[32] which de facto amounts to a form of government-funded shari'ah.

   b. Altering western cultural symbols and behavior so as not to offend Muslims.
      - Non-Muslim females in heavily Muslim neighborhoods in France, the United Kingdom, and the Netherlands are wearing headscarves in order to avoid the taunts or jeers of their neighbors.[33]
      - The practice of flying the English flag over English prisons has been banned because it shows the cross of Saint George, which was used by the Crusaders and is thus considered offensive to Muslim inmates. The flag has also been removed from Heathrow Airport and the British equivalent of the Department of Motor Vehicles. Similarly, the Church of England is also considering removing Saint George as the country's patron saint.[34]
      - The mayor of Lille, France, held a meeting with an imam at the edge of a Muslim neighborhood in deference to his demands that she not enter "Muslim territory."[35]

   c. Changing the educational systems.
      - Riksdorfer Elementary School, by German court ruling, must teach its mostly Muslim students an Islamic curriculum.
      - In Milan, school officials are acceding to Muslim parents' demands that their children be put in Muslim-only classes to insulate them from the secular atmosphere of the democratic West.[36]

3. *Radical Muslims are using European democratic freedoms and social welfare programs to advance their extremist cause.*

- Mosques and madrasas that advocate extremism in Norway and the Netherlands receive government subsidies.[37]
- The four July 21 London bombers had collected more than £500,000 in welfare benefits.[38]
- Muhammad Metin Kaplan, while on German welfare, set up the Islamist group Caliphate State and was extradited to Turkey for planning to fly a plane into Kemal Ataturk's mausoleum.

4. *The ghettoization of European Muslims (the fact that they are not integrating) is a threat to western culture. Most of whatever assimilation is taking place consists of European communities accommodating their Muslim populations rather than the other way around.*

- Illustrative of the nonassimilation of Muslim populations is the fact that 80 percent of Pakistani Britons marry their relatives.[39]
- Many Muslims in Europe are alienated, which breeds violence: a Hamburg cell was instrumental in executing 9/11; the shoe-bomber was British; and a London School of Economics graduate ordered Daniel Pearl's execution.
- Immigrants to Europe bring numerous customs that are flagrantly inconsistent with the western commitment to human rights.[40]

Recent European initiatives to "fight back" by banning the burka in France and prohibiting the use of full-face veils in public places in Belgium (with similar measures being contemplated in other European countries as well), though understandable, suggest a looming confrontation between human rights, security considerations, and "national values," a confrontation that will likely exacerbate the challenges of integration.[41]

Beneath the surface of these challenges lies yet another dynamic that also bears mentioning—that of indifference. As expressed by Maria J. A. van Hoeven, Minister of Economics and former Minister of Education, Culture, and Science for the Netherlands:

Until a few years ago, the Netherlands was known as a tolerant country, in the sense that everyone was welcome and it was taken for granted that everyone would retain their own language and culture. My assessment is that we have taken this a bit too far. Our famous tolerance has degenerated into indifference. This makes people feel excluded—sometimes literally because they do not speak the language—so that they retreat into their own bastions and cultivate their own truths.[42]

AMERICAN LEANINGS

Such concerns are not limited solely to Europe. In the United States, despite its more effective integration policies, one finds the beginning of similar, albeit less threatening, trends:

- In 1997, Nike was forced to recall more than 38,000 pairs of shoes with the word *air* written in flames, because some Muslims said the writing appeared to resemble the word *Allah* in Arabic.[43]

- Seattle has instituted gender-separate, Muslim-only swim sessions in its municipal pools.[44]
- The Massachusetts Supreme Court ruled that Muslim prisoners must be served special foods for religious holidays, including ox and camel.[45]
- In January 2008, Harvard established women-only workout hours at one of its campus gyms to accommodate the request of six female Muslim students.[46]
- School District 122 in Ridgeland Township, Illinois, banned pork from its lunchroom menus to accommodate Muslim students.[47]

Implicit in all such measures is the belief among pious Muslims that Islamic religious imperatives inherently trump the needs or wants of "unbelievers." As author Mark Steyn has put it, "What happens when a Western world so in thrall to platitudes about boundless 'tolerance' allows the forces of intolerance to carve it out from the inside?"[48] In Europe at least, the continued tolerance of intolerant Muslims could ultimately threaten the civil liberties and individual rights that European culture has so painfully achieved over the centuries.

During the same period when the earlier-mentioned Muslim attacks against the United States were taking place, America intervened militarily to assist Muslims on no fewer than four occasions in Bosnia, Kosovo, Somalia, and Kuwait. The results in each of these interventions are well-known, but lost in most tellings of Somalia are the more than 100,000 Somali lives that were saved as a result of the humanitarian aspects of that intervention.[49]

By the same token, many Americans can recall the pictures of Muslims overseas dancing in the streets immediately following 9/11. Yet even as they were dancing, then President Bush was visiting the Islamic Center in Washington to declare his support for Islam as a "religion of peace" (in order to minimize a possible backlash against Muslims in the United States). Conservative columnist Charles Krauthammer notes:

In those years since Sept. 11—seven years during which thousands of Muslims rioted all over the world (resulting in the death of more than 100) to avenge a bunch of cartoons—there's not been a single anti-Muslim riot in the United States to avenge the massacre of 3,000 innocents. On the contrary, in its aftermath, we elected our first Muslim member of Congress and our first president of Muslim parentage.[50]

American Muslims have experienced a number of difficulties ranging from infringements on their civil liberties to seemingly onerous treatment by customs agents when reentering the country. Most of this has been driven by the fear of a second attack. It is important to recall that ever since the War of 1812, the United States has historically been an open country. After 9/11, it could no longer afford that luxury. It is natural that the pendulum of reactive consequences may have swung a bit too far, but it will eventually swing back to a more acceptable midpoint, so long as no further attacks take place. If a second attack bearing Muslim fingerprints does take place, it is not only American Muslims who will have to worry. The civil rights of all Americans will be at risk as the United States gravitates toward a police state, seeking greater security in an increasingly insecure world.

Meanwhile, the respective concerns that Muslims and non-Muslims have will require that each puts on the hat of the other and views the situation from the other's perspective before significant progress toward a cooperative relationship will be possible. As challenging as this might sound, there are signs that such a rapprochement could still be possible.

A DOOR AJAR

The grievances are many and run deep, but the door is by no means closed to the possibility of improved relations. Indicative of this openness are the following polling data relating to Muslim perceptions of the West:

- Muslim respondents frequently suggest their societies are "eager to have better relations with the West." In Saudi Arabia, Morocco, and Lebanon, for example, the percentage who say a better understanding between Western and Muslim cultures concerns them outnumbers that of those who say that it does not by a margin of 2 to 1.[51]

- The most frequent responses to the open-ended question of what the West can do to improve relations were (1) demonstrate more respect/consideration; (2) do not underestimate the status of Arab/Muslim countries; and (3) make an effort to understand Islam as a religion, and don't downgrade what it represents.[52]

- When asked what Muslims could do to improve relations, one of the top responses was "improve the presentation of Islam to the West and present Islamic values in a positive manner."[53] Muslims also tend to agree with Americans about those aspects of Muslim societies that they admire least, with "extremism" and "close-mindedness to the ideas of others" ranking high on the list.[54]

- One of the top reasons for the resentment of most Muslims is the perceived immorality and cultural depravity of the West, yet when asked what can be done to improve relations, they typically make no mention of this and instead focus on political grievances: "What Muslims request for better relations has nothing to do with asking people of the West to change who they are, but rather what they do: to respect Islam and Muslims and make concrete changes in certain aspects of foreign policy."[55]

- In numerous interreligious dialogue encounters between Muslims and conservative Christians, common ground is often found in moral concerns relating to children, family values, television's influence, and the like.

- According to a February 2008 WorldPublicOpinion.org study, a clear majority of Iranians favor taking steps to improve U.S.-Iranian relations, including direct talks (57%), greater cultural/educational/sporting exchanges (63%), increased trade (64%), greater access to one another's journalists (70%), and more tourism between Iran and the United States (71%).[56]

- American Muslims, by a nearly 2 to 1 margin (63%–32%), don't see any contradiction between being a devout Muslim and living in a modern society.

Furthermore, most of them have a positive view of American society in general and like the communities in which they live.[57]

Western perceptions of Islam vary considerably from one country to the next, but American views generally improve in proportion to (1) the degree of engagement that exists between those countries and the United States and (2) the degree to which individual Americans have established personal relationships with Muslims from the countries in question.[58] The above-mentioned Pew poll confirmed that 56 percent of those who knew a Muslim had a favorable opinion of Muslims, as compared to 32 percent of those who did not. About 45 percent of Americans know someone who is a Muslim, even though Muslims account for less than 1 percent of the total population. As summed up in the March 2009 ABC News/*Washington Post* poll:

The broad relationship between knowledge and sentiment . . . is positive. Overall, people who feel they understand Islam, or who have a Muslim friend, are 22 points more apt to view the religion favorably and 17 points more apt to see it as peaceful, compared with those who lack a basic understanding or a friend who's Muslim.[59]

ON-THE-GROUND REALITIES

Most indicators show that Americans generally support the idea of reaching out to Muslims, but doubt was shed in the summer of 2010 with the controversy surrounding the proposed building of the mosque and cultural center near Ground Zero in New York City. The debate that ensued over religious freedom on the one hand and respect for hallowed ground on the other was intense; but while a majority of Americans opposed a mosque near Ground Zero, most would describe U.S. Muslims as patriotic citizens.[60] Moreover, Muslims in America feel safer and freer than anywhere else in the western world.[61]

The appointment of a Special Envoy to the Organization of the Islamic Conference (OIC) by President Bush in 2008 and the appointment of a U.S. Special Representative to Muslim Communities by President Obama in 2009 are additional indicators of American openness to improved relations. Moreover, in his inaugural address, President Obama stated, "To the Muslim world, we seek a new way forward, based on mutual interest and mutual respect."[62] And in his first official interview, which was conducted by the Arab satellite station Al-Arabiya, the President stated, "My job is to communicate the fact that the United States has a stake in the well-being of the Muslim world; that the language we use has to be a language of respect."[63] Finally, to give meaning to the idea of being a stakeholder in "the well-being of the Muslim world," President Obama has established a Global Engagement Directorate within the National Security Council that actively facilitates cooperative initiatives between the United States and Muslim countries in areas ranging from scientific research to combating disease. In April 2010, the Directorate sponsored an "entrepreneurship summit" for Muslim businesses from around the world.[64]

Most Americans and most Muslims, according to recent Gallup poll findings, share a common belief that religion is or should be a key pillar of society, that society should be informed and guided by the Bible or Qur'an, and that family values should be preserved. Common values include political participation, freedom of speech, social justice, and, notably, the eradication of extremism. Both worlds also share the same desires for economic security, employment, and the ability to provide for one's family.[65] Finally, a letter to Christian church leaders entitled "A Common Word Between Us and You" from 138 Muslim clerics and scholars in September 2007 called for interfaith dialogue and increased understanding based on Islam's and Christianity's common beliefs in love of God and love of neighbor. It sparked a welcome response from the Christian community that continues to this day.[66]

SUMMING UP

Anwar Ibrahim, former Deputy Prime Minister of Malaysia, attributes the perceived dichotomy between Islam and the West as springing from the western view of itself as a bastion of reason and enlightenment and its view of Islam as "superstitious, barbaric and dark." By the same token, the Muslim world sees the West as a "moral wasteland where the institution of the family has broken down and religion and morality have ceased to have any bearing on social mores."[67]By pointing to the past and calling attention to the present, Ibrahim offers both hope and a challenge:

If we view the past relationships between Islam and the West objectively, we cannot escape the significance of the extended periods of peaceful coexistence. These episodes are not merely confined to the annals of history, for example the well-known story of Muslim Spain. A close study of Islam in Southeast Asia today proves there is in Islam a current that is essentially an embodiment of tolerance and pluralism . . . I am convinced that if we go beyond the noise of the day and reflect more on higher ideals we will discover more of the similarities than the differences. The challenge is to conceive a common vision of the future that goes beyond our current concerns and preoccupations, advancing towards the creation of a global community dedicated to the higher ideals, of both civilizations.[68]

Sound advice, but the current reality in which the West perceives Islam as a threat to its well-being and Islam feels under siege by the West suggests the formidable nature of the task that lies ahead.

CHAPTER 5

Bridging the Cultural Divide

Amid our perceived differences, we tend to forget how the world's different religions, ideologies, and political systems were meant to serve humans, not destroy them.

—Dalai Lama

In some circles, the clash between Islam and the West is largely perceived as a clash between Islam and Christianity. If so, one cannot help but wonder why these two world religions, which share so much in common theologically, either talk past one another at best or, alternatively, resort to conflict to settle their differences. Some of this is undoubtedly attributable to the fundamental difference between the Muslim concept of life based on integration of religion and politics versus the western concept in which the realms of God and Caesar are kept separate, but the problem in actuality is more accurately a clash between Islam and secularism (rather than Christianity). The secularism of the United States, however, is significantly different from that which prevails in Europe. This is due in part to the fact that American independence predated the French Revolution.

Prior to the colonization of America, England had evolved from an absolute to a constitutional monarchy—from roots in the Magna Carta and the birth of Parliament, through the civil war and Glorious Revolution, to the establishment of political parties and the triumph of the prime minister in the 18th century. The relationship between religion and state, however, survived this evolutionary process, and America's Founding Fathers leaned heavily on their religious faith as they set about creating the American experiment. They were acutely mindful, however, of Europe's religious wars of the past and the degree to which unleashed religious passions could undermine the established order. Accordingly, they took great care to avoid a national endorsement of any particular religion. This process was consistent with the philosophy of Edmund Burke, whose idea of progress consisted of making changes at the margin while retaining the accumulated wisdom of those who had gone before.

The forces underlying the French Revolution, on the other hand, identified the corruption of the state with the Catholic Church and the divine right of kings; and in the tradition of Jean-Jacques Rousseau, discarded the old to make way for the new. So while religion became an important part of the glue that binds in America (as Tocqueville aptly noted during his visit to the United States in 1831), in Europe, it was effectively purged to make way for secular humanism.

Thus, when Americans say "secular," Muslims hear "Godless," though what is intended is "freedom to worship as you please." Muslims hear "Godless" in part because of the cultural image that we project, but they also misunderstand how religious the United States really is. The reaction of five high-ranking Muslim officials from Kashmir and the Sudan when they attended the National Prayer Breakfast in Washington, D.C., in 2004 was indicative of this misunderstanding. Following the breakfast and the two days of activities surrounding it, every one of them expressed surprise at the degree to which religious faith underpins the American democratic process. They indicated that they felt much closer to us (Americans) as a result.

The United States and its coalition partners understandably elected to pursue a hard-power response to the attacks of 9/11. However, unless this is complemented with an effective strategy of cultural engagement, the likely outcome in the long run will be an expansion of the pool of future terrorists. The stakes have simply become too high to neglect the influence of culture and, more particularly, religion in our practice of international relations.

THE CULTURAL CHALLENGE

In his *Clash of Civilizations*, the late Samuel Huntington postulated that "culture and cultural identities, which at the broadest level are civilizational identities, are shaping the patterns of cohesion, disintegration, and conflict in the post–Cold War world."[1] In some respects, he was making the same argument that conflict resolution theorists Edward Azar, John Burton, and Herbert Kelman had made before him—that conflict is based on the fulfillment of human needs, one of the most important of which is a sense of identity. The human need for self-identity is, in fact, so strong that it often takes precedence over self-preservation, food, shelter, and other basic needs. A conflict becomes intractable when identity is involved and takes the form of defining one's self in opposition to someone else. Left unattended, such a definition can lead to a need to negate that someone else.

A strategy of cultural engagement would thus require that the United States refrain from seeking to impose its culture on other parts of the world out of some misguided quest for universalism and seek instead to preserve and live out its own identity, while acknowledging and respecting the identities of others as it navigates its way into the future. Foremost among Huntington's recommendations is that the United States and Europe recognize that "Western intervention in the affairs of other civilizations is probably the single most dangerous source of instability and potential global conflict in a multi-civilizational world." By the same token, he also advocates a unified strategy for the West in dealing with the Muslim world and other civilizations.

To avoid major inter-civilizational wars, Huntington offers three prescriptions:

1. *The "abstention rule"*—nonintervention in the conflicts of other civilizations in order to maintain peace in a multi-civilizational, multipolar world.
2. *The "joint mediation rule"*—negotiation between core states to contain or halt fault line wars between their respective civilizations.
3. *The "commonalities rule"*—capitalizing on the values, institutions, and practices that all civilizations share in common.[2]

The commonalities rule is probably the most important to take into account when designing a strategy of cultural engagement. However, rather than limiting one's self to attributes that all civilizations share in common, seeking out commonalities between cultures should provide an adequate starting point. If the world order will largely be driven by identity-based conflicts, then what is needed is a broadening of identities. Identifying and expanding upon commonalities is one way of doing this. It helps chip away at people's prejudices and assumptions relating to other groups, which are often oversimplified and highly damaging. Harvard professor and social psychologist Herbert Kelman suggests that it is possible to maintain the core of a cultural identity without basing it on one's opposition to another group. In fact, one can construct a "shared identity" that accommodates the other group in a way that is not threatening to one's own. This is why the Children of Abraham concept is becoming so popular these days as a metaphor for inclusiveness and the exploration of commonalities.

With the scars of past conflict still fresh in people's memories, a renegotiation of identity is no easy task. But it is a necessary task and one that is probably best accomplished through education, the media, and proactive conciliatory gestures by political, spiritual, and intellectual leaders.

Especially significant in this mix are the spiritual leaders. As Huntington points out:

Whatever the degree to which they divided humankind, the world's major religions . . . also share key values in common. If humans are ever to develop a universal civilization, it will emerge gradually through the exploration and expansion of these commonalities.[3]

THE RELIGIOUS DIMENSION

The above quote is indicative of the central role that Huntington ascribes to religion as a defining characteristic of civilizations,[4] and that is not good news for the United States. As has been abundantly clear from our military interventions in Iraq and Afghanistan, we have very little ability to deal with religious differences in hostile settings. Nor do we have any ability to counter demagogues like bin Laden (and before him Milosevic) who manipulate religion for their own purposes.

It is supremely ironic that one of the most religious nations on the face of the planet should have such difficulty dealing with the religious imperatives that permeate today's geopolitical landscape. Unfortunately, we have let our rigorous separation of church and state serve as a crutch for not doing our homework to understand how religion informs the worldviews and political aspirations of those who do not similarly separate the two.

Perceived operational constraints relating to church/state separation also hinder our ability to respond effectively to the religious dimension of external threats. Because religion in the West has been so compartmentalized, government and industry typically beat a retreat whenever they hear the word, for fear of being accused of favoring one faith tradition over another. The extraterritorial application of this same mind-set in turn interferes with our ability to address the religious dimensions of overseas threats. The following commentary by Daniel Fickel, a young major serving in Sadr City, Iraq, in 2006 is suggestive of the consequences:

I feel our failure as an army and as a country to pay proper respect to the significant religious life of the people here in Iraq has been one of the most significant reasons for our difficulties with both Sunni and Shia extremists. We have used great energy to push our idea of the separation of church and state upon a people for whom God is an ever-present entity that cannot be separated from any aspect of life. We have further attempted to marginalize religious leaders who have a direct line to the loyalty of the people. Our own culture led us to expatriate Iraqi leaders who shared our institutional disdain for religions outside of our mainstream, and these leaders reinforced our own ideas. We had few people to challenge us and change our direction. . . . So far our efforts have lacked a focus on the necessary religious component that motivates many militiamen; we have also failed to address the religious leaders who influence these groups.[5]

And in the words of Canon Andrew White, Vicar of Saint George's Anglican Church in Baghdad, who reminisced in 2008:

I cannot forget the Iraq before the war, and the fear and oppression that were experienced every day. I cannot forget either the mistakes made after the war. The con-
tinual lack of engagement with the religious community and the continued belief
that the secular position of Iraq would supersede was dangerous and naïve.[6]

Even more recently, from Army Lt. Col. Michael Bush, who has served in
a number of overseas assignments, including peacekeeping operations in
Kosovo and stability operations in Iraq:

In all of these environments I have watched subordinates, peers, and even superi-
ors who projected arrogant attitudes based purely on being American—a citizen of
the world's only super power, and if you don't like, then get over it. Their attitude
was far from being diplomatic, let alone showing any sort of empathy for the local
nationals' religion, faith, denomination, or sense of spirituality.[7]

Lieutenant Colonel Bush's examples are clearly more the exception than
the rule, but they are indicative of the more general challenge of engaging
effectively with other cultures and faith traditions. The looming specter of
religious extremism married to weapons of mass destruction only makes
more urgent the need to bridge this gap. One approach for doing so that
shows unusual promise is a new form of engagement called faith-based diplomacy.

FAITH-BASED ENGAGEMENT

At the macro level, faith-based diplomacy simply means incorporating
religious considerations into the practice of international politics. At the
operational level, it involves making religion part of the solution to intractable, identity-based conflicts that escape the reach of traditional diplomacy. Typically these conflicts include an ethnic, tribal, or religious
dimension.

A distinguishing characteristic of faith-based diplomacy is the fact that it
is more about reconciliation than the absence of conflict. It is about restor-
ing respectful relationships between the parties through a broader array
of roles than those normally associated with traditional diplomacy—from
impartial observer to message carrier, empathetic advocate, or activist.[8]
Common to all forms of its practice is the commitment to capitalize on the
positive role that religious leaders and institutions can play in building
trust and overcoming differences. They can serve as instruments of change
by exercising their moral authority, their commitment to nonviolence, and
their ability to inspire their communities.

Beyond the temporal power of religion lie the efforts of spiritually motivated laypersons living out their personal callings. Whether they do so

independently or with the loose sponsorship of a church or ecumenical organization, they operate with a degree of autonomy that sets their efforts apart from those of ecclesiastical institutions. The roles and characteristics of such individuals are described in considerable detail in *Religion, the Missing Dimension of Statecraft*, which also includes a range of case studies that demonstrate how religious peacemakers, properly trained and supported, can add a critically important dimension to the work of diplomats and NGOs in addressing ethnic conflict and other problems of communal identity.

It should be noted, however, that faith-based diplomacy is not well-suited for government practitioners. In the West, constraints relating to separation of church and state get in the way; and elsewhere (in addition to the West) a government's political agenda inevitably compromises the kind of balanced neutrality that is normally required to succeed. Thus the task must fall to religious leaders themselves or to NGOs that are equipped to handle it. It then becomes a matter of government reinforcing the process or building upon it as circumstances permit. As straightforward as this may sound, it is important not to overstate religion's utility to government. In some situations, religion will be an unstable partner for statecraft as church and state go their separate ways over issues relating to justice or injustice.

PRACTICAL EXAMPLES

Illustrative of how religion can work to good effect in difficult circumstances is the widely acclaimed collaboration between the lay Catholic Community of Saint Egidio and official diplomats in resolving the brutal civil war in Mozambique that ended in 1994. The final breakthrough to peace evolved from the Community's recognition that it would have to do something to resolve the conflict if the humanitarian assistance it was providing was to have any useful effect. Accordingly, they set out to win the trust of both sides and soon engaged them in peace talks.

Early in this process, it became apparent to these religious peacemakers that if they were to succeed in their quest, they would eventually need the overt backing of the international community to monitor a cease-fire agreement or to guarantee fair multiparty elections. Accordingly, in the 9th round of talks, they invited diplomats from five countries and the UN to sit in as official observers. In the 10th round, they passed the baton to these diplomats who, in turn, brought the resources of their respective nation-states (and the UN) to bear. Today there is peace in Mozambique with a democratically elected government, all because official diplomacy was able to build upon the trust established by a religious third party.

Less widely known is the role played behind the scenes by the Italian and American governments in providing arms-length logistical support throughout. Thus government both reinforced the process and capitalized on the final outcome.

Finally, adding to the reasons that religious engagement is so important is the fact that almost everywhere there is conflict—from Afghanistan to Kashmir to Nigeria to Chechnya to Xinjiang—one finds a religious dimension to the hostilities. Whether it is a root cause of the conflict, as it probably comes closest to being in the Middle East, where there are competing religious claims for the same piece of territory, or merely a mobilizing vehicle or badge of identity, as has typically been the case in the Balkans, religion is nevertheless central to much of the strife taking place in the world today. This should come as no surprise when one considers the fact that nearly four-fifths of the world's population identifies itself as religious and that religious allegiances often transcend those relating to nationalism or ethnicity. Where religion is part of the problem, it must also be part of the solution.

Without tracing and untangling the religious threads in a conflict, its deeper causes will likely remain unresolved and reemerge at a later date. To some extent, this is what happened in the Sudan when civil war between the Islamic north and the Christian/African Traditionalist south erupted in 1983, 11 years after a 1972 peace agreement that had settled an earlier 16-year civil war following independence from Britain in 1956. The reasons underlying these conflicts were the same in both instances and involved a countrywide imposition of shari'ah.

It was to address this problem through faith-based diplomacy that the International Center for Religion and Diplomacy (ICRD) visited Sudan in 1999. There were a number of NGOs working there at the time, but almost all of them were engaged in the south, bringing needed relief under very trying circumstances to those who were suffering in the zones of conflict. The ICRD elected to pursue a different strategy, one that would address the causal aspects of the conflict by focusing on the north and establishing working relationships with the Islamic regime. From that vantage point, attempts would then be made to inspire the Sudanese government to take steps toward peace that it wouldn't otherwise consider.

A watershed moment in this effort took place in November 2000 when the ICRD in partnership with the Sudan Council of Churches and the International People's Friendship Council (the Sudanese equivalent of a western Chamber of Commerce, having loose ties to the government) convened a meeting of 30 religious leaders and scholars from the Muslim and Christian communities in order to address the religious aspects of the conflict (in addition to those religious issues that were contributing to social tensions more generally). Underlying this initiative was a commitment to address a fundamental question: what steps can an Islamic government take to alleviate the second-class status of non-Muslims in a shari'ah context?

The fact that non-Muslims in Muslim-majority countries are often treated as second-class citizens (or worse) runs counter to the standard set forth by the Prophet Muhammad in the Charter of Privileges that he granted the monks of St. Catherine Monastery at Mount Sinai in 628 c.e.:

This is a message from Muhammad ibn Abdullah, as a Covenant to those who adopt Christianity, near and far, we are with them. Verily I, the servants, the helpers, and my followers defend them, because Christians are my citizens; and, by Allah! I hold out against anything that displeases them.

No compulsion is to be on them. Neither are their judges to be removed from their jobs nor their monks from their monasteries. No one is to destroy a house of their religion, to damage it, or to carry anything from it to the Muslims' houses. Should anyone take any of these, he would spoil God's Covenant and disobey His Prophet. Verily, they are my allies and have my secure charter against all that they hate.

No one is to force them to travel or to oblige them to fight. The Muslims are to fight for them. If a female Christian is married to a Muslim, it is not to take place without her approval. She is not to be prevented from visiting her church to pray. Their churches are to be respected. They are neither to be prevented from repairing them nor the sacredness of their covenants. No one of the nation (Muslims) is to disobey the covenant till the Last Day (end of the world).[9]

On the face of it, the principles of this charter are binding everywhere and for all time. Current realities in countries ranging from Egypt and Sudan on the one hand to Pakistan and Saudi Arabia on the other, however, are indicative of the distance yet to be traveled in meeting the spirit, if not the letter, of the Prophet's guidance.

The Khartoum meeting had incendiary potential in light of the deep grievances involved, but it ultimately produced a breakthrough in communications between the two faith communities and yielded 17 consensus recommendations to support interreligious cooperation in human rights, education, employment, and humanitarian assistance (all areas in which religious minorities did not enjoy the same rights as Muslims).

The meeting's successful outcome was attributable in large measure to the faith-based nature of the undertaking. Each day the proceedings began with prayer and readings from the Qur'an and the Bible. This was preceded earlier in the morning by an informal prayer breakfast for the international participants and local Muslim and Christian religious leaders. Finally, and perhaps most important, the ICRD brought with it a prayer team from California—halfway around the world—whose sole purpose was to pray and fast for the success of the deliberations during the four days of the meeting. These elements, coupled with appropriate breaks in the proceedings to accommodate Muslim prayer times, provided a transcendent environment that inspired participants to rise above their personal and religious differences and work together for the common good.

Another aspect of the faith-based diplomacy that was brought to bear involved the numerous one-on-one conversations between the ICRD and the first vice president (who ran the country), the foreign minister, and other top-level officials during the 18 months leading up to the meeting about steps toward peace that the Sudanese government should take. These discussions were largely of a realpolitik nature—seeking to persuade them that whatever was being suggested was in their own best interest to do—but occasionally laced with helpful references to the Qur'an, or to how the Prophet Muhammad would have dealt with a similar situation, or to how Jesus might have reacted (westerners are generally unaware of the deep reverence that most Muslims feel for Jesus). This kind of faith-based dialogue never failed to elicit an open and engaging response.

A STRUCTURAL APPROACH TO PEACE BUILDING

In 2003, and stemming from the meeting's recommendations, the ICRD, along with its indigenous partners, facilitated establishment of the Sudanese Inter-Religious Council (SIRC), which for the first time in that country's history provided a forum where key Christian and Muslim religious leaders could meet on a monthly basis to surface and resolve their problems. In the first few months of its existence, the Council was able to accomplish more in the way of concrete actions to advance the interests of non-Muslims than the churches had been able to achieve working by themselves over the previous 15 years. Most of these were minor in nature but nevertheless important in pointing the way toward improved interaction and cooperation between Muslims, Christians, and African Traditionalists.

Among the Council's more significant accomplishments are the role it played in (1) mobilizing religious leaders to arrest widespread rioting following the death under seemingly suspicious circumstances of John Garang, former civil war leader of the southern forces; (2) defusing an emotionally charged legal issue between the Episcopal Church and the government; and (3) facilitating the payment of compensation to the Catholic Church (from the government of Sudan) for a major church property that the government had unlawfully confiscated some years earlier.

A year following the establishment of the Council, the ICRD took the lead in creating the Committee to Protect Religious Freedom, which brought needed accountability to this highly sensitive area. Prior to the Committee's establishment, there had been no mechanism for investigating alleged violations of religious freedom to determine what had actually taken place. Nor had there been any capability to rectify a problem once the facts became known. In executing its mission, this committee establishes fact-finding teams, conducts interviews and surveys, documents instances of actual violations, and produces reports on its findings to concerned parties and government authorities along with any recommendations for corrective measures that should be taken.

What is remarkable about the establishment of these two institutions is that it took place in the context of an Islamic dictatorship. Not only did the Khartoum regime permit the establishment of an independent body that had as part of its mandate the task of holding the government accountable for its religious policies, but it also agreed to the appointment of a Muslim leader for the Council who had been a long-standing critic of the government. Finally, it agreed to take seriously the recommendations of the Council. Darfur notwithstanding, which is an intra-Muslim conflict, the government has honored this commitment in the form of land and funds to permit the building of new churches and to provide restitution for the past seizure of church properties.

In some respects, the eventual failure of the 1972 peace accords was attributable to the fact that nothing was done following that agreement to cement new understandings at the grassroots level. The efforts of the Inter-Religious Council and its subordinate Committee to Protect Religious Freedom will address this earlier oversight as they work to establish a lasting culture of peace. If these two bodies can continue to meet their objectives, this will stand as a solid example of the kind of peace-building initiatives that NGOs can undertake to good effect.

It is better that they do it imperfectly than that you do it perfectly. For it is their war and their country and your time is limited.

—T. E. Lawrence

CULTURAL DIPLOMACY

Cultural diplomacy at the broader level offers yet another set of options for meaningful engagement. This form of diplomacy promotes people-to-people contacts and represents an exercise of what Harvard professor Joseph Nye has labeled "soft power." More precisely, it involves "exchanges of ideas, information, value systems, traditions, beliefs and other aspects of culture"—such as art, sports, science, literature, and music—with the intention of "fostering mutual understanding."[10] The goals of cultural diplomacy are political (such as improving relations between countries or projecting a positive image of one's own country), but the activities that actually take place—the free exchange of ideas, events, and peoples—are usually nonpolitical.

Yet another form of cultural diplomacy, albeit of a more personal nature, is that which can sometimes take place at the people-to-people level between adversaries. The following firsthand account by a Pakistani American is illustrative.[11]

An Afghan Encounter

The year is 2007, somewhere near Jalalabad. The three American soldiers had again sneaked away from their fortified bunker. To protect their identity, they will be called X, Y, and Z. They would not reveal names or units for a simple reason: what they did several times a month was against regulations.

X, Y, and Z befriended some of the local Afghans by showing no fear. Mad with cabin fever and a perverse desire to meet the people whose hearts and minds they were allegedly trying to win, the three musketeers would slip out of camp in traditional Afghan garb with scarves tied around their necks and walk unarmed down to the village where the locals burned garbage and barbecued lamb kabobs. No guns, no hostile intent. Just a brazen "we're friendly, we're unarmed, we want to meet you, we're not afraid" attitude. Without any command of Dari or Pashtu (the local languages), they were armed only with a few photos of their families and friends.

The surprised Afghans welcomed the unarmed, unthreatening men from the American heartland (at least one said he was from Oklahoma). For some time, male communion had been slowly weaving invisible bonds through the nonverbal communication of sign language and grunts of satisfaction from eating fresh lamb and Afghani bread and family talk.

"Why do you think we would harm these men?" one of the mujahideen asked. "You think we are just cruel savages? They came in peace. They treat us as their equals . . . so they are our friends. We would protect them."

"But what is the difference between these Americans and the others?"

"Do you see a military uniform, do you see them pointing a gun at us? . . . These people came here because they want to know us and we want to know them."

"What about the other Americans? And those who are not military but are harassed and kidnapped in these areas?"

"We would fight with them. They kill our people, run, and hide in their camps. They are afraid. They are our enemies. These foreigners are rude and make fun of us. . . . They try to make us like them."

The sandy-haired Oklahoman wanted me to say something to the Afghans: "Tell these guys we have the same values. We understand them. If someone were attacking our country and killing our people, we would do exactly the same thing as they are. It is only natural."

"How would you feel if these guys were killed tomorrow?" I asked the Afghans.

"We are used to seeing loved ones killed," one replied. "So I think we will deal with it . . . but I pray to Allah for their safety."

I asked the two other American soldiers if they shared the Oklahoman's view. With a cautious look, one answered, "I realized here for the first time the greatness of our country, and at the same time I know that we stop being Americans once we get involved in destroying the 'other' . . . the Iraqis, terrorists, all that stuff. We stop being Americans when we convince ourselves that all these men are out there to kill us, so we have to kill them first."

Intrigued, I pressed, "I wonder how many in our military feel the way you do?"

"I didn't think this way when I arrived. . . . It's just that I sit here and look at these people, and, at first, I was angry and thought of them as primitive, but they are just trying to survive. . . . Hell, we criticize them for not following Islam when we are not following the values of America and our religion."

I tried to get more information about the Americans, but they were not in a mood to provide any further clues that might help identify them. Three villagers accompanying the Taliban had been quiet the whole time, so I asked them if they agreed with the Taliban.

"The Taliban are simple and poor people. We love them and fight with them because they fight for the honor and dignity of our people."

The rogue Americans demonstrated two powerful qualities that endeared them to the Afghans—courage and a willingness to trust in their hospitality, characteristics for which Afghans are well known themselves.

Contrast the above with an Afghan Taliban commander's testimony during the meeting with senior Taliban leaders in the mountains of Pakistan (described in the preface). This commander indicated that he had been strongly opposed to the Taliban until one day when he and his wife were out for a stroll, they were stopped by American soldiers who made them hold their hands in the air, while frisking them and subjecting them to extensive profanity in the process. Because of the humiliation he was made to feel in front of his wife, he went over to the other side. Although he is relatively young—probably in his mid-thirties—he exudes the confidence of a natural leader and commands a band of some 350 fighters in Kunar, a province in northern Afghanistan. He is fluent in four languages, including English, and is addressed by his fellow commanders as "Engineer," a laudatory title in his culture that is reserved for those who are known for getting the job done.

There are many other members of the Taliban who have "gone over" because of errant U.S. bombs that have killed family or friends, but these incidents, while tragic, are part of the natural fog of war. However, gratuitous insults in a culture where honor is held in high esteem are both short-sighted and self-defeating (as those on the receiving end of this commander's ability to "get the job done" will undoubtedly attest). This is but one of numerous examples where respectful engagement would have yielded a far different outcome.

It goes without saying that if one is engaged in war, it should be waged smartly. The overriding challenge, though, is to avoid war in the first place. That is the challenge to which the admonitions of Sun Tzu, John Boyd, and this book are dedicated.

Although one is hard-pressed to find examples of cultural diplomacy that have directly led to breakthroughs in relations between the countries involved, that is probably too great a burden to impose on such initiatives. Realistically, the best that one can hope for is to lead the way toward improved relations. That alone would more than justify the cost, time, and energy of such efforts.

CULTURAL CONFLICT RESOLUTION

Resources for peace and conflict resolution can be found in every religion. They also exist within most cultures. Unsurprisingly, there is significant overlap in the degree to which indigenous cultural practices (often preceding the advent of major world religions) have become subsumed in the dominant religious traditions. This type of cultural engagement combines or complements official and unofficial diplomacy with traditional cultural rituals and practices in much the same way that faith-based diplomacy bridges religion with politics.

In this form of engagement, the parties to a conflict are encouraged, usually by members of their own tribe or culture, to resolve their differences through indigenous approaches. Governments can also adopt these methods themselves to create a participatory process, as has been done in Rwanda, or they might choose to serve merely as a facilitating agent (providing the venue, financial assistance, and/or logistics support). Below are representative examples of indigenous approaches from which governments can draw in resolving conflict.

Traditional Arab Conflict Resolution

Many pre-Islamic Bedouin cultural practices were later embedded into Islamic traditions, including rituals designed to resolve conflicts and disputes. These tribal and traditional norms and values, or *urf*, came to be implemented with explicit reference to religious precepts and practice, thus creating a seamless interface between the cultural and the religious. For instance, tribal leaders often use the Qur'an in administering the oath to parties in a dispute.

The Sinai Bedouin tribes even developed a special "team" within the tribe that specializes in 13 types of dispute resolution.[12] Among other categories, this team includes judges of war and peace, honor, women's issues, and camel issues.[13] Palestinians have their own method of dispute resolution that derives from the practices of Bedouin tribes in the Sinai and Negev deserts.[14] There are three principal stages to this process. First, the offender's family pays a sum to the victim's family. Accepting the sum means there will be no revenge exacted. Next is the *hudna* (temporary truce) phase in which the negotiations begin. Finally there is *sulh*, or reconciliation, when the parties decide the final outcome supported by a public ceremony (*sulhah*).

During the *sulhah*, the parties express remorse and forgiveness and read verses from the Qur'an and stories from the Hadith relating to forgiveness and patience.[15] One example of such a verse comes from the Hadith: "But forgive them, and overlook their misdeeds: for Allah loveth those who are kind."[16] There are also symbolic practices, such as handshakes between the families during the ceremony, as well as visitations by the family of the perpetrator to the family of the victim, where they drink a special kind of bitter coffee together. The family of the offender also hosts a ceremonial meal.

Further, there is a symbolic way of expressing humility by offering the victim's family the opportunity to kill the offender. The victim's family is also empowered by this gesture through the opportunity to assume the moral high ground by choosing not to kill. One way in which this unfolds is during a visit by the offender to the home of the victim in which he takes off his shirt and places a dagger in it, symbolically offering his life.[17] There is a similar tribal practice among North African Muslims in which the offender lies on the ground beside a sheep, and the victim's family approaches him, with the option of either killing him or the sheep. By killing the sheep, the member of the victim's family restores his family's dignity.[18]

Shiite Muslims have also used traditional methods of peaceful dispute resolution, such as those used by Hezbollah among fellow Muslims. Hezbollah has capitalized on such methods to deal with vendettas and cycles of violence among rival clans, including mediation, shuttle diplomacy, negotiating restitution and financial compensation, protecting the accused from revenge killings, and other symbolic gestures.[19]

Traditional Justice in Rwanda

In Rwanda, tribal courts (*gacaca*—pronounced ga-cha-cha) have been used by the government alongside the regular court system to help expedite justice and reconciliation following the 1994 genocide. In 2001, the regular court system had an overwhelming backlog of cases; and the judicial process was moving at a glacial pace. At the time, only 6,000 of the 110,000 genocide suspects had been tried in the regular courts. According to a local official, "At this rate, it would take about 200 years before all suspects have their day in court."[20] So the government established a supplemental court system based on *gacaca*, a practice that predates European colonialism in the country. A pilot system was initiated in 2002, after 11,000 traditional courts were set up alongside the 13 conventional courts that were already hearing these cases (as well as the UN tribunal in Tanzania that was trying some of the top planners and executioners of the genocide). After the pilot *gacaca* program was deemed a success, the system was introduced on a nationwide basis in 2005.

Gacaca means "grass" in Kinyarwanda, and its name comes from the traditional practice of sitting on the grass to discuss and mediate personal and community problems. Elders (the *Inyangamugayo*, or "people of integrity") lead villagers through a process to resolve village conflicts that was originally used to deal with minor infractions like cattle theft or domestic disputes between husband and wife. The elders are not elected, but instead are chosen because of their respected reputations and standing in the community.[21] The *gacaca* courts established to hear genocide cases were not quite the same, because the judges are elected and the *Inyangamugayo* is replaced by a jury (although this jury is made up of community members). There is also an assembly of community members who serve as witnesses to the proceedings.

The process has been criticized for various shortcomings, but many Rwandans see it as an effective path to "restorative justice," capable of achieving a kind of reconciliation that is rarely attained through the traditional legal system. Symptomatic of the feelings underlying this approach is the attitude of one Rwandan who lost family members during the slaughter and who is "counting on the traditional courts . . . to lift the veil of anonymity on the killers and hold those who ordered the killings accountable."

THE MEDIA

Cultural engagement through the media has also been used to good effect in any number of situations. In East Timor, for example, it was used to promote participation in the referendum for independence. Former UN public information officer David Winhurst describes a "commercial" for that referendum that was broadcast on local television. It showed an East Timorese elderly woman chewing on some leaves and spitting (a common practice in East Timor) while talking about how she planned to vote. The video went something like this: While chewing on the leaves, the woman said, "I might vote for independence [spit]. Or I might vote against it [spit]. But no matter how I vote, it's my right and no one can take it away from me [spit, spit]."

THE BOTTOM LINE

If much of the foregoing sounds tangential to the hard realities of national security, the Soviet experience in Afghanistan attests to its relevance. A May 10, 1988, letter from the Central Committee of the Communist Party of the Soviet Union to all party members, explaining the reasons for their imminent withdrawal of forces from Afghanistan (which began five days later; see appendix A) captures this aspect: "Our approach did not take into account the Country's multiple forms of economic life and other characteristics, such as tribal and religious customs."[22]

The relevance of culture to national security has also been confirmed by American military commanders. Prior to 9/11, for example, Adm. Charles Abbot, Deputy Commander in Chief of the U.S. European Command, noted in a 1999 address to military chaplains, "The way the world has evolved, it has become crucial to better understand the religious and cultural histories of peoples involved in conflicts."[23] Several years later, Lt. Gen. Peter Chiarelli, then U.S. Commanding General of the Multi-National Corps in Iraq, commented, "I asked my brigade commanders what was the one thing they would have liked to have had more of, and they all said cultural knowledge."[24]

Treating culture as a defining element of national security, however, is far more easily said than done.[25] Databases containing facts and details about other cultures are all well and good, but there is an existential dimension to values, mind-sets, and beliefs that can only be fully understood through respectful engagement with those who are living them out. Despite the language barrier, this is precisely what the U.S. soldiers in mufti sitting around the campfire with their Afghan foes were doing. Cross-cultural understanding on this level will be crucial to any hope for a peaceful future in the years to come.

III

Decision

CHAPTER 6

A New Framework for Analysis

The first, the supreme, the most far-reaching act of judgment that the states-
man and commander have to make is to establish the kind of war on which
they are embarking; neither taking it for, nor trying to turn it into, something
that is alien to its nature. This is the first of all strategic questions and the
most comprehensive.

—Carl von Clausewitz

It should be recognized at the outset that this war with *irhabis* is first and
foremost an intelligence war. Intelligence will be pivotal to any future success, as will effective partnerships with Muslim countries, which know far
more than we about the religious underpinnings of the struggle. As British military historian John Keegan observed in his recent book of essays
Intelligence in War:

The War on Terrorism may be a misnomer, but it would also be foolish to pretend
there is not a historic war between "crusaders" as Muslim fundamentalists char-
acterize the countries that descend from Western Christendom, and the Islamic
world . . . The challenge to the West's intelligence services is to find a way into the
fundamentalist mind and to overcome it within.[1]

Good advice, except the term "fundamentalist mind" that Keegan uses
is itself a misnomer—a convenient but misleading shorthand used by sec-
ularists who don't understand or empathize with people who take God
seriously and who want to live by His book as a source of guidance for at-
taining eternal life. There is no single "fundamentalist" mind. The term
itself emerged as a reaction to modernity from a collection of essays by

American and British conservative Protestants in the 1910s entitled *The Fundamentals: A Testimony to the Truth*. These essays were a theological response to the propagation of liberal theology, Darwinism, socialism, atheism, and other "isms" that were seen to undermine the authority of the Bible. What resulted was a definition and defense of traditional Protestant teachings. Those who accepted these teachings were referred to as fundamentalists.[2]

Biblical fundamentalists view scripture as their compass for living. In this sense, the term *fundamentalism* also describes the vast majority of observant Muslims. Muslims embrace the Qur'an and Muhammad in the same way that observant Christians embrace the Bible and Jesus—as the word of God. The Qur'an, as God's word for Muslims, neither denies nor cancels previous revelations. Rather, it is viewed as the last brick in the one House of God. "We believe in Allah and that which is revealed unto us and that which was revealed unto Abraham and Ishmael and Isaac and Jacob and the tribes, and that which was vouchsafed unto Moses and Jesus and the Prophets from their Lord. We make no distinction between any of them, and unto Him we have surrendered."[3]

The closest equivalent term to fundamentalism in Islam is *salaf,* meaning "those who preceded." *Salafis* are Muslims who want to live their faith as closely to the original practice of Islam as possible. Wahhabis (*Ahle Hadiths*), for example, are *Salafis;* but not all *Salafis* are Wahhabis. Nor are all Wahhabis the same. Wahhabi practice in Qatar is different from that in Saudi Arabia which is different from that in Pakistan and the United States. *Salafi* guidance is taken directly from the Qur'an and the *Sunnah*—the teachings and example of the Prophet. Amish, Mennonite, and other monastic communities in the United States, who live according to their interpretation of the Gospels, offer an analogy. *Salafi* fundamentalists are radical monotheists, like certain ultra-Orthodox Jews, who consider the nation-state a form of idolatry. Some *Salafis* condemn headstones in cemeteries and the celebration of birthday parties, even the Prophet's, as nascent idolatry. Thus, a major fraction of *Salafists* are apolitical quietists concerned with personal righteousness until they feel threatened in their identity,[4] as the Amish did when the U.S. government proposed that they send their children to public schools and tried to force them into the social security system.[5]

Marine Gen. Anthony Zinni, former Commander-in-Chief of the U.S. Central Command, has said that we have a vocabulary problem. Like the Eskimos who have eight different words for snow, we need a finely developed vocabulary to describe the varieties of Islam, including those whom we misleadingly label "fundamentalists." He is right.

NATURE OF THE THREAT

Carl von Clausewitz, the celebrated and still iconic Prussian military thinker, provides U.S. civilian and military policymakers with an admonition worthy of reflection. What is the true nature of this war? Or is "war" really an adequate term for what is actually happening? Chairman of the U.S. Joint Chiefs of Staff Adm. Michael Mullen has said, "We can't kill our way to victory."[6] If this is so, then this is not a shooting war in any usual sense of the word.

The abrupt transition from the Westphalian framework of nation-states, which took hold in 1648, to today's transnational terrorist networks having no apparent geographic cohesiveness has created a confused response from those most threatened. This is due in no small part to the West's long-held allegiance to the assumption that nation-states will behave rationally in seeking to maximize their power. This model provided a level of predictability that enabled public officials to construct their national agendas. Even the communist concept of a highly controlled economy implicitly assumed a state-centric framework.

COLD WAR DISTINCTIONS

Based on the complementary concepts of sovereign states and rational behavior, two security principles emerged as the cold war pillars of western security: containment of Soviet global encroachment through (1) applying an ever-shifting mix of carrots and sticks to influence proxy states and (2) deterring a direct attack against the West by the Soviet Union itself. The security that this strategy provided largely evaporated with the attacks of 9/11, which significantly eroded the sovereign-state basis for future security calculations. Overnight, the threat to the West became nonstate actors with nonstate soldiers and non-national borders. Suddenly, the world's most powerful state found itself vulnerable to asymmetric threats from a largely dispersed and somewhat invisible enemy.

The cold war strategy of containment lost its credibility in light of terrorists' disregard for state borders or finances. The same held true for the concept of deterrence. Because the terrorist's reward comes in the afterlife instead of the here and now, deterrence as practiced in the past would have little, if any, effect on suicidal behavior.[7] Thus, the contest became a struggle for hearts and minds that in *irhabi* eyes would ultimately lead to a world dominated by Islam under the control of a global caliphate.

A TRAP TO AVOID

Because the cold war led to security planning around a single global threat, once that threat disappeared, our foreign service, intelligence services, and national security community were left high and dry in terms of their basic organizing principles. The entire U.S. attack submarine force, for example, had been sized and shaped around the Soviet submarine threat. The sudden disappearance of that threat led to intense scurrying to find alternative missions to justify this formidable capability.

When terrorism in the name of Islam appeared on the scene in the 1990s, it effectively poured new wine into the old wineskin and was treated in much the same manner as the earlier Soviet threat. Although geographically quite limited and far from formidable, terrorism's significance was hugely inflated, as it continues to be into the present. The resulting mindset led to chronic overreaction to isolated threats (like the shoe-bomber), while obscuring a central truth that the Byzantines had discovered some 13 centuries earlier—that most Muslims are not jihadi militants, while those who are tend to fight other Muslims much more than they do non-Muslims.

Islamic religious fervor may occasionally generate dangerous attacks against non-Muslims, but it more frequently divides the militants of the different sects who seek to impose their own specific doctrine on other Muslims. In the present, as in Byzantine times, there is endemic violence not only between militant Sunnis and different kinds of Shia but also between violent *Salafists* and more moderate Sunni *Salafists* (and non-*Salafists*) as well as between extreme and mainstream Shias.

We are allied with most Muslim governments against the extremists. Only Iran and Syria have governments that openly support violent militants, while Pakistani authorities are ambivalent at worst. With these exceptions and running counter to Huntington's "clash," Muslim governments are in the front ranks of the struggle against extremist violence. Thus, artificially inventing a single, global Muslim terrorist threat in our own minds and policies represents a strategic error of major consequence. Religious extremism in the name of Islam exists, of course; but it is geographically scattered, and it very largely victimizes other Muslims. Israel has grown 5 times in population since statehood relatively unmolested by such terrorism (which has killed far fewer Jews than do road accidents in just a few intersections around Tel-Aviv).[8]

EMERGENCE OF A NEW STRATEGY

The disquieting tendency of some western policymakers to cast illiberal Islamic movements in the same mold as the communist insurgents of the cold war on the basis that the Islamic world is gripped by an intolerant and militant ideology that must be contained and forcibly defeated is wrong on two counts. First, Islamist activism (Islamism) includes a number of different streams that are by no means uniform in their thinking. And second, a cold war analogy fails to do justice to the new and critically important differences that underlie today's threat.

Analysis by the International Crisis Group concludes that there are three distinctive and often competing forms of Sunni Islamism, each with its own worldview and approach to change: (1) *political* Islamists, who give priority to political reform and invoke democratic norms in addressing problems of social injustice and poor governance; (2) *missionary* Islamists, whose overriding focus is on the individual moral and spiritual well-being of Muslims as the most effective counter to the forces of unbelief; and (3) *jihadi* (*irhabi*) Islamists, who, en route to establishing a global ca-liphate, advocate armed struggle against one (or more) of several targets: impious Muslim regimes, non-Muslim occupiers of current (or former) Muslim lands, and the West.[9]

All three of the above forms of activism represent attempts to reconcile tradition and modernity in some form. However, by lumping them all to-gether, branding them as radical, and treating them as hostile to the West, one risks the possibility of inspiring them to band together in opposing a common foe. In such an eventuality, it is highly likely that the *irhabis* would soon co-opt the nonviolent modernist streams. In short, Islam is not a monolith. The West needs a discriminating strategy that capitalizes on the diversity of Islamist outlooks and which, to the extent possible, iso-lates, or at least marginalizes, the *irhabis*.

In the wake of 9/11, a war-fighting strategy was enacted consisting of three complementary pillars: (1) protecting the homeland, (2) attacking ter-rorists and their support systems, and (3) supporting Muslims who reject violent extremism. A new form of deterrence is also beginning to take shape that keys to the reputation and credibility of the terrorist organizations among Muslim communities. If the *irhabis*' activities can be successfully branded as un-Islamic, then their support base will wither and attacks will diminish.[10]

Extensive bombardment in Afghanistan is now giving way to commu-nal engagement. Rather than confining the enemy as before, with some variant of containment or deterrence, U.S. forces are addressing with some success the communal foundations of the terrorist networks through trust-building engagements with the local populations. Recent Afghan opinion polls showing reduced support for the Taliban suggest that the new strat-egy is beginning to work.[11] However, more will be required if the United States hopes to reverse the Taliban's momentum. The ideas behind the guns set forth in chapter 3 will have to be addressed through state-to-state in-teractions, including religious engagement, which is what this book is largely about.

AMERICA'S CHALLENGE

The United States has been on a steep learning curve since 9/11 and has thus far avoided a second successful attack against the homeland. Those who have contributed to this success deserve great credit. However, one gets the uneasy feeling that little thought has been given at the top of government to how the United States can reposition itself to deal more ef-fectively with the causal factors underlying the religious rage that is con-tributing to such attacks.

KING FOR A DAY

If one were hypothetically to become "King for a Day," what might one do to meet the political challenges of religious engagement? A useful first step would be to broaden our basis for understanding the religious dynamics at play and to optimize our opportunities for responding effectively. Here, we could begin by considering which of our existing national assets might be redirected to help deal with the problem. That should then be followed by developing new capabilities to bridge any remaining gaps.

EXISTING ASSETS FOR RELIGIOUS ENGAGEMENT

Existing assets that can be redirected to formulate a more effective framework for discernment and action include the American Muslim community, military chaplains, and nongovernmental organizations (NGOs). Properly engaged, the American Muslim community could help bridge relations with Muslim communities overseas, many in areas of strategic consequence to the United States. However, not only has this community not been fully recognized as the strategic asset that it is, but it has at times experienced mistreatment to the point where it has felt little incentive to cooperate.

Military chaplains are uniquely positioned to help deal with the religious dimension of external threats in the sense that they (1) already bridge the church/state divide, (2) are accustomed to working with people of other religions, and (3) typically command strong interpersonal skills. With expanded rules of engagement and the necessary training, they could work effectively with local religious leaders and NGOs and apply the resulting insights in advising their military commanders on the cultural implications of future decisions. Taken together, these capabilities could significantly enhance the conflict-prevention capabilities of the military commands. While some progress has been made in this direction, there is clearly room for more.

Finally, NGOs, for their part, provide flexible, apolitical capabilities that can enhance a government's ability to deal with the transnational dimension of today's threats. In other instances, they may offer the only capability for dealing with specific kinds of threats, such as those that are religious in nature (owing to the political restrictions that often impede a western nation's ability to respond).

NEW CAPABILITIES

In terms of new capabilities, strong consideration should be given to realigning the executive branch of government so that it can deal more effectively with religious challenges. For at least 15 years, the State Department has been aware that it has a blind spot when it comes to dealing with religion,[12] yet it remains firmly bound in its straightjacket of dogmatic secularism. A number of other offices in the executive branch are equally mis-aligned for dealing with religious imperatives. Exacerbating this state of bureaucratic paralysis are the perceived constraints relating to separation of church and state that discourage creative thinking in this area. These need to be examined closely, with an eye toward freeing up policymakers, diplomats, and military commanders to deal with the religious dimensions of external threats, without fear of violating the establishment clause in the process.

Also missing is an effective capability for intervening in unsettled situations soon enough to prevent conflict before it breaks out. Priority should be given to developing and supporting well-qualified teams of experts that can be sent to potential trouble spots on an early warning basis to prevent festering situations from getting out of control. Critics might counter that this is something that the ambassador's country team should be able to handle.[13] Perhaps so, but most country teams are fully occupied with the daily challenges of doing business in a foreign setting and, in any event, lack some of the professional disciplines (especially those relating to religion) required to deal adequately with the nuanced tasks of prevention.

THE OVERRIDING NEED FOR ENGAGEMENT

Finally, many policymakers and foreign policy practitioners inadequately appreciate the potential utility of organic approaches in addressing problems of religious extremism. To be sure, there are the never-ending complaints about the failure of mainstream Muslims to stand up to the extremists (most of them ill-founded). Missing completely, however, is any willingness to deal directly with the extremists themselves or to encourage reform from within. Indeed, in the United States, rather than engaging extremists, there has been a deep-seated inclination to isolate and demonize them—an unfortunate tendency that was on full display in the Clinton administration's policies toward Sudan and later with the Bush 43 administration's dealings with Iran.

The U.S. predilection for imposing *unilateral* economic sanctions against countries that offend our sensibilities in one way or another (usually to placate domestic political or economic grievances) is yet another manifestation of this unfortunate tendency, despite the fact that such sanctions have almost always failed to elicit the intended response. In fact, a strong case can be made that the application of such sanctions has typically inspired the leadership of targeted countries to flaunt U.S. policies even more than they did before their imposition.[14] Thus far, the Obama administration appears to recognize that absent engagement, there is almost no leverage to move events in a positive direction.

Direct communication with an adversary is not something to be undertaken lightly, but on those occasions when it seems beneficial, it should be accompanied by a predisposition to hear and validate whatever legitimate aspirations the other side may present. Here, serious consideration should be given to a *strategy of reconciliation* in which steps are taken to address and heal to the extent possible any wounds of history that may be contributing to the impasse. Far easier said than done, but armed conflict is becoming an increasingly ineffective means for securing our national interests.[15]

Key to whatever strategy is pursued will be optimizing the opportunities for success, which brings us to the decision phase of Boyd's OODA Loop. Much of the remainder of this book will deal with the decisions needed to implement the recommended capabilities discussed in this chapter.

IV

Action

CHAPTER 7

Realigning the Wheels of Government

All that spiritual courage and energy wasted in war could have prevented it, if properly used.

—Roger Martin du Gard[1]

In 1994, two of the country's finest strategic thinkers, Edward Luttwak and Stanton Burnett, collectively came up with the following observations, which were set forth in *Religion, the Missing Dimension of Statecraft*:

1. The impact of Enlightenment prejudice on the scientific study of politics and international relations has created a "learned repugnance" toward contending intellectually with anything religious or spiritual.

2. American diplomats, raised in the Enlightenment secularism of the realist school, are unprepared to consider the spiritual aspects of problems and possible solutions.

3. Many future conflicts, both international and within states, will have religion as the defining characteristic of at least one of the contending communities. The character of said conflict will be misunderstood if religion is not accurately taken into account.

4. Blindness to spiritual elements has frequently led U.S. diplomacy to hope and action when despair and inaction would have been more appropriate. Optimism may be an attractive American characteristic, but ignorant optimism can be deadly.

5. The failure of the CIA to conduct or support a single research proposal relating to the religious dimension of Iranian politics leading up to the revolution in 1979 is symptomatic of the distortion caused by defining struggle solely in terms of conventional western political and economic categories.

6. American policymakers and diplomats should be keenly interested in understanding the potential role of spiritual factors in the resolution of conflict, an idea that may seem hopelessly idealistic to practicing politicians or diplomats unfamiliar with the historical record of past instances in which such forces have been brought to bear to good effect. They do not need faith in faith, but faith in history and analysis.

7. An inability to see, understand, and make common cause with religious/spiritual forces will involve even higher costs in the future because of an increase in the number of conflicts and instances of political turmoil in which religious phenomena will constitute an important part, either of the problem or of the possible solution (or both). U.S. diplomacy, by consciously widening its vision to include the influence of religious convictions, could achieve far greater agility and effectiveness.

8. It is clearly urgent that the varied inhibitions that continue to obscure and distort both official and unofficial analysis whenever religion is involved be overcome.

9. One should not perpetuate administratively the misconception that religious institutions and leaders ipso facto constitute only a marginal factor, a diminishing force, or a purely political (or social, or economic, or ethnic) phenomenon in religious guise.

10. One administrative remedy that could be helpful would be to assign "Religion Attachés" to diplomatic missions in those countries where religion has particular salience in order to monitor religious movements and maintain contact with religious leaders, just as labor attachés have long been assigned to deal with local trade unions. Intelligence organizations that already have specialists in many functional areas could usefully add religion specialists as well.

11. The characteristic desire of U.S. diplomats to improve the quality of their service gives hope that they will be enthusiastically open to the considerations of this study.

Over the course of the seven years that it took to produce the above-mentioned book, the Berlin Wall fell and ethnic conflict emerged in many of the areas where it had previously been suppressed by the bipolar dynamics of the cold war. With this resurgence of dormant antagonisms, the approach that the book advanced of linking religious reconciliation with official or unofficial diplomacy (as illustrated in seven case studies of past instances where this has taken place to good effect) was thought by many readers to represent an important expansion of diplomacy that could enhance its efficacy in dealing with identity-based conflicts.

Book sales soared, as did requests for public appearances to discuss this new idea. Among the latter were requests to speak at the State Department, the Foreign Service Institute (FSI), and various other forums where active or retired ambassadors and Foreign Service officers (FSOs) were present. To their credit, when confronted with the above findings relating to religion and U.S. foreign policy, these Foreign Service veterans, rather than growing defensive, admitted to having a blind spot. The following comments from former U.S. Ambassador John McDonald in his endorsement of the book are indicative:

I must acknowledge, with considerable remorse, that . . . diplomats are not sensitive to the importance and power of the spiritual factor in negotiations. I certainly ignored these issues in all my years as a negotiator.

As a United States career diplomat for 40 years, I urge my fellow diplomats to make the study of religions an integral part of their professional training and to recognize the importance of spirituality in dealing with international conflicts.[2]

Because 15 years have now passed since that collective admission, with next to nothing of an institutional nature done to fill this gap, one can only surmise that either the will to do so or the knowledge of how to do so (or perhaps both) is missing.

Taking these in order, the will to act must come from the top. Ideally, both the President and the Secretary of State should champion the idea of incorporating religious considerations into the practice of U.S. foreign policy (In a contest in which religious legitimacy trumps all else in the minds of one's enemies, why should they do any less?). Moreover, if U.S. diplomacy were to broaden its vision in this area, it would achieve far greater suppleness in a critical arena.

At the presidential level, insistence that the National Security Council (NSC) systematically include religious imperatives in its calculations would go a long way toward filling the gap. The current mandate of the Obama administration to have the White House Office of Faith-based and Neighborhood Partnerships work with the NSC to foster interreligious dialogue will probably be inadequate to the task. Interreligious dialogue as it is typically practiced often amounts to no more than a sterile exchange of views about differing belief systems. Unless such interactions are accompanied by a commitment to meet on an ongoing basis in order to develop relationships, build trust, and pursue an action agenda that benefits both parties, nothing much will change.[3]

Rather than counting on an amorphous strategy of facilitating interreligious dialogue, the NSC staff should be realigned in a way that will enable it to ask the penetrating questions that can help prevent critical missteps such as that of the Coalition Provisional Authority in Iraq when it failed to take into account Grand Ayatollah Sistani's views in its game plan for rebuilding the country—an oversight that led to a still-birth of the plan and significant embarrassment for the Coalition.

Higher up the ladder, the President's appointment letters for new ambassadors should specifically require that they pay close attention to religious issues and take steps to anticipate and deal with related problems in this sphere in the execution of their duties. The Secretary of State should likewise make the understanding of religion and how to deal with it a priority within the State Department. As a first step, the Department should be re-aligned to develop the institutional capacity to incorporate religious considerations into its policymaking calculations in the normal course of doing business.

BUREAUCRATIC REFORM

The U.S. government (USG) has already singled out the Muslim world for ongoing engagement in a State Department document titled "U.S. National Strategy for Public Diplomacy and Strategic Communication," released in June 2007.[4] One of the objectives outlined in that strategy is as follows: "With our partners, we seek to isolate and marginalize violent extremists who threaten the freedom and peace sought by civilized people of every nation, culture and faith." Among the listed methods of achieving this goal are "actively engaging Muslim communities and amplifying mainstream Muslim voices" and "demonstrating that the West is open to all religions and is not in conflict with any faith."[5]

The strategy specifically targets "key influencers," with clerics appearing first on the list of those groups "whose views can have a ripple effect throughout society." With regard to religious leaders, the document states:

The unique role of religion in the current war on terror requires that greater efforts be made to engage in dialogue with the leaders of faith-based communities. Moral and religious leaders such as clerics, imams, rabbis, monks and priests can foster tolerance and mutual respect among religions and their followers.

USG officials should seek opportunities to participate in events that resonate with local populations, including visits to important religious and cultural sites and hosting events such as *iftar* dinners to demonstrate respect for different faiths.[6]

Special efforts should be made by USG officials to highlight mainstream Muslim voices that condemn extremist violence.[7]

While the strategy of giving religious considerations a higher priority in U.S. foreign policy is unquestionably sound, nowhere in the Department's organizational structure can one find that priority reflected in any meaningful way.[8] The following are offered as several possible approaches for incorporating this "missing dimension."

The Religion Attaché

Given the State Department's current organizational structure, it may be most useful to begin with a bottom-up approach. And here, the idea expressed earlier of assigning a Religion Attaché to those overseas missions in countries "where religion has particular salience" merits attention (such as Israel, Nigeria, Egypt, Iraq, and Saudi Arabia, to name only a few). Twelve years after this idea was first advanced in *Religion, the Missing Dimension of Statecraft,*[9] former Secretary of State Madeleine Albright recommended in her insightful book *The Mighty & the Almighty* that the State Department "should hire or train a core [*sic*] of specialists in religion to be deployed both in Washington and in key embassies overseas."[10] Clearly, the idea of engaging religion specialists has a degree of staying power, at least among those who are not totally captive to the current system.

Chief among the religion specialist's responsibilities would be that of developing relationships of trust with local religious leaders and groups, reporting on relevant religious movements and developments (including the emergence of religious demagogues who might pose a challenge to the existing order), and helping the mission or headquarters deal more effectively with complex religious issues. Just as Cultural Affairs Officers have programming responsibilities, Religion Attachés would also plan suitable programs appropriate to their budgets. Not only would these specialists require special aptitudes and the appropriate training for dealing with the "nonrational" complexities of religious issues, but they would also need to be able to understand (1) religious motives and priorities, (2) the specific language of local religious expression, and, above all, (3) how faith inspires action.

As things currently stand, the responsibilities for dealing with religious issues typically reside with the Cultural Affairs Officer, the Political Officer, or the Ambassador. But regardless of where the responsibility lies, today's reality is that complex religious issues often get pushed aside by "more pressing" business, hence the need for a new position empowered with special qualifications, not unlike those required for labor, agriculture, and science attachés.

The Religion Attaché concept was examined at some length in the February 2002 edition of the *Foreign Service Journal;* and it was determined that a cadre of 30 such attachés could handle America's global requirements in this area at an annual cost of $10 million.[11] This cost, which pales in comparison to the billions being spent annually to deal with the symptoms of Islamist extremism, would represent a cost-effective way to enhance our ability to understand and deal with the underlying causal factors. The article also anticipates and specifically addresses the most likely bureaucratic concerns that would arise from establishing such a position.[12] Some of these same concerns were captured in later commentary by former U.S. Ambassador Kenton Keith:

The idea of a religion attaché, per se, would raise enough red flags throughout the foreign policy establishment that its good intention would be smothered. Also, there would almost certainly be an effort by domestic U.S. groups to own the religion attaché. Our experience with labor attachés, who have been controlled by the AFL/CIO since the early days of the Cold War, is enough to demonstrate the dangers of creating such positions with the inevitable pressures from interested groups in the U.S., including Congress.[13]

If the "red flags" have to do with church/state separation, this concern would appear to be co-opted by the mandate to engage with the Muslim world as set forth in the State Department's public diplomacy (PD) strategy mentioned earlier. On the other hand, if they have to do with creating a new position of any kind, it should be noted that the Foreign Service (and PD in particular) has been facing staffing shortages for quite some time.[14] Because of this, many junior officers have been moved into midlevel PD positions without adequate training. At times, their only experience in the Foreign Service will have been in the consular section.[15] In short, for those embassies that are understaffed, establishing a new position, with adequate funding and training to support it, would clearly help to ease this burden.

Ambassador Keith's second point about the possibility of domestic groups trying to "own" the Religion Attaché position is a legitimate but not insurmountable concern. With regard to the labor attaché position, both the American Federation of Labor (AFL) and the Congress of Industrial Organizations (CIO) shared the U.S. foreign policy objective of combating the influence of international communism in foreign labor movements during the cold war. The principal difference between them was in their approach, with the AFL focusing on the "negative" goal of eliminating communists from foreign labor movements (which at times ran counter to U.S. attempts to engage Eurocommunists on a tactical level in Italy and elsewhere), and the CIO concentrating on the "positive" goal of encouraging the growth of "non-political trade unionism, labor-management co-operation and modern working practices."[16]

The underlying goal of both unions was consistent with U.S. foreign policy objectives, however, and the extent of their influence was not a secret. This influence extended all the way to the Secretary of Labor. According to a 1987 interview with Philip Kaiser, former Assistant Secretary of Labor for International Labor Affairs (1949–53), "The only time in recent history, or maybe since the beginning of the Labor Department in 1913, that you had a Secretary of Labor who had no relation to the trade union movement was when Raymond Donovan [President Reagan's Secretary of Labor] was head of the Department."[17]

Thus, while it is true that domestic labor unions often competed over the appointments and control of Labor Attachés, the argument that this should militate against the creation of a Religion Attaché position would depend on two assumptions: (1) that Religion Attachés would be subjected to comparable pressures from domestic religious groups and (2) that this sort of influence would be harmful to U.S. foreign policy. With regard to the first condition, it would seem that an embassy's economic officers would be in far greater danger of being "owned" by U.S. corporations. Whatever safeguards are currently in place to prevent this from happening could also be used for Religion Attachés.

As for the second condition, one could argue that the partnership between labor unions and the U.S. government was generally good for U.S.

foreign policy. The government and the unions shared many of the same policy objectives and were working toward similar ends. The same could be said of domestic religious organizations that have a conciliatory agenda. Although outright control of the Religion Attachés by religious organizations of any kind would be highly problematic, if the Attaché's connection to domestic religious groups in the United States was limited to facilitating mutually beneficial goals, there should be no conflict of interest.

How could former Secretary of State Madeleine Albright's recommendation that the State Department hire or train a corps of religion specialists for deployment in Washington and in key embassies overseas be accomplished, if not through the establishment of a new position? How one fills such a position, however, is a question that deserves thoughtful reflection. There are several options: (1) establish a separate career track within the Foreign Service for religion specialists and hire additional FSOs possessing the right background qualifications, (2) establish a religion subspecialty within the Foreign Service training pipeline to provide interested candidates with the necessary specialized training, (3) hire outside experts who would serve on a contractual basis, (4) again, with the appropriate training, engage Foreign Service Reserve officers to perform the function, or (5) use qualified Fulbright Fellows on a volunteer basis to do the job. Each of these options has strengths and weaknesses that would have to be weighed accordingly.

Foreign Service Reserve officers, for example, are officers with special skills who are given short-term temporary assignments and work where they are most needed. The following excerpts from a 2006 Government Accounting Office (GAO) report, however, suggest that something longer-term is needed:

Staffing challenges in public affairs sections at posts in the Muslim world are exacerbated by shorter tours of duty and fewer officers bidding on public diplomacy positions than in the non-Muslim world. According to data provided by State, the average tour length at posts in the Muslim world is 2.1 years, compared with 2.7 years in the non-Muslim world. . . . Furthermore, as a result of the security concerns mentioned above, tours at many posts in the Muslim world are for only 1 year, without family members. Of State's 20 so-called unaccompanied posts, 15 are in the Muslim world. . . .

Shorter tours contribute to insufficient language skills and limit an officers' ability to cultivate personal relationships, which, according to a senior public diplomacy officer, are vital to understanding Arabs and Muslims. Another senior State official, noting the prevalence of one-year tours in the Muslim world, told us that public affairs officers who have shorter tours tend to produce less effective work than officers with longer tours. In Pakistan, we were told that the public affairs officer views himself as a "management consultant," in part because of his short tour in Islamabad. Furthermore, the department's Inspector General observed that the rapid turnover of American officers in Pakistan was a major constraint to public diplomacy activities in the country.[18]

There is no country on the face of the planet where it is more important to get our message right than in Pakistan. Clearly, high turnover in the embassies and the loss of institutional knowledge that goes with it only adds to the difficulty of engaging effectively.

Whether the religion specialists are designated as Religion Attachés or some other title is far less important than the fact that embassy staffing would include the requisite expertise to take religious imperatives fully into account in the conduct of our relations with that particular country. This position would also go a long way toward ensuring that foreign policy mistakes resulting from ignorance or the conscious exclusion of religious factors are minimized, if not eliminated altogether.

Yet another, perhaps less controversial, way to meet this need would be to assign someone with the requisite religious qualifications to the political section of the embassy staff in much the same manner that Pol/Mil (Political/Military) officers are assigned to selected embassies. Pol/Mil officers serve as specialists and are required to draft or at least sign off on all embassy cables having military implications. They are also present at all meetings with foreign officials where military questions are on the table. In short, they are chief counselors (and occasionally hold that title) to the Ambassador and the embassy on military issues. More important, they are also a part of the Ambassador's country team, even though they report directly to the Political Officer. This idea would entail giving the new "Pol/Rel" officers status and responsibilities comparable to those of Pol/Mil officers, which, in turn, would finesse any concerns about untoward influence from external sources.

Occupants of these positions would also provide on-the-ground assessments of the religious aspects of conflicts that could help create the kind of framework needed for effective peace building and conflict resolution. Over time, the flow of religious reporting that takes place would begin to sensitize the entire bureaucracy to religion's importance, as would the presence in the mission of someone specifically assigned to the topic. More important, to the extent that insights of religion specialists can shift the embassy's focus from reaction to prevention, the cost-effectiveness of our overseas involvements would be enhanced accordingly.

Religion Attachés (or their equivalent) could also assume the responsibility for the mission's religious freedom reporting requirements, deepening those connections in addition to developing others. Working closely with the political and cultural officers, they could improve America's image with important religious groups and leaders while at the same time acquire valuable insights into their motives and objectives.

Because it will take some time for the bureaucracy to address this need once the decision has been made to do so, consideration could be given to bridging the gap in Muslim countries by recruiting qualified American Muslims or other suitable experts to perform the function, while serving as special assistant to the ambassador.

Adjusting the Structure

Adjusting the organizational structure itself is a more complicated undertaking, not well suited to casual contemplation. One possible approach for increasing departmental focus and attention on religion-related issues is that employed by former Secretary of State Condoleezza Rice in July 2005, when she institutionalized democracy promotion in the department by:

- Renaming the Under Secretary for Global Affairs the "Under Secretary for Democracy and Global Affairs." This name change underscored the importance that the Secretary placed on advancing the President's freedom agenda.

- Launching a comprehensive review of U.S. democracy promotion strategies and associated funding, with a goal of enhancing and intensifying activities in that area.

- Creating a new Deputy Assistant Secretary for Democracy within the Bureau of Democracy, Human Rights, and Labor to streamline and centralize democracy promotion efforts.

- Creating a new advisory committee that could provide the Secretary with expert advice on democracy promotion.

- Transferring reporting responsibilities of the Bureau of International Narcotics and Law Enforcement (INL) to the Under Secretary for Political Affairs. This transfer promoted a closer link between INL and the regional bureaus, while allowing the Under Secretary for Democracy and Global Affairs to focus more intensively on expanded democracy promotion responsibilities (in addition to already assigned responsibilities for programs related to democracy and human rights, including the Office to Monitor and Combat Trafficking in Persons and the Human Smuggling and Trafficking Center).[19]

From the above, it follows that parallel actions could be taken to institutionalize the consideration of religion in U.S. foreign policy. Four possible options for doing so can be found in appendix B, with the two most promising involving consolidation of the religion function under the Under Secretary for Political Affairs (who would be retitled the "Under Secretary for Political and Religious Affairs"). If either of these two are adopted, the Under Secretary for Political and Religious Affairs should be given a seat at the table in National Security Council meetings to further ensure that religious considerations are given their just due in U.S. foreign policy and national security deliberations. Each of the remaining two organizational alternatives—tying it to the public diplomacy function or expanding the Office of International Religious Freedom—suffers from a greater likelihood that religion would ultimately end up marginalized within the bureaucracy.

Although the State Department has not yet seen fit to realign itself to accommodate the new realities (see Figure 7.1), some progress is being made on an informal basis through the efforts of a recently formed Religion and Global Affairs Working Group (RGA), a department-wide forum within

Figure 7.1
State Department Organizational Alternative

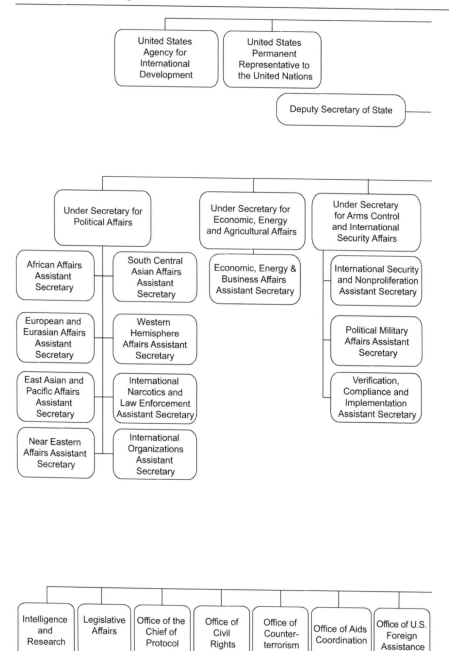

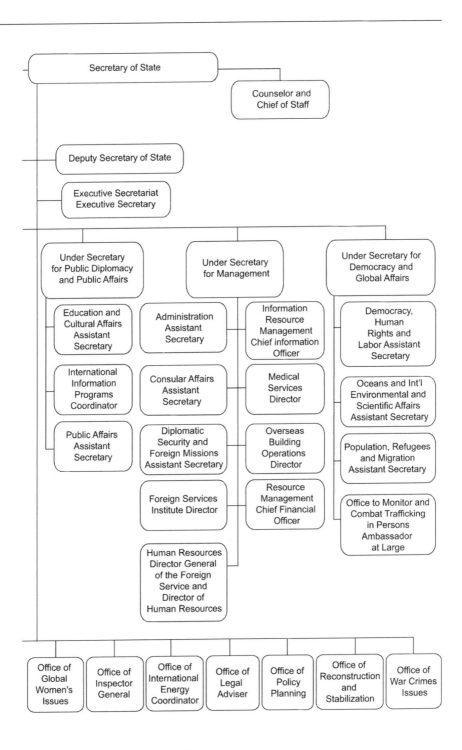

the Office of International Religious Freedom that connects State Department officers who are trying to think creatively about new strategies for engaging religious leaders and communities in support of U.S. foreign policy objectives. Thus far, the RGA has been conducting briefings by outside experts and has developed an Internet site that provides insights on religious-political issues to State Department and U.S. AID officers around the world. Building on the RGA's concept, a White House/NSC-based Interagency Working Group on Religion and Global Affairs has also been formed. As its first task, it is conducting a comprehensive review of how U.S. government agencies are relating to religious communities and faith-based institutions overseas, with an eye toward identifying needed improvements. Although these informal bodies are ad hoc and under-resourced, with any luck they will soon begin to influence the formal structure and, over time, lead to the institutional realignment that is long overdue.

In this same vein, it is interesting to note that no less than the pioneers of the Enlightenment have seen fit to establish a Religious Center housed in their Ministry of Foreign Affairs. In the words of French Foreign Minister Bernard Koucher, "We have incorporated the demography, ecology and pandemics in strategic thinking, why not religion? All the wars that I have known have carried varying degrees of religious stories."[20] This center will centralize French foreign policy decision making on religious subjects.

EDUCATIONAL REFORM

In theory, all FSOs are supposed to receive cultural training. In reality, staff shortages and the rapid turnover in foreign assignments often leave FSOs inadequately prepared.[21] Although the FSI has provided some coverage of religious matters for decades in its area studies courses, it was not until 2008 that courses with a specific focus on religion first appeared. Currently, a one-day course, *Islam—The Rise of Religion in Eurasia*, is offered several times a year, as is a three-day course called *Islam in Iraq: Religion, Society, and Politics*.[22] Finally, a five-day course, *Islam: Formation, Institutions, Modernity, and Reform*, is being offered three times a year.[23] In contrast to the robust Soviet studies programs that proliferated the academic landscape during the cold war (FSI included), the crucial religious dimension underlying today's foremost security challenge has until now been largely ignored. Thus, the critical challenge confronting the U.S. Foreign Service is to ensure that its thinly stretched diplomatic corps is provided sufficient training to develop a sophisticated understanding of the role of religion in international affairs that will enable it to interact effectively with religious leaders and institutions.[24]

To give religion the priority it should command in the training of State Department diplomats and policymakers, two major changes will be required. First, a separate subspecialty should be established within the FSI for specialized training in religion and statecraft. This subspecialty would apply to those who are interested in serving as Religion Attachés (or their equivalent); and, depending on which structural option is adopted, the Deputy Assistant Secretaries for Religion or religion specialists in the office of the USPD. The selection process for those FSOs who wish to specialize in religion should focus on candidates who already have some background in theology, religious studies, cultural anthropology, or other relevant disciplines.

Second, a four to six week course on all major world religions, including the key cultural elements and practices associated with them, and the resources and methods available within each for facilitating faith-based conflict prevention and resolution between and among religions should be provided for all FSOs who are on the political affairs and public diplomacy career tracks, as well as for the relevant desk officers in the Washington bureaus. As former Ambassador Kenton Keith has recommended, "In posts where religion is an important component of our bilateral relationship, diplomats should be given adequate educational background and training, and they should be required to pass a qualification test before being assigned."[25]

Past training in this arena has generally reflected a one-dimensional focus on the negative aspects of religion rather than its potential for peacemaking. Resources permitting, one could alternatively make this training an in-depth, nine-month course modeled on that provided for rising economic officers.[26] A regional focus could also be provided within such a subspecialty so that the training is targeted for those parts of the world in which the capability will be brought to bear.[27] For instance, those foreign affairs professionals who are focused on the Muslim world could receive extensive specialized training on diplomacy in an Islamic context. The curriculum, which would also include intensive language instruction, should be developed by the FSI in consultation with experts in religion and diplomacy from academia and civil society.

Among such experts, the U.S. Institute of Peace (USIP) stands out as a leader in innovative research and education in the areas of religion, violence, conflict resolution, and peacemaking. Not only could it ably assist the FSI in developing its religion-related curriculum, but, more than that, it could systematically sensitize the national security community within the executive branch to the critical importance of religion in diplomacy and international security, including, in addition to the State Department, the intelligence community, the Department of Defense, and National Security Council staff. Beyond the executive branch, it could also educate the congressional authorizing and appropriating committees and their professional staffs as well as the Congressional Research Service. In short, USIP is a critically important asset, the full impact of which has yet to be felt.

In contrast to the paucity of courses relating to religion at the FSI, traditional academia offers more comprehensive training in this arena for prospective FSOs. In the Washington, D.C., metropolitan area, for example, key institutions such as American University (AU), George Washington

University (GWU), and Georgetown University (GU) have specific programs to prepare students for careers with the State Department. All of
these schools have well-staffed religious studies/theology departments; and
students preparing for international service are encouraged—in the cases of
GWU and AU—to take courses in religious studies on an elective basis.

Georgetown goes a step further with its School of Foreign Service, specifically mandating in one of seven course tracks (the track involving politics and culture) that students take classes in comparative religion and
regional studies. Since the 1970s, most private and public colleges and universities have had academic departments of religion, religious studies, or
combinations of these and theology. Consequently, prescient or well-
advised students who intend to pursue careers in the Foreign Service have
had considerable religion-related training opportunities available to them.
Following the events of 9/11, most of these institutions have strengthened
their curricula on the subject of Islam.

It is important to note here a related observation by Father Ryan Maher,
Associate Dean at Georgetown University:

The majority of Georgetown students I know are fairly knowledgeable about religion. They can talk intelligently about Christianity, Islam, Judaism, Hinduism and
Buddhism. The glitch is that they talk from the perspective of anthropologists and sociologists and historians. These are valuable perspectives, but they are not enough.
Of course we need to raise young people who can be smart, savvy, sophisticated
participants in international affairs. What we also need are young people who can
be all of those things while at the same time knowing and understanding what it
is to live one's life with a commitment rooted in faith.

Father Ryan concludes that what hobbles American higher education when
it comes to educating people for careers in international affairs is not that
we do not know about religion; it is that we do not understand faith and
its life-shaping power.[28] This suggests that while FSOs in general should
have a reasonable grounding in comparative religions, the selection process for Religion Attachés should give strong consideration to those who
have had meaningful exposure to theology in their backgrounds.

THE CONGRESSIONAL DIMENSION

The U.S. Congress is politically and culturally more comfortable dealing
with religion than is the executive branch (which, when addressing situations that include a religious dimension, is often intimidated by the possibility of violating the provisions of the establishment clause). However,
because incorporating religion into the formal committee system would be
impossible owing to the structural difficulties of addressing crosscutting issues, consideration should be given to creating a staffed working group or
specialty caucus that includes representation from the relevant committees

and which has both a policy and communications capacity. Not only would this provide Congress with the means to act in its own right, but it would also enhance its capability to hold the executive branch accountable in this highly critical area.

CONCLUSION

Cultural awareness, while highly important, may be inadequate to the task when religious affiliation and spiritual orientation trump all other attributes. Moreover, the importance of religious knowledge extends not just to knowing one's enemies, but to knowing one's potential allies as well. In either case, U.S. diplomats cannot risk violating or offending religious mores without jeopardizing their professional effectiveness along the way; thus the need for a sound professional grounding in this sphere.

A potential drawback to enlisting Religion Attachés or their equivalent is the possibility of perpetuating the prevailing tendency to treat religion as a thing apart (and therefore more appropriately the province of experts). One of the vulnerabilities of the prevailing secular mind-set is the belief that religious knowledge can be leveraged without a deeper understanding of how religious faith inspires adherents to action. Not only is religion gaining influence on the world stage, it is becoming pivotal to understanding the newly emerging structures of international politics. This point was indirectly confirmed by Defense Secretary Robert Gates in his address to the Association of American Universities in April 2008:

There is little doubt that eventual success in the conflict against *jihadist* extremism will depend less on the results of individual military engagements and more on the overall ideological climate within the world of Islam. Understanding how this climate is likely to evolve over time, and what factors—including U.S. actions—will affect it thus becomes one of the most significant intellectual challenges we face.[29]

CHAPTER 8

Addressing the Operational Implications of Church/State Separation

Only religion can possibly stop the violence being done in its name.

—Joan Chittister

There are few issues that generate as much controversy as those surrounding the separation of church and state in the United States. For decades, scholars and jurists alike have struggled to negotiate a proper balance between respecting religion, while protecting it from the state, and preventing "excessive entanglement" that could be interpreted as governmental endorsement of one particular faith tradition over another. Indeed, the aversion to entanglement has reached the point where today one hears laments from religiously minded citizens who complain that the concept of religious freedom as set forth in the First Amendment to the Constitution has morphed from its original intent of providing "freedom of religion" to providing "freedom *from* religion," as though every atheist has a "God-given" right to live in a religious-free atmosphere.[1] More important, that same aversion has contributed significantly to the marginalization of religion at the policy level.

The pertinent portion of the First Amendment states that "Congress shall make no law respecting an establishment of religion, or prohibiting the free exercise thereof."[2] This provision was created in response to the long-suffering experiences of colonists held subject to religious controls, both in their homelands and in the new colonies.[3] When understood in this context, it becomes clear that the intention of the authors was to prevent infringement of the federal government on state or individual religious beliefs and practices, not to expel all things religious from government as many interpret it today. Another way of looking at it is that the separation clause guaranteed that churches would continue to be seen as a force for good, untainted by the corruption of politics. In short, the U.S. Constitution neither mandates ignorance about religion nor proscribes its public practice. The challenge has thus not been one of banishing religion from politics but of negotiating the boundaries within which they can compete.[4] Despite the ambiguity and tensions, religion has clearly had a strong influence on American politics from the birth of the republic to the present.

EXTRATERRITORIAL ASPECTS

Related to these domestic constraints is a concern over the degree to which they should extend to our overseas involvements. More specifically, can the United States actively use taxpayer funds to address the religious dimension of external threats like Islamist extremism if doing so might seemingly violate Supreme Court interpretations of the establishment clause of the Constitution? To a considerable extent, the long-standing reluctance of U.S. government officials to allow religious considerations to influence their professional judgments has carried over to many of our military leaders as well. Indicative of this aversion is the following response from a military commander to his chaplain's suggestion that the command provide indirect support to an NGO that was actively addressing the religious dimension of the same threat which the command itself was confronting:

During the past few months I have had some in-depth discussions with my Commander and others on the staff here. Without going into lengthy details, our staff tells me that they are prohibited from interacting with and supporting organizations which have religion associated with them. It seems as though I am the only one on the staff that is willing to interact with an organization associated with religion. My Commander has directed me to spend more time ministering directly to our headquarters staff and less time focused on strategic religious issues.[5]

The mind-set reflected in the response is not uncommon, but it is by no means all-pervasive. One who has not fallen prey to placing religiously affiliated groups out-of-bounds is Gen. David Petraeus, current Commander of International Security Forces in Afghanistan. In his earlier assignment as Commanding General of the Multi-National Force–Iraq, prominent on the briefing charts that he used when testifying before the U.S. Congress was the task of engaging the religious leaders in his theater of operations.[6] Further, he also provided the kind of indirect support mentioned above to the Foundation for Relief and Reconciliation in the Middle East, a faith-based NGO that has played an instrumental role in bringing key Iraqi Shia and Sunni leaders together to stem the sectarian conflict that was running rampant at the time and that threatened to sabotage U.S. efforts to stabilize the country.[7] With so much at stake, it only makes sense to bring to bear every asset one has at his or her disposal, including those with a religious dimension. That is exactly the kind of license that General Petraeus took yet again when he engaged the Sunnis in turning the corner against al Qaeda in Iraq.

Existing case law relating to the extraterritorial application of the establishment clause does not provide a clear picture of what is or is not specifically permitted when operating overseas. Although the clause itself could be construed as limiting U.S. action internationally in the same way that it does domestically, the overriding priority of national security–related considerations appears to offer considerable room to depart from domestic norms. Despite the lack of clarity in this arena, a quick review of the salient case law will provide a sense of the extent to which there is legal room to maneuver.

CASE LAW AND SCHOLARSHIP

It was Thomas Jefferson, with his more secular perspective than most of the other founders, who described the First Amendment as effectively creating a "wall of separation between church and state."[8] Although a seemingly clear and straightforward characterization, extensive related legal challenges over the succeeding centuries suggest that it is anything but. The following represent some of the more recent cases and scholarly contributions:

1. *Lemon v. Kurtzman*, 1971. In this case involving a domestic program, it was decided that government funding or action must meet what came to be known as the "Lemon test," that is, it (a) must have a secular purpose, (b) must neither advance nor inhibit religion, and (c) must not result in excessive government entanglement with religion.

2. "The Religion Clauses of the First Amendment and Foreign Relations," a two-part lecture by Harvard Law School professor John Mansfield, written under the auspices of the Center for Church/State Studies of the DePaul University College of Law and delivered March 13 and 14, 1986. In this lecture, Professor Mansfield argued that the apparent constitutional preeminence of the executive branch in the conduct of U.S. foreign policy, coupled with an accompanying need for presidential "room to maneuver" (by creating exceptions to nonestablishment rules), tends to undermine the force of the establishment clause in foreign relations.[9] He also highlighted the idea that "there should be found implicit in the Constitution recognition of the importance of respect for the ways of foreign nations."[10]

3. *Lamont v. Woods*, 1991. In considering the application of the establishment clause to a U.S. AID program for Catholic and Jewish schools abroad, the court decided that the principal goal of the establishment clause is to prevent governmental advancement of religion regardless of place.[11] At the same time, it suggested that "the government should be permitted to demonstrate some compelling reason why the usually unacceptable risk attendant on funding such an activity should, in the particular case, be borne."[12] This case was noteworthy for three reasons:

   a. The ruling was worded to suggest that different interpretations might result when national security considerations are at stake.

    b. It implicitly endorsed the distinction of the Lemon test between pro-
moting secular ends and those that could have the effect of advancing
religion.

    c. It drew a distinction between individual rights and restrictions on
the competency of Congress to enact laws (consistent with the constitutional prohibition against Congress making any law respecting the
establishment of religion).

4. *Hein v. Freedom from Religion Foundation,* 2007. Building on item 3c above, the
Supreme Court in *Hein* made it more difficult for the lower courts to enforce
establishment clause restrictions on government funding of religion by ruling
that unless a legislative body has explicitly directed that a specific religious
organization or activity be funded, individual citizens do not have a right as
taxpayers to bring suit in federal court alleging that such funding violates
the provisions of the establishment clause. In other words, taxpayers do not
have sufficient standing to challenge executive branch activity to promote
religious entities or causes.[13]

As noted by Walter Weber of the American Center for Law and Justice
during a probing discussion of *Hein* with several other attorneys at the
Pew Forum on Religion and Public Life in Washington, D.C., "The issue in
these cases is, who can sue? The normal rule is you can only sue—at least
in federal court—if you are someone who is injured."[14] And, "I think that's
the way the government is set up, is [*sic*] the things that are individual
rights, the individuals get to sue; the things that are structural, we're trusting to political enforcement."[15]

When one couples this narrowed standing with the wide-ranging authority granted the President under Article II of the Constitution to conduct foreign relations and development assistance and the fact that the Secretary
of State is authorized by rule to waive establishment clause restrictions relating to international development "where the Secretary determines that
such waiver is necessary to further the national security or foreign policy
interests of the United States,"[16] it would appear that there is, in fact, considerable legal room to maneuver in engaging religious leaders and activities overseas in the execution of U.S. foreign policy, whether diplomatically,
through provision of financial assistance, or by force of arms.

THE CONSEQUENCES OF AMBIGUITY

The Supreme Court has yet to rule on how the establishment clause applies beyond U.S. borders, but it appears reasonable to conclude from the
foregoing that if the religious initiative in question includes a national security dimension and can be shown to have a secular purpose, it will in
all likelihood go unchallenged. That aside, it is nevertheless the case that
U.S. government officials, including many military commanders, are often
reluctant to address issues relating to religion because of (1) their discomfort stemming from our long-standing secular political and legal traditions,

(2) the chilling effect of ambiguous policy, and (3) the adverse impact on their careers if their actions are not supported by the chain of command.

First Amendment–related restrictions are also interfering with initiatives by U.S. AID and other civilian agencies to win Muslim hearts and minds by rebuilding war-damaged mosques and the like. In other words, civilian attempts to stem the influence of the extremists are being undercut by these perceived legal barriers.[17] Religious excess demands religious counterargument, which requires the kind of religious leverage the United States has been forsaking as a result of these policies.

Until the reluctance to engage is squarely addressed, we will run the continued risk of making uninformed foreign policy choices and having to fight with one hand tied behind our back. Indicative of the latter (and as pointed out in a Center for Strategic and International Studies [CSIS] report of August 2007) is the fact that following 9/11, and after much deliberation, the State Department's legal branch advised that outreach efforts should "limit direct engagement with religious issues."[18] This same cautionary stance was repeated in the Department of State's 2007 *U.S. National Strategy for Public Diplomacy and Strategic Communication*, which urged government officials to be "extremely cautious and if possible, avoid using religious language, because it can mean different things and is easily misconstrued."[19]

COMMON SENSE CONSIDERATIONS

Our military and civilian officials need the freedom to work with influential Muslim religious authorities and scholars in order to counter the extremism that threatens our national interests. Yet there have been any number of instances in which such attempts have been opposed on the grounds that they violate the establishment clause. With so much at stake in thwarting the designs of the terrorists, this is clearly a case of the tail wagging the dog. As recently noted by former U.S. AID lawyer Colum Lynch, "Our legal position is too conservative. We've got a war on terror. The lawyers are concerned about excessive entanglement with religion. Well, we're already entangled."[20] Implicit in this statement of the obvious is the fact that there is no risk-free way to engage the problem of terrorism. The sooner our inherently risk-averse bureaucracy recognizes this fact, the better off everyone will be.

Lawmakers who give credence to legislative intent should note the original goal of the framers of the First Amendment. There was no discussion of extraterritorial applications of the establishment clause.[21] It is also noteworthy that the First Amendment placed limits on Congress but not on the states, a number of which had state-established churches and laws supporting religion, for example, Congregational Connecticut and Anglican Virginia. Since the amendment did not include a disestablishment clause, many states continued to support their established churches through laws and tax dollars long after the ratification of the Bill of Rights. Massachusetts, for example, retained ties between religion and state until 1833—more than 40 years after ratification of the First Amendment—and it did so without incurring the wrath of the federal government, since its connection with the church violated neither the Constitution of the United States nor that of Massachusetts. Thus, limiting the rights of states, and specifically their right to establish and support a particular religion, was simply not a goal of the First Amendment.

Not until ratification of the Fourteenth Amendment following the Civil War in 1868 did the First Amendment's provisions extend to the states. This resulted from the Republican Party's determination to protect the endangered rights of recently freed African Americans by extending to the government of every state the protections granted to individuals by the federal government (through the Bill of Rights).[22] If the framers of the First Amendment were unconcerned about individual states establishing the religion of their choice, is it not unlikely that they would have been concerned about influencing the religious choices of other nations? A case could thus be made that this extrapolated apathy should open the door for U.S. officials to engage freely with religious actors and institutions in other countries.

MEETING THE NEED

To remove the perception that there are legal impediments which limit our ability to act, the President should immediately task the Department of Justice to provide the legal case for a policy of religious engagement as a component of U.S. foreign policy. A bipartisan endorsement of this policy by the congressional leadership would be helpful as well.

CHAPTER 9

Developing a Preventive Engagement Capability

> I hate war as only a soldier who has lived it can, only as one who has seen its brutality, its futility, its stupidity.
>
> —Dwight Eisenhower

In 1992, a widely heralded Georgetown University report that looked ahead to "The Foreign Service in 2001" stated that "the decision for the United States to intervene in foreign conflicts will be based more often on complex moral or ethical grounds" and went on to predict that within a decade, more diplomacy will be "preventive and interventionist" in nature.[1] Conspicuous by its absence was any mention of the word *religion*, either as a source of ethical ideas or as a potential contributor to reconciliation between protagonists. Unsurprisingly, this omission has carried through to the present. One reads lengthy realpolitik articles on smart power these days without any reference to the *R* word whatsoever, not even as a source of current or prospective problems.[2]

International recognition of this same need for prevention was institutionalized in 2000 with the establishment of the International Commission on Intervention and State Sovereignty. This initiative by the Canadian government was in response to former UN Secretary-General Kofi Annan's challenge to the international community to determine when external intervention in the affairs of individual states is warranted, under whose authority it should take place, and how. The central theme of the commission's report was "the responsibility to protect," and prevention was singled out as the most important dimension of this responsibility.[3]

Although understanding conflict situations before determining how to respond to them might seem an obvious precondition, recent military experiences in Iraq and Afghanistan underscore the difficulty of engaging foreign cultures and dealing with unfamiliar political, social, religious, and economic realities. In view of the cultural complexity that surrounds so many of today's conflicts, a new approach to planning is needed that involves greater effort on the front-end in order to gain a deeper understanding of the social dynamics underlying the problems to be addressed and of the political context within which solutions must be found.

In most situations where the potential for armed conflict exists, one finds an intense competition between political movements in pursuit of power and those that already have it. Failing to understand the cultural and social dimensions of these situations at the outset can lead to reactive, ill-conceived policy decisions that exacerbate an already unstable situation. Because the preconceived assumptions that typically inform our policy choices overseas seldom accurately reflect the actual situations on the ground and because of our proven reluctance to engage militarily at an early stage, the plethora of identity-based conflicts that permeate today's geopolitical landscape makes all the more acute our need for an effective conflict prevention capability. The consequences of such conflicts are enormous and, in addition to loss of life and limb, include (1) destroyed assets and infrastructure, (2) a weakened workforce due to death and disease, (3) the exorbitant costs of raising capital (owing to increased political risk), and (4) draconian safety and security costs. Thus, while the after-the-fact expenses of nation building are vast, the benefits of preventing such conflict in the first instance are equally immense. Clearly, in the military (as in medicine) preventive beats proscriptive any day.

Developing a conflict prevention capability, however, represents a formidable challenge in light of the difficulty of (1) proving its effectiveness (how does one prove something did not happen because of something one did?) and (2) mustering the political will required to take action now in order to prevent something from taking place in the future, when current politicians and policymakers may no longer be in office. In short, prevention will not come naturally in a democracy where crisis is the normal prerequisite for intervention. There are at least three reasons, though, why such impediments must be overcome if the nation is to remain secure.

First and foremost, the specter of religious extremism married to weapons of mass destruction demands no less. Second, based on the huge expense of our post–cold war involvements in Bosnia, Kosovo, Kuwait, Afghanistan, and Iraq, it appears that interventions to halt violent conflict that can adversely impact our vital interests are becoming increasingly cost-prohibitive. Finally, the fact that terrorist organizations opposed to the United States and its foreign policies find conflict environments well-suited to meeting their needs for basing, training, and equipping their members only adds to the need for preventing such conflicts in the first instance.

Formulating an effective prevention capability will first require a high fidelity understanding of (and ability to relate to) the social, cultural, and political realities of critical trouble-spots where the potential for conflict exists. And for this kind of enhanced situational awareness, a new vehicle will be needed in the form of Conflict Prevention Research Teams (CPRTs).

CPRTs would consist of social science professionals, regional experts, and situational-dependent combinations of experts from various other disciplines (such as psychology, demography, geography, archaeology, history, criminal justice, health management, and organizational development), who would operate as neutral researchers in areas where instability could conceivably lead to open conflict. The purpose of the CPRTs would be to inform the U.S. policy process with insights that can help prevent conflict. In some respects, they could also be viewed as providing advance reconnaissance for suitable Track Two initiatives.

Involving five or more civilian personnel, the four-fold mission of these teams would be (1) to "map" the existing social, political, and cultural networks and determine their influence in the country or region of interest; (2) to conduct sufficient local field research to acquire a clear understanding of what is taking place; (3) to develop working relationships with key local figures whose insights can help inform that research; and (4) to advise the U.S. government, international and regional organizations, and possibly the NGO community on appropriate measures to improve stability. Organizationally, CPRTs could operate under the auspices of an organization like the U.S. Institute of Peace (USIP) and while deployed maintain an autonomous-appearing presence in order to minimize their U.S. affiliation/ profile. Alternatively, a more neutral peace research institute or an NGO like the International Crisis Group could also serve as the organizational umbrella.

In some respects, the CPRTs could be viewed as the preventive equivalent of the Defense Department's Human Terrain Teams (HTTs), which with some success have been advising Army combat units on local cultural and political dynamics (with an eye toward winning the hearts and minds of the people). However, the CPRTs, with their civilian structure and preventive focus, would not be subject to the same academic criticisms of "militarizing anthropology" or "anthropologically aiding subjugation" that have plagued the HTTs.

The size and composition of the CPRTs would vary based on the need; and over the course of their existence, both might change as subject matter experts (SMEs) on the particular area in question or other relevant specialists are added to accomplish specific additional tasks. In other words, the goal of CPRTs would be to understand the cultural landscape in areas where conflict threatens and to recommend appropriate actions for promoting stability and peace.

The specific political goals of a CPRT would be influenced by a target country's form of government. Under a dictatorial regime and the right circumstances, for example, a CPRT's research might be oriented toward assisting the regime in transitioning to a more representative form of governance. In weaker states or transitional regimes, where the risk of civil violence is high, the CPRT might work toward developing a dialogue among competing political movements that could lead to more inclusive governance. In situations where religious or ethnic strife appears likely, the CPRT might help facilitate reconciliation through research that leads to the formation of useful new structures such as interreligious councils.[4] In the aftermath of civil violence, the CPRT might pursue some of these same measures (and others) in reestablishing a fully functioning society.

In addition to administering the CPRTs, USIP (or some organizational equivalent) could conduct training programs to familiarize U.S. government and NGO officials with the role of CPRTs and how they can improve stability in countries at risk. It could also sponsor research on "best practices" and "lessons learned" relating to early warning/response mechanisms and various other elements involved in developing a "culture of prevention."

SOCIAL SCIENCE RESEARCH

The field of social science is composed of a set of interrelated academic disciplines: sociology, anthropology, political science, economics, and psychology. There are a number of subject areas, such as religious studies and communications studies, in which the more relevant cross sections of these disciplines can also be applied to acquire useful insights. Such interdisciplinary initiatives have also been used to good effect in area studies programs.

The social science disciplines generally seek to describe or explain social life by collecting facts that one knows with certainty (data or observations) in order to learn things one doesn't know with certainty (theories or hypotheses).[5] In other words, social science seeks to describe the life of a society by identifying its underlying dynamics through proven methods of data collection and analysis.[6] These disciplines overlap greatly but vary in the topics on which they focus, the goals of their research, and the methods they use to collect and analyze information.

Anthropology and political science are the two disciplines thought to be most relevant to conflict prevention and resolution. Whereas the former tends to focus on the description of a conflict situation, political science is much more interested in the causes of conflict. Accordingly, they differ in the methods they use in conducting research and analysis. With the pervasive resurgence of religion in international affairs, however, experts in theology and/or religious studies should be accorded equal prominence in situations where religion is a major factor. Here, it is insufficient to treat religion as a mere subset of anthropology. What is needed are religion experts who have a visceral appreciation for the power of faith to move people to action. Among the possible sources of such people, faith-based NGOs and selected ecclesiastical bodies would be leading contenders.

The parent organization for the CPRTs could ensure that the research is conducted in an ethical manner and that its applications are confined to conflict prevention. It could also select the relevant researchers, provide them with a team structure, help coordinate their logistical support for conducting field research, sponsor workshops to share the results of that research with U.S. policymakers and appropriate others, assist in the development of helpful policy recommendations, and ensure that the information is made available to the policy community and, where helpful, to the public more generally.

THE CPRT CONCEPT

Building the Team

Building a multidisciplinary research and analysis team to conduct field research in countries at risk will not be a simple task. As the foregoing suggests, it is not merely a matter of identifying an anthropologist, a sociologist, a political scientist, and an area expert. It is instead a question of identifying academics with the right combination of skills, knowledge, and experience to be relevant to the specific need at hand. Toward this end, literature reviews could be conducted to help identify and enlist the participation of appropriate social scientists for the specific research in question. Additionally, the organizing institution should be experienced in working in unstable areas to help facilitate the recruitment of any local researchers that may be required.

An effective way to organize team security is through the use of security officers experienced with living in communities outside of U.S. embassies and military bases. These security officers will live with the teams and provide security throughout the operation. They will emphasize low-profile security measures to ensure the team's safety, including that of any local researchers who might be involved. The approach that security professionals take to ensure the safety of the team will vary according to the on-the-ground realities. In most situations, providing team members with Hostile Environment Awareness Training (HEAT) would be a useful first step.[7]

The guiding principle of the research team should be to blend in with the population and provide benefits to as many locally relevant groups as possible. Such an approach can help make the security of the research team a priority for the local population as well. In many instances, the team's own efforts to prevent conflict from erupting will act to reinforce its own security as well. In insecure areas, an extra layer of security is often prudent, but it should be low-key, defensive, and not openly threatening to the local population. Wherever possible, the team's presence should not in any way compromise the population's security.

Academic research experts would be most comfortable working with an organization that allows them intellectual freedom, does not directly associate them with the U.S. government, and allows them to use the collected data to publish independent studies. Peace research institutes provide just such an environment.

Methodology

Some of the initial analysis should be conducted by well-trained staff in the field to ensure the accuracy and currency of the baseline against which future progress will be measured. Once engaged in the task itself, the CPRTs may deploy to the field for months at a time, depending on the kind of research to be conducted and the time required to complete it.

It is important to take into account the "reactive error" that can arise in response to the role and makeup of the team that will be used. This occurs when the team stimulates the subjects of the research to behave differently than they otherwise would.[8] This kind of error is very common in areas where conflict is imminent because people are constantly confronted with shifting rules relating to identity and behavior. As a system of social order breaks down, it is no longer clear what one can say and to whom without the possibility of violent repercussions. Conducting the needed research through individuals who closely identify with the interviewees is often the most effective way to mitigate this problem.

Significant reactive error is common when Americans conduct research in less-developed countries, because they are seen to be potential sources of money and power. For that reason, in many of the places where preventive research would be conducted, an important part of the job will consist of designing research for local researchers to conduct and training them in how they should conduct it. Research by locals can also provide another potentially helpful perspective on the situation in question and help the principals identify errors in their own research. The job of recruiting and managing local research teams in areas where conflict is likely is a highly specialized task that should be assigned to someone with the skills and experience to safeguard both the local researchers and the subjects of the research. Throughout the research project, a group of at least five academics experienced in conducting field research in zones of conflict should serve as an ethics and accuracy review board, providing advice and informed guidance to the research team.

When their research is completed, the teams will return to Washington to present the results of their research in workshops attended by the policymaking community and selected nongovernmental organizations. These presentations will provide the basis for discussing the possible courses of action. Depending on the importance of the situation to U.S. national interests, the research findings may also be presented to high-ranking members of the executive and legislative branches. Finally, if it so chooses, the organizing institution can publish the research results to encourage public discussion and build widespread support for appropriate preventive measures.

A POSSIBLE TARGET

To illustrate the potential utility of CPRTs, a hypothetical case study relating to Bosnia will be presented since that region is growing restless once again and may be ripe for a CPRT intervention. First, a little background.

When Adm. William Owens was Commander of the U.S. Sixth Fleet in the early 1990s, he received a message from the President of the former Yugoslavia requesting more port visits by U.S ships to help keep the lid on as things were beginning to heat up. The request was vetoed by the State Department on the grounds that Yugoslavia was a European problem and ought not to involve the United States.[9] Although the ship visits might not have made a significant difference in view of the deeper issues at play, one nevertheless wonders what might have been, considering the $53 billion that America and the international community spent on Bosnia alone between 1992 and 1998.[10]

If a CPRT had entered Yugoslavia during that time period, it would have seen rising tides of ethnic nationalism fueled by Serbian moves for political dominance, including the use of social tactics designed to incite chaos.[11] The CPRT would have also found a nonfunctioning economy, with unemployment running as high as 30 percent owing to government intrusion into private enterprise and government cooperation with the massive and growing black market. It would have seen the competition for resources exacerbating ethnic divisions and leaders adopting nationalistic agendas and using religious rhetoric to unite their communities and denigrate their rivals. Further, it would have found a society on the edge—unsure of what was going to unfold but keenly aware of Serbian moves to consolidate power and build up its armaments. Clearly, the situation had deteriorated to a point where it was well beyond the ability of a CPRT to influence. Perhaps five years earlier. . . .

Even today's situation would pose a substantial challenge for one or more CPRTs. In important respects, Bosnia-Herzegovina, Croatia, and Serbia all suffer from varying degrees of economic, social, and political dysfunction. Once again, the potential for violence lies just beneath the surface in a milieu of fear and suspicion that has survived the Dayton Accords. As one Serbian Orthodox priest observed, "[The children] will grow up to kill again."[12] Because of disparate features of ethnicity and religion, policy solutions that might be appropriate in one region or area will, in all likelihood, be inappropriate in another. In short, one size won't fit all.

In Bosnia alone, the most recent official census data (1991) shows an ethnic breakdown of 46 percent Muslim, 33.1 percent Serb, and 18.4 percent Croat.[13] A more recent estimate shows a population breakdown of 48 percent Bosniak (Bosnian Muslim), 37.1 percent Serb, 14.3 percent Croat, and 0.6 percent other.[14] Although the literacy rate is high, at 96.7 percent,[15] acute social and cultural differences are superimposed on complex geopolitical demographics. These differences include the fact that a significant number of people in the region are of mixed ethnicity, which makes for a highly complicated challenge. Adding to this are the facts that for the first time in decades, the people of Bosnia are living completely segregated lives, the educational system is propagating ethnic stereotypes, unemployment is as high as 40 percent,[16] and religious extremism is on the rise. Finally, negative emotions bound up not just in recent history but extending back to past empires—be they Byzantium, Ottoman, or Hapsburg—contribute to a miasmic memory that acts to undermine compromise.

Background

Under the Dayton Peace Accords, Bosnia-Herzegovina remained an internationally recognized state within its prewar borders consisting of two semiautonomous entities: the Federation of Bosnia and Herzegovina occupied by Bosniaks and Bosnian Croats and the Bosnian Serb Republika Srpska, with each controlling about half of the country's territory (see Figure 9.1). Overarching these entities is a central Bosnian government with a rotating presidency supported by a European Union–led peacekeeping force (EUFOR). Each of the entities has its own parliament and government, with wide-ranging powers.

Most powers are vested in the entities, but the central government has responsibility for foreign policy, foreign trade, monetary policy, and customs policy (in addition to several other lesser functions). Decisions of the central government and parliament are nominally taken by a majority, but any of the three major ethnic groups can block a decision if it views that the decision as being against its vital interests. As mandated by the earlier pre-Dayton Washington Accords, the federation is further subdivided into 10 cantons, each of which has control of policy in critical areas like policing and education.

Finally, the UN-appointed Office of the High Representative (OHR), created by the Dayton Accords, oversees civilian peace implementation efforts. The OHR is supported by the Peace Implementation Council (PIC), an umbrella group of 55 countries that exerts influence through a steering board consisting of representatives from a number of key countries and institutions, including the United States, Russia, France, Germany, Britain, Italy, Canada, Japan, Turkey, and the EU Commission and presidency. The OHR also serves as the EU's Special Representative in Bosnia.

Figure 9.1
Bosnia and Herzegovina

At a December 1997 PIC conference in Bonn, Germany, the PIC granted the High Representative powers (known as the "Bonn powers") to fire and take other actions against local leaders and parties as well as to impose legislation in order to implement the peace agreement and more generally bring unity and reform to Bosnia. Since that time, the international community has been pressing hard to enhance and empower Bosnia's central government. Specific accomplishments toward this end have included (1) merger of the armed forces and intelligence services of the two entities and (2) creation of new central government institutions such as border and customs services and a state prosecutor's office in the Ministry of Justice. Such changes, while supported by Bosniak politicians, have been strongly opposed by Bosnian Serb and Bosnian Croat politicians. The Bosniaks basically seek a state of their own in which they are dominant (as Serbs are in Serbia and Croats are in Croatia), while the latter two groups seek total autonomy.[17]

Bosnia's cumbersome governing structure has severely hampered progress toward a viable nation-state, whether it be centrally controlled like France or federated in nature like Belgium or Switzerland. Large and expensive bureaucracies, coupled with long-standing problems relating to rampant corruption, have hampered Bosnia's economic growth as well. It is estimated that Bosnia's public sector constitutes 50 percent of the country's GDP.[18] Although Republika Srpska also suffers from high-level corruption, its less-cumbersome governing structure (having none of the cantons that comprise the federation) has enabled it to move more quickly on economic reforms. Nevertheless, the largely dysfunctional economic picture is exacerbated by antagonisms between wealthy elites and the numerous and growing poor classes within the respective populations—made worse by the recent global economic crisis. Further complicating the march toward sovereignty is the fact that Bosnia is said to suffer from a "dependency syndrome" dating back to the Ottoman Empire, which gets in the way of taking the kinds of initiatives required for it to stand on its own.[19]

Current Realities

At the political level, there is considerable debate about the future role of the international community in Bosnia. The PIC appears eager to end the direct international oversight of Bosnia through the OHR. This may be partly due to "political fatigue," after having played such a prominent role in the country for over 13 years. Since 2007, the High Representative has been reluctant to use his wide-ranging powers to impose legislation or to fire obstructionist officials, owing to a lack of political support for such actions by leading countries within the PIC. In January 2009, the High Representative resigned, expressing frustration at the ineffectiveness of the OHR's powers.

Ironically, the Dayton Accords created the decentralized political system that the international community has been working so hard to centralize. Tension between the international overseers and the various nationalist parties has been an ongoing fact of life from the beginning. Although Bosnia claims to seek the creation of a unified, multiethnic state, its political institutions support ethnic partition at every level of government.[20] By the same token, the country's disjointed domestic institutions have been undermined by (1) a poorly functioning protectorate (the OHR), which has been characterized by international organizations as working at cross-purposes, and (2) the OHR's failure to persevere in implementing needed reforms when challenges arise. In short, the consequences of decentralizing before consolidating central authority continue to hinder movement toward a mutually agreeable arrangement. In light of continuing ethnic tensions and other realities, the Swiss model is probably the most promising option to pursue.

There is a distinct catch-22 aspect to the nation-building challenge in Bosnia. Creating a more centralized and efficient Bosnia can happen only if the entities are weakened, which, in turn, will create fear among the Serbs that they will lose Republika Srpska and hope among the Bosniaks that they will gain accordingly. In other words, the Serbs want the internationals to leave them alone and to leave Bosnia while the Bosniaks have no incentive to facilitate their departure as long as they believe those internationals may eventually give them what they want, a centralized Bosnia that they will dominate.

Approach

In summary, 15 years after the Dayton Accords brought an end to the conflict resulting from the breakup of the former Yugoslavia, Bosnia and its people are still struggling to find a path for reconstruction and reconciliation. The root causes of the war have not been properly addressed, among which is the ongoing instability arising from politicians actively exploiting ethnic and nationalistic differences; and the international community seems unable to create conditions for a sustainable peace. The country itself is in a mild state of paralysis that is preventing it from moving toward peace and prosperity. The most critical challenge—that of rebuilding human relationships across ethnic and religious lines—remains largely unattended and ignored. Were things to deteriorate to the point where widespread violence erupted, EUFOR could easily be overwhelmed, requiring a U.S. and/or NATO military response, at a time when their respective forces are severely stretched in other parts of the globe. In addition, neighboring Serbia and Croatia could be pulled into such a conflict, which, in turn, could also implicate NATO, since Croatia joined the alliance in April 2009. Serbia's recent movement toward European integration could also be halted, and conflict between Serbs and Albanians in Kosovo could revive.

With so much at stake and Bosnians once again talking about the possibility of war, the insertion of one or more CPRTs to assess the situation and develop recommendations would be timely and potentially quite helpful. In view of the political gridlock at the top, a grassroots focus may be the most fruitful starting point. Here, it would be important to note the following:

1. Because of the different ethnic perspectives involved (and accompanying points of view) , at least three CPRTs should be engaged, one operating out of Sarajevo for the Bosniaks, another out of Mostar for the Bosnian Croats, and the third out of Banja Luka for the Bosnian Serbs.

2. The CPRTs should operate as independently as possible from the OHR and the PIC in order to avoid any specter of bias.

3. They should integrate as much as possible with the local communities in whichever entity they are operating (as opposed to Bosnia as a whole).

4. Where possible, the CPRTs should consider engaging expats who may be living among the locals to serve as liaisons between the teams and the communities.

5. Bosnian NGOs play a significant role in Bosnian society, performing a number of functions that one would normally expect local governments to perform. They are highly trusted and could be of great assistance, both in providing insights and in possibly serving as members of the CPRTs themselves.

6. At prescribed intervals, the CPRTs should communicate with one another to compare notes and determine if there are any areas in which the separate entities/ethnic groups are pursuing similar agendas, thereby facilitating an indirect dialogue between those whom they are assessing.

7. Because of the high stakes involved and the need to move quickly, CPRTs could report any potential opportunities for cooperation directly to U.S. officials working in the PIC (in addition to Washington policymakers in later briefings back home).

8. Each CPRT should engage local experts, including religion specialists familiar with Islam, Catholicism, and Orthodox Christianity, since the populations are still mixed and numerous disputes occur between locals representing all three faiths. Before attempting an assessment of the current situation, each team should have an advance familiarity with what the situation was like in its assigned area prior to the breakup of Yugoslavia.

9. A key role of the CPRTs would be to consolidate existing information regarding the successes and failures of the international community, national and local governments, NGOs, and religious bodies throughout the country.

Relevant Disciplines

The array of CPRT professionals that could be engaged to work with NGOs and local governmental agencies is quite broad and extends beyond the bounds of sociologists, political scientists, and economists. To be sure, the use of sociologists, especially those with an understanding of the political dynamics, would be a potentially fruitful beginning. The diverse nuances of culture and religion in pan-Yugoslavia, however, would require the use of other social scientists (in addition to political scientists and economists), such as cultural anthropologists, psychologists, and geographers (who would be particularly helpful, since this field incorporates cross-disciplinary associations relating to human, environmental, and regional geography). In addition, team members trained in comparative religious studies and theology would be valuable in working with local religious leaders and clerics to enhance cooperative and irenic possibilities by helping to bridge the religious differences. By identifying and working with religious leaders in the region who understand the need for peace and reconciliation, CPRTs could help begin the process of marginalizing the more radical and disharmonious fringe elements.

Challenges

Economic

- Economic disparity is growing between the two entities, as privatization in the Serb republic is taking place at a faster rate (driven in part by a recent influx of Russian investment). Many Serb companies are thus able to outbid Bosniak or Croat companies, even in the Bosniak/Croat parts of the country. This, in turn, fuels nationalist tendencies. A CPRT could recommend measures to accelerate the privatization process throughout the country in addition to finding ways to connect other foreign investors with Bosnian firms.

- Because Bosnia's "informal" sector is so large (as much as 50% of GDP), measures will need to be taken to help legitimate informal businesses incorporate easily and to press illegitimate businesses either to shut down or become incorporated. Much of this situation relates to high taxation and overly burdensome regulations, both formidable deterrents to entrepreneurship that will most certainly have to be taken into account. CPRTs could provide important guidance in this area as well.

Political

- To minimize corruption and political patronage, government spending and redundant government offices need to be cut. The CPRT could generate recommendations to help restructure the government's institutions and the budget in order to decrease opportunities for pork barrel politics and to keep as much money as possible in the investment-seeking private sector. For example, there are 160 government ministers and 11 different employment agencies in the Bosniak/Croat federation alone. It also takes 60 days to start a business, as opposed to one week in Kosovo and one day in Macedonia.

- Under the Dayton Accords, each constituent is identified according to his or her ethnic or national identity. The result is that politicians use ethnicity to appeal to voters and acquire support. Constituents identify with these appeals and approve of nationalist politicians, in part because of the financial rewards they get in return, thus fostering a self-reinforcing cycle of financial kickbacks in the political system. Decreasing government spending would be a useful first step in addressing this problem. Finally, enlightened electoral reform could create a system in which ethnicity is not taken into account, but that will not happen until ethnic tensions are mitigated.

- The roles of the multiple presidents need to be reduced through constitutional reform, even if a federated state structure is adopted. Not only do they contribute to nationalist tensions, but they also result in an inefficient bureaucracy. With appropriate safeguards, consideration could even be given to a rotating presidency, much like what was attempted in Yugoslavia before the breakup.

The Prime Minister, in any event, should be granted greater power in running the ministries.

- Any major change in government structure or expenditures would have to be carefully crafted and complemented with an economic agenda that serves the three constituencies equally. A major obstacle here is the fact that as long as renewed conflict is a possibility, Bosnian leaders will not want to do anything that could limit their power or access to capital. Thus, for politicians to accept such changes, they will have to view the potential benefits of change as clearly outweighing those of the status quo.

NGOs

- Many NGOs have focused on building up civil society through educational programs and encouraging democratic participation, while also providing child care, psychosocial support, education opportunities, and the like. NGOs have also helped provide a useful source of employment for Bosnians through the various programs that they implement. However, by offering services normally provided by either the private or public sector, NGOs are ipso facto enabling the government and economic sectors to develop without taking these services into account. The CPRTs would thus need to evaluate and develop recommendations for streamlining NGO operations throughout the country, in much the same way as they would for streamlining superfluous government agencies.
- Donor revenue to the region has been steadily declining since 1998, making it all the more important for the CPRT to develop recommendations for streamlining that will maximize the benefits of EU and American donor funding. Dependence on the NGO sector over the past decade has meant that as revenues decline, unemployment rises, and gaps are created in community services, such as health care, child care, and education, hence the need for the national government and private sector to take over such responsibilities on an ongoing basis. An NGO economy is a vulnerable economy.

Nationalistic, Ethnic, and Religious Tensions

- There is an ongoing concern that the internal and external boundaries for each ethnic group and the nation itself may change. This fosters intense nationalism in a heavily competitive atmosphere. Thus, the nation's leaders need to pledge that they will not violate one another's borders. Membership in the EU or NATO would go a long way toward alleviating such fears.
- Mustafa Efendi Ceric, the Grand Mufti and foremost spiritual leader of Bosnia's Muslim community, has said, "The Serbs committed genocide against us, raped our women, made us refugees in our own country . . . and now we have a tribal constitution that says we have to share political power and land with our killers. . . . We Bosnian Muslims still feel besieged in the city of Sarajevo."[21] The CPRT needs to survey the opinions of key religious leaders throughout the country and encourage them to promote reconciliation and love of neighbor. The Interreligious Council formed by World Religions for Peace in Sarajevo in 1997 could play a critical role in this effort.

- Bosnia is undergoing an Islamic revival. Dozens of new mosques have opened, increasing numbers of men are sporting long beards, and more women are opting to wear the hijab. Analysts indicate that the Saudis have invested $700 million in Bosnia since the war, mostly in mosques, thus heightening the fear of creeping Wahhabism.[22] This infusion of mosques was precipitated by the earlier Shiite takeover of Iran, which so concerned the Saudi royal family that they gave Wahhabi "missionaries" a free hand to spread their anti-Shiite faith all over the world.

- Similarly, church attendance for Catholics and Orthodox Christians is also on the rise. Unfortunately, churches often enflame nationalism more than they curb it. Here, the CPRT could identify churches and mosques throughout Bosnia that are in difficult financial straits and possibly facilitate western financial support for them from churches or mosques in the United States. Through such partnerships, western-based mosques and churches could encourage their Bosnian counterparts to resist nationalistic impulses.

- Even in communities where Serbs, Croats, and Muslims live next to one another, some of them opt to send their children to school in different time shifts to prevent interethnic contact. Community leaders (religious and business) should encourage integrated schools, and teachers should be trained in fostering interethnic and religious understanding and respect. Illustrative of the challenge is the fact that some publicly funded schools have introduced Islamic education as early as kindergarten, thus pressuring non-Muslim parents to pull their children out of class at the outset. In this case, legal action could be taken to prevent one-sided religious education in publicly funded schools.

- It has been proven in India and elsewhere that mixed ethnic participation in civic associations is one of the best deterrents to ethnic conflict. This is something that a CPRT could encourage and help facilitate through recommendations that encourage external pressure and funding. A useful device here would be to require international organizations like the UN or NATO to award grants for services that favor those applicants who provide multiethnic submissions.

- There are religious bodies in Bosnia that actively promote interfaith tolerance, such as the Catholic order of Franciscans in northern Bosnia and selected moderate Islamic leaders. Such leaders should be identified and provided with foreign assistance to promote their approach on a wider scale. Moreover, there are numerous opportunities for religious leaders to work within their own faith traditions to curb ethnic tensions within the churches and mosques.

- Religious leaders should also be encouraged to play a more visible role in cooperating with other faiths in the community.

- Orthodox, Catholic, and Muslim religious leaders from outside the country should be brought to Bosnia to conduct lectures on tolerance and reconciliation at colleges, civic forums, and houses of worship. These leaders should also work with and encourage local religious leaders to cooperate with one another. Local religious leaders are often reluctant to do so on their own for fear that members of their church communities will retaliate. Having foreign religious leaders serve in this capacity would provide Bosnian religious leaders the opportunity to ride their coattails.

International Support

- The EU, United States, and other allies like Turkey and Norway need to formulate a common policy for Bosnia. This could be encouraged through a U.S. special envoy to the region with whom a CPRT could work in developing a comprehensive strategy.

Left unattended, the situation in Bosnia could easily deteriorate, with unpleasant consequences (as it has on more than one occasion in the past). However, with the kind of thoughtful assessment that a CPRT could provide and effective intervention based on that assessment, the potential deterioration could conceivably be reversed to the benefit of all.

CONCLUSION

The above case study illustrates the prospective roles that CPRTs could play in difficult situations. Although the depiction of these roles is by no means exhaustive, it does suggest the need for a capability of this nature to provide the kind of in-depth understanding that will be needed to support enlightened foreign policy choices.

CHAPTER 10

The American Muslim Community: An Asset-in-Waiting

I warn you of extremism in the religion for indeed those that came before you were destroyed due to their extremism in the religion.
—Prophet Muhammad (PBUH)
Hadith 4049, Al Sunan al-Kubra

The events of September 11, 2001, created a new global environment in which international security became the overriding challenge for most western policymakers and foreign policy practitioners. The implications of this sudden transformation have been especially obvious in the United States, where the resulting policy changes and institutional realignments have been felt at many levels of government. These legislative and executive branch shifts, designed to enhance national security while balancing safety with normalcy, have had far-reaching consequences for many Americans, especially for those who are Muslims.

AMERICAN MUSLIM GRIEVANCES

A perceived erosion of civil liberties, coupled with sometimes onerous treatment at the hands of customs agents and other security officials, has created no small degree of concern within the American Muslim community (AMC). A disquieting trend that has developed as a result of this was captured by respected Muslim commentator Geneive Abdo in the *Washington Post* in 2006. Her conclusions were based on numerous interviews conducted across the United States over the course of the previous two years:

A new generation of American Muslims—living in the shadow of the Sept. 11, 2001, attacks—is becoming more religious. They are more likely to take comfort in their own communities, and less likely to embrace the nation's fabled melting pot of shared values and common culture.

Part of this is linked to the resurgence of Islam over the past several decades, a growth as visible in Western Europe and the United States as it is in Egypt and Morocco. But the Sept. 11 attacks also had the dual effect of making American Muslims feel isolated in their adopted country, while pushing them to rediscover their faith.[1]

This trend may be abating; but either way, American Muslims have achieved a degree of integration with their society that is rare in the West.

American Muslims are more educated and affluent than the average U.S. citizen,[2] a status that contrasts dramatically with Muslim populations in Europe, where the forces of isolation are stronger than those of integration (largely because of their deprived socioeconomic status). American Muslims are thus better positioned than their European counterparts to integrate more effectively with the rest of society. By a 2 to 1 margin, Muslim Americans see no conflict between being a devout Muslim and living in a modern society.[3] This has clearly been a significant contributor to the relative absence of "homegrown" Islamist radicalism or widespread discontent among Muslim Americans such as that which led to the London and Madrid bombings and the riots in France. However, as Salam al-Marayati, executive director of the Muslim Public Affairs Council, has noted:

Although the vast majority of American Muslims do not live in economically depressed physical ghettos, many live in a psychological ghetto caused by the lack of acceptance they feel from their neighbors and colleagues, especially in the post-Sept. 11 era. This psychological ghetto may prove the largest challenge in the war on terrorism.[4]

He goes on to suggest that only by including American Muslims in serious discussions about national security can the walls of pluralism keep at bay the appeal of radical ideologies. In other words, American Muslims need to feel like partners rather than suspects.

ENGAGING A NEGLECTED PARTNER

If properly engaged, the AMC could quickly become America's most formidable asset in its struggle with extremism in the name of Islam. Beyond the assistance it can provide in rooting out militants at home and facilitating improved relations overseas, there is another equally compelling reason to enhance the status and role of American Muslims. If the AMC perceives itself to be a persecuted, ignored, or marginalized community, this plays directly into the hands of the radicals. However, if American Muslims see themselves as partners actively engaged in the U.S.

policy process, they could become this country's most effective ambassadors to the Muslim world. Before one can hope to secure the cooperation of the AMC in pursuing such ends, however, its legitimate misgivings and concerns will have to be addressed. Foremost among these is the double standard practiced by many western observers, who tend to define Islam by the actions of its extremists, while treating their own extremists as exceptions to the faith.

By the same token, before U.S. policymakers will be willing to temper current restrictive practices, they will need to be convinced that America's best interests will be served by doing so. First and foremost, they will need compelling assurances that the government's needs for greater political and financial transparency will be met. Beyond that, they will need to understand in fuller measure the benefits that could accrue from a cooperative relationship. It was toward this end (and others) that the Washington-based International Center for Religion and Diplomacy (ICRD), in partnership with the Institute for Defense Analyses (IDA, the Pentagon's leading think tank) and the International Institute of Islamic Thought (IIIT) in Herndon, Virginia, convened a conference involving 30 American Muslim leaders and a like number of U.S. government (USG) security officials and foreign policy practitioners in March 2006. The overriding purpose of the conference was to determine how both sides could begin working together for the common good. More specifically, the conference goals were to

1. identify and mitigate those factors standing in the way of a constructive partnership between American Muslims and their government;
2. engage the AMC in bridging relations between the United States and the Muslim world;
3. inform U.S. foreign policy and public diplomacy with a Muslim perspective;
4. support American Muslim efforts to play a leadership role in the further development of their religion.

The first goal is fundamental to achieving the other three, and the problem itself stems from three sources: (1) post-9/11 legal, immigration, and security reforms (in addition to negative rhetoric in the media) that have singled out Muslims as a potential threat; (2) USG investigations of Muslim organizations, including raids on offices and seizures of records, that have stretched out over a number of years without good-faith efforts to achieve closure in a timely manner; and (3) a feeling among American Muslims that they do not have sufficient political space to express their concerns or to influence domestic and foreign policy. As succinctly captured by *Newsweek* columnist Anna Quindlen in 2007:

Instead of trying to understand and therefore counter the mind-set of those who hate us, and to rally our allies in their communities, American jingoism has produced an ugly strain of anti-Muslim thought and chatter. That has hampered intelligence gathering, since Arab-Americans are loath to cooperate with government agents who solicit them as sources but treat them as suspect.[5]

Achieving the second goal will involve capitalizing on the extensive paths of influence that the AMC has to Muslim communities overseas, many of them in areas of strategic importance to the United States. The potential benefits of American Muslims acting as agents of change and outreach with their Muslim counterparts in other parts of the world are enormous.

The third goal will require the deliberate appointment of qualified American Muslims to key advisory bodies and policy-relevant positions in government to help shape U.S. policy choices that more effectively anticipate the likely reactions of Muslim audiences around the world. American Muslims cannot explain, let alone defend, policies with which they disagree or, even more importantly, have played no role in making. Past failures to understand and deal with the religious dynamics that were taking place in Iran, Lebanon, Iraq, and elsewhere have cost the United States dearly. The stakes are simply too high to continue on this basis.

Finally, it may be possible for American Muslims to provide a leadership role in guiding the future intellectual and spiritual development of Islam. Beyond bridging modernity with the contemporary practice of Islam on a daily basis (a challenge that still puzzles much of the rest of the Muslim world), they enjoy greater freedom of thought than other Muslim communities around the globe. The ready-made vehicle for exerting this kind of leadership is the long-dormant Islamic principle of *ijtihad*, mentioned in chapter 3, that provides for the periodic reexamination of Islamic values in light of major changes in the external environment. Another way of thinking about it is that the expression of Islam must adapt, even while the essence remains the same. Or as expressed by one prominent American Muslim imam, "What we need to do is borrow those attributes from the West that we admire and reject those that we don't. That is the wave of the future."[6]

The conference acknowledged at the outset the need to cooperate in bridging the gaps in understanding and mitigating their detrimental effects. Accordingly, concerted efforts were made to foster open communication and to develop sound working relationships as a first step toward building bridges for future cooperation. Toward this end, the conference recommended that the USG should

1. increase American Muslim involvement in the design and implementation of U.S. public and official diplomacy, especially with regard to media projects directed at the Muslim world more generally;
2. include American Muslim representatives in U.S. delegations to international organizations and in other high-level bodies and advisory committees;

3. work with American Muslim educators and community leaders to establish cultural competency training programs for government agencies at the federal, state, and local levels;

4. appoint more Muslims to high-profile positions, including political appointments that may or may not be directly related to public diplomacy or foreign policy;[7]

5. recruit young Muslims into law enforcement and other government careers.

Some action has taken place on each of these fronts but not nearly enough to realize the full potential of engaging American Muslims as agents of change and outreach to the world Muslim community. It is encouraging to note, however, that as a result of that conference (and a follow-up conference one year later), the doors at the Departments of State, Defense, Justice, and Homeland Security have opened wider to the inputs of Muslim citizens.

On the other side of the ledger, the conference recommended that American Muslims

1. establish an American Muslim Advisory Council to advise the government on (a) policy issues affecting the Muslim community and (b) measures to improve USG-American Muslim relations;

2. create a directory of American Muslim institutions and individuals who can exert influence in specific geographic areas overseas and thereby help facilitate the emergence of tolerant religious, civil, and political institutions in the Muslim world;

3. create and make widely available a directory of American Muslim experts who can provide technical and policy advice to USG agencies and who can represent the American Muslim viewpoint in the mainstream media;

4. establish programs to encourage greater Muslim involvement in local government and to foster a positive image of government service, including law enforcement, as a viable career option for young American Muslims;

5. open Track Two dialogues with Islamic opinion leaders overseas to build trust, especially in the areas of educational reform, political freedom, and humanitarian relief.

Thus far, the recommended advisory council has been established and given the title American Muslims for Constructive Engagement (AMCE). Under the auspices of the AMCE, which includes an impressive cross section of American Muslim leaders, the directory of experts recommended in item three was completed and promulgated.[8] The idea of a separate directory defining various paths of influence overseas, however, was abandoned, owing to the highly sensitive nature of the relationships involved. It was decided instead that these paths could be developed on a situational basis as the need arises (and an adequate level of cooperation exists).

Most of the potential benefits of the AMCE, especially in the area of policy development, have yet to be realized, largely because of insufficient engagement by the USG. Here, it is strongly suggested that the Muslim roundtable that used to meet about seven years ago under the auspices of the State Department's Policy Planning Office (and which the Secretary of State often attended) be revived in a slightly different form to include AMCE representation and the participation of the Under Secretary for Public Diplomacy and Public Affairs (perhaps as a co-convener).

To expand on the increased access to federal departments mentioned earlier, it is recommended that the AMCE proactively seek out and participate on a regular basis in those USG bridging initiatives that are already under way. For example, every two months the Civil Rights Division of the Department of Justice convenes interagency meetings with Muslim, Sikh, Arab, and South Asian civic and religious leaders to deal with existing civil rights issues and/or problems relating to their faith communities. The FBI and Department of Homeland Security are actively reaching out in similar fashion.

EMPOWERING CHANGE

Subsequent to the above conferences, Americans, by electing President Obama, expressed their desire for a new tone in U.S. discourse with the rest of the world. Clearly, one of the more damaged and vulnerable relationships out there today is that between Islam and the West. Yet even using such a broad categorization suggests a monolithic frame of reference that ignores the wide presence and active participation of Muslim communities in the western world more generally and in the United States in particular. It also assumes that the two groups are fundamentally incompatible in nature.

Since the beginning of his presidency, President Obama has been attempting to repair the damage caused by the hostile characterization of Muslims that has taken place in the United States and that of Americans that has taken place in the Muslim world. He seems to understand that if the tension is to be neutralized, someone has to take the first step in healing past indignities and in showing respect for the other side. That appears to be what he has been attempting to do, with a goal of opening a dialogue that can lead to reconciliation and the achievement of common goals.

Some of the hostility among Muslim populations around the globe has religious roots. If one considers the *umma* (the body of Muslims worldwide) to be of direct concern, then violent acts committed against members of the *umma* in one part of the world may warrant retribution from members in another. This is not to say that all Muslims share this belief to the point of hostility. However, there is strong evidence to suggest that the war in Bosnia, particularly the sense of injustice stemming from the western arms embargo imposed on the Muslim population while they were being massacred by the Serbs, was a major turning point in triggering today's Muslim global consciousness. As British Muslim Ed Husain has noted on a personal level:

Between '91 and '94, when people from Arab countries who had taken political ref-uge in Britain . . . came and said to us that, "Look, two hours away from London's Heathrow Airport, you've got people who are being slaughtered in the thousands despite being European Muslims for 600 years. What chance do people like you and I, who are brown skinned, black-haired, have in the long term here in Brit-ain. . . . Bosnia politicized me."[9]

The sentiment of kindred suffering has also inflamed Muslims on the issues of Israel-Palestine, Iraq, and Afghanistan. Without compromising America's major policy stances relating to its unconditional support for Israel or its condemnation of Iran's perceived nuclear weapons develop-ment, President Obama appears committed to addressing some of the long-standing grievances felt by Muslims around the world. Among these are the suffering of the Palestinian people and the need for a two-state so-lution in the region, the need for Israel to cease building new settlements in the contested areas, and the need to withdraw from Iraq and Afghani-stan so that Iraqis and Afghans can chart their own course for the future. It remains to be seen whether or not any of these initiatives will bear the intended fruit; but measurable progress on even one would represent an important step forward on the part of the West. The task of eliminating the radicals who are threatening Muslims and non-Muslims alike and who have sullied the reputation of Muslims the world over, however, is one for which Muslims themselves must bear the greatest burden.

Improvement in mutual understanding and future interaction will re-quire no small degree of reciprocity from the Muslim world. The challenge in this arena is sobering and was succinctly captured in an article titled "Islam's Trajectory" by David Forte, professor of law at Cleveland State University and author of the book *Studies in Islamic Law:*

There is a great mystery in Islam. Islam should have been the first civilization to have abandoned slavery; it was the last. Islam should have been the first to estab-lish complete religious liberty; today, non-Muslims suffer egregious persecution in Muslim lands. Islam should have been the first to establish social equality for women. Instead, women who stray outside the family's code of behavior are mur-dered with impunity. Islam should have been the foremost civilization to observe the humanitarian laws of war, but its empires have been no different from others; some claim they have been worse. Today Muslims slaughter innocent civilians precisely because they are innocent.[10]

He then goes on to point out that the founder of every great religion sets its message off on a trajectory that is carried through human history. Over time, the religion's followers inevitably deflect that trajectory from its original path. This holds true for every religion that has ever commanded a following. In the case of Islam, Forte goes on to say:

As we take the Qur'an, as most moderate educated Muslims interpret it, we find the following: Christians and Jews are respected as Abrahamic brothers in faith and will enjoy the favor of God on the last day. There is no compulsion in faith for any person. A person who abjures Islam will suffer God's disapproval, but may not be harmed in this world.[11]

On a semirelated note, when shari'ah was first introduced in Arabia some 1,400 years ago, it was a liberating force that provided significantly better treatment for women, slaves, and prisoners, among others, than was customary at the time. With the passing of the centuries, however, most of the rest of the world not only caught up with shari'ah but passed it by with the introduction of universal human rights.

THE LEADERSHIP CHALLENGE

When speaking with Muslims in Malaysia and other parts of the world about the possibility of American Muslims playing a leadership role in the further intellectual and spiritual development of Islam, the response has been uniformly favorable. Indeed, there is an undercurrent in Muslim circles suggesting that the "sun of Islam" is going to rise in the West. Consistent with this sort of expectation was the view expressed by a British Muslim who sees American Muslims as

intelligent and deeply erudite and connected to a sense of prophetic Islam, connecting themselves right back to the Prophet Muhammad. And they embodied that persona of compassion, of justice, of love, of humanity. . . . American Muslims are deeply patriotic and deeply proud of being American and being Muslim. Here we don't have that. You'd be hard pressed to find Muslims in the north of England saying that they're British Muslims. It just doesn't happen.[12]

Thus, the stage is set for the American Muslim community to begin addressing the embarrassing list of failings mentioned by Professor Forte. A good beginning would be for American Muslims to start by asking themselves, "If I were caliph for a day, what could I do to smooth the rough edges and move things toward a more inclusive world in which everyone can take pride?" In the final analysis, moderation in Islam can only come from within.

Finally, the earlier mentioned conferences also recommended a set of actions to be pursued on a joint basis:

1. Engage Muslim parliamentarians and opinion leaders from overseas in policy-relevant activities, and facilitate the participation of Muslim opinion leaders in visiting scholar programs of U.S. educational and policy institutions.

2. Establish American Muslim expert groups that can be made available upon request to advise and assist Muslim governments overseas in activities relating to education, civil society, good governance, and public health.

To date, there has been no discernable progress on either recommendation, owing to a lack of follow-through. This may change, however, as a result of the Obama administration's establishment of a new Office of the United States Special Representative to Muslim Communities, which is already engaging Muslims around the world on a people-to-people basis. Only time will tell how effective this office will be, but there is no question that the American Muslim community could greatly assist U.S. interests overseas through the kinds of recommendations that emerged from the deliberations of the two conferences.

Western engagement of Islamic societies through American Muslim channels could go a long way toward improving relations. All that would be required is for our King for a Day to task the Under Secretary of State for Public Diplomacy and Public Affairs to make it happen.

CHAPTER 11

Military Chaplains: Bridging Church and State

> There is only one radical means of sanctifying human lives. Not armored plating, or tanks, or planes, concrete fortifications. The one radical solution is peace.
>
> —Yitzhak Rabin

In early 2001, the U.S. Navy initiated a training program in religion and statecraft for all Navy, Marine Corps, and Coast Guard chaplains. The purpose of this training, which took place under the sponsorship of the Chief of Navy Chaplains, was to enhance the conflict prevention capabilities of the sea service commands, which are typically at the forefront of our country's overseas involvements. Among other avenues of inquiry, this training explored in considerable depth the benefits that would accrue from military chaplains (1) establishing relationships of trust with local religious leaders and (2) serving as advisors to their military commanders on the religious (and cultural) implications of command decisions that were either being contemplated or implemented.

The training, which was conducted around the world by a four-person team of religion and conflict resolution experts,[1] was well received by the chaplains, with about a third of them enthusiastic about the possibility of an expanded mandate, another third quite willing to give it a try, and the remainder protesting that it wasn't why they had "signed up." Based on their performance during the program, it became obvious that with the right kind of training, the two-thirds who were supportive represented a formidable capability that could be brought to bear to good effect, especially in situations where religion was a significant ingredient in the security equation. Capitalizing on this capability, however, was going to require two important steps. First, the line officer community would need to expand the rules of engagement (ROE) for its military chaplains to include these new functions.[2] Second, the Chaplain Corps would have to adjust its personnel policies to support the new ROE by providing chaplains who want to participate in this manner with the opportunity to do so, perhaps through the development of an appropriate training subspecialty within the corps.[3]

Although the stakes skyrocketed with the attacks of 9/11, neither of the above measures has proven easy to address. During the course of the 2001 training program, for example, it became clear during visits to various military commands that even if the chaplains were willing to take on the added functions, the line community was going to take further convincing. Illustrative of this challenge was one Marine general's response to the idea of expanding the chaplain's functions in which he slammed his fist on the table and said, "The role of my military chaplains is to attend to the spiritual needs of the men and women of my command. Period!"

With the line community in mind, an article was published in the *U.S. Naval Institute Proceedings* that described the training which had taken place and made a strong case for capitalizing on the formidable potential of military chaplains in addressing the nation's preventive agenda.[4] Although the article had no apparent effect at the time, it is encouraging to note the progress that has taken place during the intervening years. Much of that progress, however, has been ad hoc in nature, and there is still a great deal yet to be done. As a review of history will make clear, though, changing the role of military chaplains is neither unprecedented nor a particularly novel idea.

HISTORIC BACKGROUND

The modern chaplaincy traces its roots to medieval Catholicism in 742 C.E. when the Council of Ratisbon authorized the use of church officials to perform ecclesiastical rituals in a military setting:

We prohibit the servant of God in every way from bearing arms or fighting in the army or going against the enemy, except those alone who because of their sacred office, namely, for the celebrating of mass and caring for the relics of the saints, have been designated for this office; this is to say, the leader may have with him one or two bishops with their priest chaplains, and each captain may have one priest, in order to hear the confessions of the men and impose upon them proper penance.[5]

During the reign of Charlemagne from 768 to 814 C.E., the chaplain's role expanded from merely attending to the spiritual needs of the troops to providing divine endorsement of the righteousness of the cause for which they were fighting.

In 1095, Pope Urban II assigned Bishop Adhémar of Le Puy to be his personal representative in the First Crusade. As the Papal Legate, Adhémar not only acted as spiritual leader of the Crusade, but he also organized relief for poor pilgrims and appealed to the West for more crusaders.[6] Until his death from disease at the siege of Antioch, he also played a key role in maintaining the cohesiveness of the Crusade, settling numerous disputes that arose between the various Christian generals involved.[7] Later Pope Innocent III (1198–1216) and Pope Gregory IX (1227–1241) refined the spiritual duties to (1) encourage proper Christian behavior on the battlefield and in camp and (2) promote the fighting spirit of the soldiers through inspiring sermons.[8] In the mid-1600s, the duties shifted according to the changing dynamics of the Reformation and in colonial America even went so far as to include the role of soldier-priest when fighting against the Indians.[9]

AMERICAN REALITIES

The American experience included a similar ebb and flow with respect to the scope of chaplain activities. Even before the formation of America and its army, one finds their use in colonial militias like that headed by Capt. John Mason, a British Army major who immigrated to New England in 1632 and who led an expedition from the colony of Connecticut against the Pequot Indians in the wake of some prior skirmishes. Since Mason's force was responsible for the Mystic Massacre in 1637, which led to the death of nearly every man, woman, and child of the Pequot tribe, it would appear that mercy was not high on the agenda. Later in 1725, Capt. Henry Dwight, a Massachusetts militia leader, enlisted a chaplain to provide moral authority in matters of discipline, drunkenness, and general fitness for duty (in addition to performing church services for the soldiers and their families).

During the Revolutionary War, George Washington's first order to his army reflected his religious leanings:

The General most earnestly requires and expects a due observance of those articles of war established for the government of the army, which forbid profane cursing, swearing, and drunkenness. And in like manner, he requires and expects of all officers and soldiers, not engaged in actual duty, a punctual attendance of Divine service, to implore the blessing of Heaven upon the means used for our safety and defense.[10]

These views were reconfirmed during his Farewell Address from the presidency when he stated that "reason and experience both forbid us to expect that National Morality can prevail in exclusion of religious principle."[11] On July 29, 1775, the Second Continental Congress authorized the assignment of chaplains to the U.S. Army.[12]

From then until the present, there has been constant change both in the total number of chaplains (including going out of business altogether on at least two occasions) and in their duties. Over time, the latter ranged from normal clerical functions to those of teacher (of nonreligious subjects), doctor, psychologist, and morale builder.

Following World War II and into the cold war, chaplains became increasingly involved in civic action and humanitarian assistance projects.[13] During Vietnam, the role further evolved from morale builder to moral advisor, especially with respect to combating drugs, alcohol abuse, and racism. The later "pacification efforts" even led to chaplains ministering beyond the boundaries of their flocks. The roots of the newly recommended role of religious liaison (in which chaplains interact with local religious leaders) trace their origins to this Vietnam experience.[14] Thus, as the geographic reach of the United States has grown over time, so too has the scope of the chaplain's mission.

TODAY'S CHALLENGE

The chaplain's role became even more expansive following 9/11, as some chaplains took creative license in advancing humanitarian projects and others even began interacting with indigenous religious leaders and/ or serving as cultural advisors to their commanders. However, the pendulum soon swung back to a more cautionary stance in response to concerns within the chaplain community about the possibility of being perceived as intelligence agents in religious garb, a perception that could clearly compromise their noncombatant status. There was also concern that the parent religious organizations, which endorse their clergy for service as chaplains within the armed forces (and retain a degree of control over their conduct once assigned), might oppose this expanded role.

Each of the above concerns has been carefully addressed in the latest revision to Joint Publication 1-05, which provides doctrinal guidance for the religious support of joint military operations. Among other things, JP 1-05 stipulates the parameters that are to govern the chaplain's roles as principal advisor to the joint force commander on religious affairs and as a key advisor to the commander on the impact of religious factors on military operations. It specifically prohibits any activities that might compromise the chaplain's noncombatant status such as functioning as intelligence collectors, engaging in manipulation or deception operations, identifying targets for combat operations, serving as lead negotiators for the command in given situations,[15] or even removing one's chaplain insignia. These prohibitions, however, do not preclude chaplains from participating in operational planning or in providing command and staff with religious insights that can contribute to an enhanced situational awareness. The latter, which is particularly important when it comes to deterring conflict, will often derive from the relationships of trust that chaplains establish through their networking with local religious leaders, NGOs, private voluntary organizations, international organizations, and the interagency community (e.g., embassy country teams, U.S. AID officials, and provincial reconstruction teams, among others).

Of paramount importance, military chaplains can contribute to preventing conflict and mediating differences through the religious legitimacy they bring to communications with other clerics. These channels are often preferred over others by indigenous religious leaders and typically represent the only avenue available for conducting religious engagement.[16] With one foot in the religious world as a member of the clergy and the other in the secular as a military officer, chaplains are well suited to serve as intermediaries between military and religious leaders in zones of conflict and during postconflict stabilization. Nonetheless, chaplains should always approach this task cautiously, not only out of concern for their own safety, but for the safety of the religious leaders with whom they meet. The risks are real and must be anticipated.

"Chaplain Liaison in Support of Military Engagement" is defined in JP 1-05 as "any command-directed contact or interaction where the chaplain, as the command's religious representative, meets with a leader on matters of religion to ameliorate suffering and to promote peace and the benevolent expression of religion."[17] The overriding requirement that governs this kind of engagement is that it be directed by the commander and that it be in concert with strategic intent.

TOMORROW'S CHALLENGE

There have been any number of instances in which U.S. military chaplains have engaged with local religious leaders in Iraq and Afghanistan in projects ranging from organizing and celebrating community religious services to coordinating mosque renovation projects and forming religious councils. Almost all of these efforts have contributed to improved dialogue, increased trust, or reduced violence.[18] Quite apart from any policy or doctrinal considerations, it seems clear that the role of chaplain liaison has already become a living reality. Moreover, the liaison function itself may become a stepping stone to an even more expansive mission statement in the future, as implied by the theme of a 2009 international conference on "The Role of the Chaplain in Reconciliation and Healing in Post-Conflict Reconstruction."[19]

In some respects, a future move in this direction would actually represent a revisiting of the past. During a time of tremendous chaos immediately following World War II, U.S. Army chaplains played an instrumental role in stabilizing and rebuilding shattered societies in both Germany and Japan. They did this through addressing the immediate and potential long-term effects of the conflict by recognizing loss, promoting reconciliation, facilitating the rebuilding of institutions, and working toward social transformation.[20] Certainly, the dual functions of bridge building and serving as agents of reconciliation seem tailor-made for today's chaplains operating in today's environment.

One consideration that should be taken into account when assessing the liaison function is the fact that chaplains rotate assignments rather frequently. In the Navy, there is the added complication of abbreviated port visits, which do not provide much opportunity for developing relationships with religious leaders ashore. Trust takes time, so it is important that chaplains record whatever progress they make in developing it so their successors can build upon what has gone before. A secure Web site could facilitate this kind of information transfer and provide an effective vehicle for recording "lessons learned" and "best practices" for the benefit of others. Such measures notwithstanding, the quality of relationships inevitably relates to personal chemistry, which also takes time to develop, hence the desirability of the more permanent presence that Religion Attachés would provide.

The enlightened use of military chaplains is a function of the military commander's discretion. Yet little religious education is provided to prospective or current military commanders either at the service academies, the command and staff colleges, or the various war colleges. As a consequence, U.S. military commanders in the field are essentially "winging it."[21] In the absence of a formal requirement to engage religious leaders, a military unit's interaction with them—and the chaplain's role in this activity—has basically been a function of the instincts and judgment of the unit commander. The stakes in this process were expressed rather bluntly in a 1996 issue of the *Naval War College Review*:

An operational commander, however well-trained in the military issues, who is ignorant of or discounts the importance of religious belief can strengthen his enemy, offend his allies, alienate his own forces, and antagonize public opinion. Religious belief is a factor he must consider in evaluating the relationship with allies, and his courses of action.[22]

To gain the full benefits of a broadened mandate for military chaplains, the commanders for whom they work must have a basic (if not nuanced) familiarity with the religious imperatives at play within his or her area of responsibility. Because an enlightened understanding of the underlying religious environment can make the difference between failure and success, it is important that military commands understand and be able to deal with this aspect of any conflict in which they become involved. In short, the same kind of energy, commitment, and investment should be devoted to Islamic and Middle Eastern regional studies as was applied to Soviet studies during the cold war.

Pentagon planners should review the current training requirements for military officers, with an eye toward determining what additional training in religion should be added at each stage in the officer's development to ensure that military commanders can think both strategically and tactically about the influence of religious factors in their decision making. Some cultural and religious instruction is already provided for most military units prior to deploying overseas, but it varies in quality and timeliness and often suffers from its "once-over-lightly" nature.

Related training for military chaplains, although further along, is still a work in progress. As a result of the Base Realignment and Closure process, the services have co-located their training for chaplains at the Armed Forces Chaplain Center (AFCC) at Fort Jackson, South Carolina. There, the Army, which is strongly committed to the expanded role for military chaplains, has created a Center for World Religions that will eventually provide its chaplains with training on the impact of religion on joint, interagency, intergovernmental, and multinational operations. It will also develop strategies and capabilities for conducting chaplain liaisons in support of military engagements.[23] The Air Force and Navy (including the Marine Corps) do not have a similar program, but it is probably only a matter of time before the Army's center provides such training for all of the services (including, at some point, members of the line officer communities).

As mentioned previously, the military services should consider creating a religion and culture subspecialty for those chaplains who are willing (and able) to serve in the expanded capacity.[24] A challenging curriculum for those who are so motivated would clearly enhance the conflict prevention capabilities of their military commands.[25] As things currently stand, however, service-wide acceptance of the religious diplomatic function is still ad hoc in nature owing to the absence of an institutionalized selection process and the training regime to support it. There is a long way to go before the desired level of effectiveness will be reached. Just how far is reflected in the following observations of a recognized expert in this area based on recent conversations with combatant commanders and military chaplains:

- Not all of the chaplains serving in Iraq and Afghanistan who provided "advice" to commanders or conducted religious leader liaisons were successful.
- Some commanders commented that their chaplains knew less about the religion of their area of operations than they did.
- Some chaplains who had no previous war experience suffered from war shock to the point where they weren't able to adequately address the spiritual needs of the troops.
- Some chaplains commented that they disliked Muslims and would not deal with them unless so ordered.

Other challenges related to using chaplains in the suggested liaison and advisory roles include the fact that (1) some religious groups that sponsor (endorse) chaplains do not view interfaith dialogue as an appropriate function, (2) the chaplain's short time in theater may limit his or her ability to follow through in meeting the expectations of local populations, (3) chaplains typically have limited language skills and cultural understanding, and (4) some chaplains may not have the maturity, knowledge, or personal disposition to work closely with religious leaders of other cultures and faiths. All of these considerations give added credence to the corresponding need for Religion Attachés (or their equivalent) in the U.S. embassies of those countries where chaplains could become involved on this basis (see chapter 7).

In contrast to the combat-related failings of some chaplains in Iraq and Afghanistan, other chaplains have initiated a number of highly effective interventions in these same theaters of operation. Most of these have resulted from the chaplains taking the initiative, securing their commanders' approval, and then following through.[26]

On some occasions, it has been the commanders themselves who have initiated the intervention. In one instance, Army Lt. Gen. Karl Eikenberry, then Commanding General, Combined Forces Command–Afghanistan (and later Ambassador to Afghanistan), directed the Navy chaplain assigned to his command to serve as the liaison between the command and the Afghan Ministry of Religious Affairs in addressing a problem that had arisen with a campaign to inoculate Afghans against polio. Some Taliban-sympathizing mullahs had spread the word that this was actually a sinister ploy to convert Afghans to Christianity "by injection," and several World Health Organization (WHO) staff had been killed as a result. The Navy chaplain not only secured the cooperation of the ministry but also communicated quietly with the subversives and was able to turn the situation around.[27]

On another occasion, a U.S. Army truck had lost its brakes in downtown Kabul and plowed into a crowd, killing several Afghan civilians. A tense atmosphere prevailed as all U.S. personnel were ordered off the streets. The same Commanding General again sent his chaplain to meet with the Ministry of Religious Affairs to deal with the problem. The chaplain was able to calm the situation, help initiate an investigation of the incident, and follow through by leading subsequent discussions relating to remuneration.[28]

In Iraq, command support for chaplain engagements with key Muslim clerics was instrumental in securing their support for a concerned local citizens program that matured into the Sons of Iraq program and facilitated a major turning point in the war known as the Anwar Awakening.[29] It has been said that chaplains are only as good as the training they receive and that the training is only as good as the policy and doctrine that supports and directs it. To the extent this is so, the new JP 1-05 gives strong reason to hope.

INSPIRATION FROM AFAR

How other countries have made use of their military chaplains can also be instructive. For example, Canada—a country that stands out in terms of its peacemaking initiatives around the world—is placing an increasing emphasis on how chaplains can assist their commands to become more aware of, and thus prepared for, cultural, psychological, and religious factors that significantly impact military operations. Canadian chaplains have also been quite active in engaging local religious leaders. As noted by a major in the Canadian Chaplain Corps:

As Canadians, deployed chaplains will discover among local religious and community leaders genuine intrigue and curiosity with respect to western thinking, beliefs and values. A desire to engage in some form of dialogue [with] reference [to] the existing conflict and/or its residual effects is also not uncommon.[30]

Official guidance issued in 2008 supported this kind of engagement by authorizing the chaplaincy to "provide Canadian Forces (CF) leadership with perspective and guidance on religious, spiritual and ethical matters in garrison and in the field." It also explicitly endorsed a role in conflict resolution:

Chaplains will require increased levels of training, education, and experience in religious understanding and reconciliation in order to contribute effectively to the conflict resolution processes internal to the CF and in operational settings.[31]

It is noteworthy that Canadian Force chaplains are already trained for and actively engaged in developing indigenous religious leader support for stability operations.[32]

Norway also makes expansive use of its chaplains, including the mandate to participate in conflict resolution activities. Norwegian chaplains in peacekeeping operations maintain constant contact with religious leaders of all faiths "as a way of contributing constructively to conflict resolution."[33]

Going back in time, one finds other examples of using chaplains in expansive roles. During the Spanish-American War in the Philippines (April to August 1898), for example, U.S. Army Gen. John "Black Jack" Pershing used his chaplain as a liaison with Catholic clergy in the north and Muslim leaders in the south to temper the hostilities.[34] Sixty-five years later, when French commanders found themselves in tight predicaments during the Algerian War for Independence, it was their military chaplains who they often sent out to negotiate with the Muslim insurgents.[35] Implicit in this action was French recognition of the unique role that chaplains can play in mitigating or preventing conflict (in addition to dealing with the human casualties after it has erupted).

CONCLUSION

In both the Philippine and Algerian examples, military chaplains played roles that extend beyond the current, evolving expansion of duties. The lesson of historical examples like these for the modern chaplaincy is this: rather than confining the chaplain's liaison role within rigidly circum-scribed boundaries, we would do well to provide greater latitude to those chaplains who are well-educated and seasoned practitioners in this arena. Even the French—the authors of secularism—understood the need to deal creatively with religious imperatives. With so much at stake, can we afford to do any less?

CHAPTER 12

Capitalizing on the Transnational Capability of NGOs

An invasion of armies can be resisted; an invasion of ideas cannot.

—Victor Hugo

The concept of national sovereignty has been steadily eroding under the onslaught of technology change and economic globalization; and the power of state-centric political bodies has diminished accordingly, with NGOs stepping in to fill the vacuum. This, in some respects, represents the continuation of a trend dating back to the creation of the League of Nations following World War I, when citizens were inspired to begin thinking beyond the interests and boundaries of their respective nation-states.[1] The later use of the new term *nongovernmental organization* in Article 71 of the UN Charter (formally establishing a consultative relationship between the UN and international NGOs) provided the political space for this new breed of organization to emerge.[2] As commonly defined, an NGO is a legally sanctioned, nonstate entity that operates on a nonprofit, independent, voluntary basis to promote the public good.

METEORIC GROWTH

Since that early beginning, the quantity and impact of NGOs has literally skyrocketed. As of 2009, the Union of International Associations determined that there were at least 27,800 functioning international NGOs.[3] It was also estimated at that time that NGOs assist more than 250 million people annually[4] and collectively disburse more money than the World Bank.[5]

Among the reasons for their burgeoning numbers and impact is the fact that NGOs provide incubators in which new ideas in almost any field of endeavor can be given collective expression, whether it be at the local, regional, or international level (or, in some cases, two of these levels, if not all three). In contrast to state-sponsored initiatives, which are typically politically constrained both in purpose and design, NGOs provide much greater freedom to pursue altruistic agendas unfettered by the normal quid pro quo considerations that accompany national self-interest. NGOs, without the political trappings of sovereignty, have a legitimacy that typically transcends governmental intervention. They are thus inherently freer and quicker to react to developing situations and opportunities. NGOs, with their neutral posture and extensive networks of local contacts, are often better informed and more able to deal with crisis situations than either national governments or international organizations.

AN EARLY EXAMPLE

There are any number of examples in which NGOs have played an instrumental role in resolving difficult situations. One of the better known is the initiative taken by Moral Rearmament (MRA) to reconcile French and German decision makers and opinion leaders following World War II. It did this through a series of intense personal interactions extending over a five-year period (1946–50) at a mountain retreat in Caux, Switzerland. Among other things, this initiative effectively paved the way for Konrad Adenauer and Robert Schumann (whose friendship owed much to these MRA encounters) to implement Jean Monet's European Coal and Steel Community Plan. This plan, by effectively integrating the war-making industries of Germany and France, ensured that neither country could ever again launch a surprise attack against the other. While MRA (now Initiatives of Change, I of C) makes no claims about having had a role in the creation or implementation of the plan, rigorous research has revealed it is highly unlikely the plan could have ever taken hold in the absence of the earlier MRA-inspired reconciliation that occurred at Caux between industrialists and labor leaders from both countries.[6]

A MORE RECENT EXAMPLE

NGOs are generally midlevel actors with linkages both up (to political leaders) and down (to local communities), which enable them to bridge identity groups as well as political divides. Their balanced neutrality enables them to promote dialogue and seek common ground between the parties where others cannot. A lesser-known but nevertheless meaningful example of how this can be done was provided by the Conflict Management Group at Harvard University when it intervened in 1995 to address a long-standing border dispute between Peru and Ecuador.

Dating back to the 1820s, Ecuador and Peru had engaged in no fewer than 34 armed conflicts over their common border, a border that had been the subject of continuing dispute since both countries gained their independence from Spain in the early 19th century. Most recently, in 1995, escalating tensions concerning the 80-kilometer-long stretch of Amazon jungle along the summit of the Condor Mountains led to a brief, but violent, conflict, resulting in the death of several hundred, mostly Peruvian, soldiers.[7] A cease-fire was called, but skirmishes continued, illustrating once again the need for a permanent resolution.[8]

At that point, the Conflict Management Group (CMG), founded in 1984 by Harvard Law School professor Roger Fisher, proposed the possibility of conducting a "facilitated joint brainstorming" session to the then President of Ecuador and the former Peruvian Deputy Minister of Foreign Affairs. The intent of the session was to facilitate better communications between the two sides, improve the management of differences, and explore more effective techniques for achieving a peaceful solution. Both countries agreed, and in April 1995, 11 carefully selected participants gathered for a week-long workshop in Cambridge, Massachusetts.

Great effort was taken to ensure an open environment for personal interaction. An informal ice-breaking dinner, for example, was held prior to the beginning of the workshop where it was made clear by CMG that participants were there to build relationships and explore possibilities, but not to engage in unofficial negotiations relating to the border dispute. The soundness of this approach soon became evident when, during participant introductions, a Peruvian senior military official said, "I have already failed the first assignment. I know very little about what my colleague from Ecuador does for a living. What I do know is that we both have handicapped daughters and we spent our time talking about that passion in our lives." That sort of bridge building remained at the heart of the workshop, which was designed to introduce participants to various skills and techniques for strengthening working relationships and enhancing communications as a precursor to developing empathy and solving problems.[9]

One example of such bridge building was an exercise in which each of the participants was invited to write a victory speech set six months in the future, outlining the major themes of a hypothetical agreement. Each participant then paired up with a member from the other side to share common themes and redraft their respective speeches to highlight similarities. Options were then explored that addressed the common interests in economic development, trade, and environmental protection.[10]

The response to the workshop exceeded the expectations of participants and facilitators alike. One participant, Jamil Mahuad, later became President of Ecuador in 1998. That year a lasting agreement was reached when Ecuador agreed to Peruvian sovereignty over the disputed region if Peru met several conditions. First, the small hill of Tiwinza, the site of several Ecuadorian military victories that falls within the disputed territory, was to be leased to the government of Ecuador as private property. Additionally, the Peruvian government would agree to build a road from Tiwinza to Ecuador within 30 months of signing the agreement. While this area amounts to only 250 acres, it holds special significance for the country, since 12 Ecuadorians are believed to be buried there.[11]

In addition to property rights, the peace agreement also called for two demilitarized ecological reserves on both sides of the disputed 50-mile strip of jungle.[12] Further, the treaty also set the terms for bilateral trade and navigational agreements in addition to establishing a committee to resolve border issues peacefully.[13]

Finally, the treaty also paved the way for approximately three billion dollars of investment in oil, power, roads, and other projects in the impoverished area. It also saved each country hundreds of millions of dollars annually in now-unneeded defense spending.[14] Although the treaty

Figure 12.1
Boundary Dispute Area—Ecuador and Peru

confirms Peru's historical claims to the frontier, both countries ultimately felt like winners.[15]

Agreement was reached on all of the above points through the efforts of the Center for International Development and Conflict Management of the University of Maryland at the grassroots level and of Argentina, Brazil, Chile, and the United States at the regional and international levels.[16] Although not actively involved in those negotiations, the contribution of the Conflict Management Group was significant as reflected in the statement of President Mahuad when agreement was finally reached: "That one-week session in Cambridge has had a lasting impact on the way Ecuador and Peru deal with the boundary problem and deal with each other."[17] In addition to the Cambridge workshop, the Conflict Management Group continued to help Mahuad improve his negotiating style leading up to the historic settlement. Two weeks prior to the agreement, Mahuad wrote Mr. Fisher stating, "I know of none who have done more to make this peace possible than you and the Conflict Management Group."[18]

NGO COLLABORATION

In the areas of conflict prevention and resolution, NGOs have any number of arrows in their peacemaking quivers, ranging from facilitating communications through back-channel meetings or unofficial shuttle diplomacy to mediating differences between the opposing parties. However, because the challenges in many conflict situations often exceed the capabilities of any given NGO to address fully, efforts are under way by such umbrella groups as the Global Partnership for the Prevention of Armed Conflict (GPPAC), the Global Development Alliance (GDA), and the International American Council for Voluntary International Action (InterAction) to promote synergistic collaboration between relevant NGOs.[19]

To be sure, some collaboration between NGOs takes place in the natural course of business without any need for external prompting, but not nearly as much as one might hope. This is largely due to the economic disincentives that often stand in the way. Beyond meeting the needs of those whom they serve in the field, NGOs also need to please their donors and their boards of directors. This, in turn, translates to an inclination to claim total credit for any success that results from their work and a corresponding tendency to go it alone.

While NGOs greatly value their independence and autonomy, many are witnessing increasing levels of success through cooperating with one another. An excellent case in point is the collaboration that has taken place in Sudan between the Mines Advisory Group from Britain, which educates people on land mines and detection; South Africa's Mine Cleaning Group, which specializes in mine removal; and the Sudan Mine Action Service. Collectively, this alliance is removing mines in Sudan and teaching the surrounding public how to identify and avoid potential land mine–ridden areas. Without their efforts, Sudanese refugees would not be able to return safely to their homes in the south.

COLLABORATION AT HIGHER LEVELS

Stemming from the original mandate of article 71, the United Nations also actively coordinates many of its activities with those of NGOs that apply for and obtain official "consultative status." In exchange for the expertise that the NGOs provide, this relationship confers on the NGOs a level of gravitas and added legitimacy that enhances their stature.

Finally, national governments often work with NGOs as well. For example, the U.S. government works quite extensively with NGOs in its development activities overseas. The U.S. military also engages them on a situational basis when doing so can help accomplish the military mission.[20] More often than not, the overlap of interests that leads to NGO engagement on this particular front involves such issues as rule of law, restorative justice, reconciliation, and conflict prevention.

CRITICISMS AND CONCERNS

Among the many positive attributes that NGOs enjoy, foremost among them is the unrivaled social space that they occupy, engaging the UN and national governments on the one hand, while simultaneously making their presence felt in local, remote corners of the world on the other. Yet they are also the subject of criticism on several fronts, including inadequate accountability for the resources they consume; unmeasured (and sometimes unverifiable) claims of success; inadequate connectivity to other organizations stemming from a never-ending competition for resources, attention, and political space; and their perceived manipulation at times by those they are attempting to influence.[21]

Indicative of these concerns is the strong rebuke issued by President Karzai on the eve of the April 2005 Afghanistan Development Forum in which he explained why his cabinet supported a draft law barring NGOs from bidding on government projects and criticized NGOs for "squandering precious resources that Afghanistan received in aid from the international community." As quoted in an Iranian Newspaper,

"We had a responsibility towards the Afghan people, as well as the taxpayers in the donor countries, to stop NGOs that are corrupt, wasteful and unaccountable," he said, while also praising the "good work" of those NGOs serving the country's development and humanitarian needs.[22]

President Karzai's stinging critique of NGOs may sound a bit disingenuous in light of the ongoing allegations of corruption directed at his administration, but that critique was five years ago; and then, as now, the slow progress in reconstruction resulted in predictable antiforeigner sentiments.

Perhaps of even greater concern than such criticisms, especially among American NGOs, is the possibility of being seen as part of a larger western hegemony. To quote from a 2006 op-ed in the *Yemen Times* entitled "NGOs: Another Wing of US Foreign Policy":

The latest catch phrase in US foreign policy is the Greater Middle East Initiative (which at least sounds more democratic than regime change). The Greater Middle East Initiative—in a nut shell—is the attempt to deal with the entire Muslim world as one, and to counter the extremist threat with a sweeping set of political and economic reforms. How will they implement such an agenda? Why through the phenomena of trans-national, apolitical, non-aligned, unsuspected, all-singing, all-dancing, saviours of the modern world—NGOs. . . .

What NGOs bring are items of the western reform agenda, and they bring them one by one. Whether they hold workshops, or lectures, or training seminars, or publish publications, they promote a solution deriving from secular capitalism. Whether the subject is poverty, or literacy, or human rights, press rights, human trafficking, or empowerment of women, or child labour, they promote a solution deriving from secular capitalism. Whatever the development project, however well it's administered, it is done in the name of, or for, an idea of secular capitalism. The problem is that Secular Capitalism did not come from Islam. The two are not the same, in fact they almost always differ. . . .

Building infrastructure, providing drinking water, sanitation, public transport, electricity, judiciary, education and healthcare are the exclusive responsibility of Government, not NGOs. Why else do we have governments—if not to administer projects that are in the collective interest and from which everyone benefits? The more we accept NGOs to do the work of government the more we tolerate governmental incompetence, and the longer we're stuck with it. The sad truth is that the kind of reform needed is a little more drastic than patchwork plasters of "development aid" or the lipstick of "democracy."[23]

Also contributing to this concern is the earlier-mentioned connection of NGOs to the U.S. military in the conduct of stability operations[24] (which are now given the same level of importance as the combat mission).[25] This involvement has led some in the NGO community to complain that "the appearance of joint operations or visits by U.S. military personnel imperil the NGO's reputation for neutrality and independence in the eyes of local communities."[26] This is not an inconsequential concern, since it is the NGO's neutrality (or impartiality) that is often its best guarantee of safety in conflict-prone areas. By the same token, the military has concerns of its own. As captured in this paragraph from a NATO Defense College paper entitled "Improving NATO-NGO Relations in Crisis Response Operations":

For many of the military, NGOs are ambiguous, non-professional actors whose choices are ill-considered. From a military perspective, there are too many NGOs in crisis areas and they are unpredictable. Moreover, since they do not have a single command, their actions are not monitored, and they can pose security problems for military forces. Many are ideologically hostile to the military. Many NGOs are not professional enough to work effectively in challenging conditions and they have not been trained to operate in dangerous areas. Their attitude is illogical: they refuse to cooperate with the military forces, they refuse to exchange information, but they are the first to want to be rescued from danger. NGOs exploit military forces for their sole objective: securing the humanitarian space. Lastly, they have money and influence that the military do not possess.[27]

Needless to say, such criticisms are not applicable to all NGOs; but in response to the concerns on both sides, U.S. government agencies and the NGO community are seeking to develop mechanisms that will facilitate more effective military/NGO partnerships. The October 2008 revision of the U.S. Army's *Stability Operations Manual* (FM 3–07), for example (which postdates the above commentary), reflects this commitment and specifically cites command-approved chaplain support as an effective instrument for facilitating unity of effort and improving relationships among diverse groups.[28]

GLOBAL APPRECIATION

More than offsetting the occasional criticisms and concerns, however, are the countless commendations that NGOs regularly receive around the world for their herculean efforts in relieving human suffering and meeting a range of critical needs. Representative of these is the prestigious Star of Sacrifice Award bestowed on Catholic Relief Services by the government of Pakistan in July 2006 for its comprehensive and timely response to a devastating earthquake the previous October.[29] As reflected in a BBC World Service poll of 32 countries in 2005, the perception of NGOs in the world today is five times as likely to be positive as it is negative.[30]

FAITH-BASED NGOS

Faith-based NGOs are less likely than secular NGOs to incur charges of governmental co-option, primarily because the religious arena is perceived to be out-of-bounds by most government practitioners. Yet they have been among the most effective of all NGOs, having led the way in the Jubilee 2000 campaign to relieve third world debt, played an important role in the creation of the International Criminal Court, shaped the discourse at important UN conferences, and intervened to good effect in numerous conflict situations.[31]

Faith-based NGOs also fill a unique niche within the field of conflict resolution and provide several distinct advantages over their secular counterparts in preventing or resolving conflict. First, when working through religious institutions as they often do, faith-based NGOs tend to maintain closer linkages with those whom they serve. Religious institutions provide penetrating access to the local community and are well positioned to reinforce accountability for any agreements that may be reached. By the same token, they also understand the national perspective on most public policy issues by dint of their access to religious networks that extend throughout the country.

One example of this extended reach can be found in the role being played by the National Conciliation Commission in the five-decade conflict in Colombia. The Commission, which was established in 1995 by the Roman Catholic Episcopal Bishops' Conference and is staffed by Catholic clergy, has gained such a degree of trust with the disputing parties—the government, paramilitaries, and leftist guerrilla groups—that it is serving as the principal facilitator of negotiations between these disputing groups. Because of the widespread presence of the church throughout Colombia and because most other organizations have been compromised to one extent or another by drug money, it remains the only social institution that has the ability to connect grassroots concerns with high-level negotiations. As a result, the Commission remains a trusted interlocutor of positions and verifier of agreements, despite the heavily polarized environment in which it is operating.

The second major advantage that faith-based NGOs offer is the sense of moral authority which they bring to policy debates, debates that are otherwise dominated by political considerations in which the human costs of policy choices are often overlooked. Thus there is often greater receptivity to their agendas. A poignant illustration of this aspect is the work in Iraq by the Foundation for Relief and Reconciliation in the Middle East (FRRME) to arrest the sectarian conflict that threatens the country's stability. Through meeting with top-level Sunni and Shia religious leaders, Canon Andrew White, the Foundation's president, has with the assistance of others been able to facilitate cooperation between them and to secure their agreement in issuing a joint Sunni/Shia fatwa (September 2008) prohibiting suicide bombings and calling upon all Iraqis to adhere to the rule of law.

Despite the fact that his efforts have had the active support of the U.S. military and the financial backing of the U.S. Department of Defense, the British Foreign Office, and the U.S. Institute of Peace, Canon White nevertheless enjoys a high degree of trust among the Iraqi people and the religious leaders with whom he is working. This trust stems from the fact that he is a religious leader himself and the fact that he has been in Iraq for over a decade, pastoring a church under extremely trying conditions. These conditions have included the murder of some of his staff and a number of threats against his own life.[32] Another helpful ingredient in garnering the trust of the people has been the principles that govern the work of FRRME:

1. Political peace tracks in the Middle East would benefit from supporting religious peace initiatives as the most effective approach for ensuring that whatever peace settlement emerges proves lasting in nature.

2. Any religious peace track needs to be owned jointly by each of the major faiths present in the region.

3. Religious peace processes need to engage both the senior leadership and the grassroots of a community in order to be fully effective.

4. Economic hardship is a major cause of persistent instability in conflict-ridden societies. Reconciliation must therefore actively involve relieving those in need at the grassroots level.[33]

A third advantage is that faith-based NGOs often have greater "staying power," commitment, and immersion in the community, resulting in a deeper understanding of the community's needs, than that of their secular counterparts. Building on this reality, former World Bank President James Wolfensohn and then Archbishop of Canterbury George Carey underscored through joint initiatives the idea that churches and faith-based organizations can be important partners in implementing economic and social reforms at the local level, especially in societies plagued with ethnic discrimination, resource-related conflicts, and widespread violence.

Finally, faith-based NGOs have an inherent ability to integrate religious beliefs and language into their conflict resolution initiatives, which can foster a greater sense of forgiveness and reconciliation between protagonists than would otherwise be possible. Recent research, however, has revealed that in some situations, faith-based organizations have been adversely influenced by the same religious and ethnic divisions that are shaping the cultures in which they are operating. Rather than transcending the schisms found in larger society, they have at times reinforced them.[34] These situations, however, are clearly the exception rather than the rule; and on balance, faith-based NGOs offer knowledge, skills, and contacts that secular diplomats would be hard-pressed to emulate.[35]

LESSONS LEARNED

Every conflict that takes place is inherently unique, driven as much by personalities as circumstances. Yet, each has broad lessons to convey. Among them:

1. Trust and integrity
   - The best hope for progress in intractable situations is to create trust on a personal level between those who are in a position to influence policy. Mistrust is the cornerstone of conflict, either among nations or between factions.
   - When convening a meeting to resolve differences between conflicting parties, the following should be considered:
     i. Engage as cosponsors of the event respected indigenous institutions that can represent the critical points of view that need to be accommodated.

ii. Seek balanced representation among the participants, both in terms of stature and numbers (keeping the latter to a manageable size).

iii. Determine in advance the desired outcome, and devise an effective strategy for the participants to achieve and "own" it.

iv. As appropriate, find ways to incorporate a meaningful spiritual dimension into the proceedings, one that can help provide a transcendent capability for overcoming the secular obstacles to peace.

- The NGO must have *credibility with the parties* to a conflict, and this is most often gained through a long-term local presence (perhaps in concert with development work, as Norwegian Church Aid has done in the north of Mali and as the Mennonites characteristically strive to do wherever they are involved) or by partnering with a local individual or institution that commands such a presence. Successful conflict prevention or peace building requires long-term commitment.

- *Transparency and cultural sensitivity* are absolutely crucial. When planning an intervention, NGOs must be transparent in their objectives, goals, and decision-making processes. Equally important, they need to provide transparency in financial matters and fundraising, taking particular care that sources of financial support do not compromise their perceived neutrality.

- *Integrity of analysis* is crucial to gaining and maintaining credibility in the eyes of other stakeholders. One must develop a sound expertise in the social problems one is addressing in order to (1) command the intellectual respect of the parties to the conflict and (2) articulate credible alternative goals and the means for achieving them. Such was the strategy of the East German Lutheran Church during that country's transition to democratic governance in 1989. One must also have a broader view of the conflict in order to properly tailor one's recommendations to the historical, political, economic, and security realities.

- *Integrity of practice* is also important. The spirit with which one pursues one's work is every bit as important as the substance of its content. For example, by emphasizing strategic nonviolence and avoiding polemics, both the Catholic Church during the 1986 People's Revolution in the Philippines and the East German Lutheran Church during its country's transition to democracy gained and maintained the critical mass of public support needed to overthrow their discredited governments.

2. Resourcefulness

- In situations involving state-sponsored oppression, consideration should be given to *using existing networks of religious communication* to mobilize large-scale support, much like the Catholic Church did in using its radio stations and newspapers to confront the Marcos regime in the Philippines.

- In third-party mediation/intervention, religious peacemakers should *capitalize on religious beliefs and symbols* in finding a common religious language of conciliation that can foster a genuine spirit of forgiveness and cooperation. When sensitively applied, such language and symbolism can aid in getting to the deeper issues, as the Conciliation Commission in Nicaragua was able to do when it brokered a peace between the Sandinista regime and the East Coast Indians in 1988. More recently, the work of the ICRD in Kashmir provides yet another example. By appealing to the reconciling principles of Jesus of Nazareth, a figure who commands the respect of all major world religions, the ICRD has been able to promote a cooperative spirit between and among next-generation leaders from the Hindu, Muslim, and Buddhist regions of that troubled state.

- Whenever possible, serious consideration should be given to including religious leaders in formal peace negotiations. Because of their unrivaled influence at the grassroots level, it is important that they feel a genuine sense of ownership in whatever political settlement emerges. Further, their presence provides a moral authority that is otherwise missing and an enhanced capability for dealing with the kinds of religious issues that often arise in such negotiations.

3. Coordination with other stakeholders

- Conflict prevention and peace building are complex undertakings that typically require action on the part of multiple actors at multiple levels. Thus, adept coordination is often required with domestic and foreign governments, international organizations, and NGOs. In high-level mediation and negotiation, it is important to keep all of the stakeholders closely informed of the proceedings and to *effectively coordinate the involvement of Track 1 and/or Track 2 diplomats*. The Community of Saint Egidio's work in Mozambique and that of the Conciliation Commission in Nicaragua are both examples of situations where these tasks were superbly executed.

- As feasible, religious peacemakers should generally *seek to strengthen and support existing peacemaking initiatives,* thereby avoiding any need to re-create a wheel that already exists and enabling them to focus more effectively on bringing the religious elements to bear. The Mennonites customarily do this to excellent effect.

- Finally, as a general rule, it is always preferable to *develop indigenous ownership* of conflict prevention and peace-building initiatives as early in the process as possible.

To the extent that faith-based NGOs constructively exploit their religious identities, relationships of trust, and far-reaching networks, they offer a vital (and too-often-overlooked) tool for conflict avoidance and mitigation. Again, the role of government in such a process is to reinforce it by lending support from afar and, as appropriate, building on the results that are achieved. Attempting to control it in any way, however, would risk discrediting the results by undermining the neutrality that is required to achieve a fair and balanced outcome.

CONCLUSIONS

Consideration should be given to establishing standing forums on an ad hoc basis at which NGOs (and possibly other grassroots organizations operating in the field) can provide information and recommendations to diplomats and/or field commanders on matters of common interest. Creating a transparent feedback loop of this nature would enable NGOs to share their expertise in ways that are empowering to them and helpful to policymakers, while respecting the NGO's neutrality.

Such partnerships, however, would not apply to NGOs involved in conflict mediation, since it is their perceived neutrality and independence that provides the credibility to negotiate peace agreements. Once an agreement is reached, though, a partnership with the military may be required to monitor the resulting cease-fire or to guarantee free elections.[36]

Because of the disincentives for collaboration between NGOs discussed earlier, consideration should also be given to requiring U.S. AID to make widely known the fact that responses to its requests for proposals (to accomplish specific objectives), which include partnering between NGOs, will be given preferential treatment in determining which proposals to fund. The opportunities to achieve helpful synergies are substantial and should be strongly encouraged wherever possible.

CHAPTER 13

Dealing with the Ideas behind the Guns

In speaking against fanaticism, let us not imitate the fanatics: they are sick men in delirium who want to chastise their doctors. Let us assuage their ills, and never embitter them, and let us pour drop by drop into their souls the divine balm of toleration, which they would reject with horror if it were offered to them all at once.

—Voltaire

THE UNEVEN PLAYING FIELD

For over a decade, defense planners in the West have been wrestling with the challenges of the *asymmetric threat*. This term is normally associated with creative, unconventional attacks by militarily weak opponents against more powerful adversaries—much like that used by bin Laden on 9/11 to rock America back on its heels. By definition, insurgents almost always resort to asymmetric warfare as a means of engagement in which they win by not losing and their adversary loses by not winning. In response to this kind of threat, the Pentagon has come up with a new strategy for "irregular warfare" that calls for a much tighter coordination between defense, diplomacy, and development.[1] This is all to the good; but whatever potential this highly promising concept may hold, there is simply not enough money in western treasuries to defend against all possible asymmetric threats. What is needed instead is an asymmetric counter to these threats, one that deals with the ideas behind the guns.

ORGANIC SUASION: THE ASYMMETRIC COUNTER

Often the human body's best weapon against disease is its own internal biological defenses. Similarly, in a context where religious legitimacy trumps all, the best antidote for religious ignorance is religious understanding. This is the basis for the concept of "organic suasion," or change and healing from within. It is the obverse of "shock and awe" and a process in which extremism is either marginalized or moderated by members of the same faith community. Civil rights reform in the United States post-1864, for example, was a hundred-year-long process of organic suasion.

For definitional purposes in this chapter, organic suasion presumes that Islam has within its own traditions and sacred texts the means to counter illegitimate warfare carried out in its name. For example, the Qur'an states, "Fight in the way of Allah against those who fight against you, but begin not hostilities. Lo! Allah loveth not aggressors."[2] These "limits" were later clarified in the "10 commands" of the first Caliph, Abu Bakr al-Siddiq:

Do not act treacherously; do not act disloyally; do not act neglectfully. Do not mutilate; do not kill little children or old men, or women; do not cut off the heads of the palm-trees or burn them; do not cut down the fruit trees; do not slaughter a sheep or a cow or a camel, except for food. You will pass by people who devote their lives in cloisters; leave them and their devotions alone. You will come upon people who bring you platters in which are various sorts of food; if you eat any of it, mention the name of God over it.[3]

Frequently referred to as "Islamic terrorism" by certain western media and policy circles, this term is rejected by most Muslims who view "Islamic terrorism" as no more than criminal activity carried out in the name of Islam. In the eyes of most Muslims, such people have no more right to call themselves Muslims than Ku Klux Klan members have the right to call themselves Christians.

Organic suasion recognizes that religious faith can be a powerful motivator for good or ill, for excess or self-restraint, for extremism or building community. Its power resides in the sincerity of those "Islamic" terrorists, who believe that their actions will make them martyrs of the faith and lead them to eternal bliss. Like Christian believers, they believe in divine revelation and a Judgment Day that will determine their place in the next life. If they can come to understand that their knowledge of the Qur'an is faulty and that their conduct will win them eternal damnation rather than eternal bliss, they may be "disarmed." This "disarming" process is also organic suasion and works best in tandem with other conditions. Examples of this inner transformation can occur on a broad societal level as well as on the community and personal levels. In the end, it is about changing attitudes. The Qur'an says that to change one's condition, one must first have a change of heart.[4] Change can come from a variety of sources and conditions external and internal to the terrorists. Foremost among them are knowledge and attitude. The cases that follow illustrate the indispensable role of these two ingredients in achieving success at every level.

ORGANIC SUASION ON A SOCIETAL SCALE

Organic suasion on a societal scale is a process that takes knowledge and wisdom, time and patience, while containing the violent manifestations of underlying social ills.

In the United States of the 1960s, agents of change had to battle a long history of racism, much of which had been rationalized by Christian proponents on the basis of scripture relating to the curse that Noah placed on his youngest son's descendents, thought to include the Negroid race.[5] Peter Gomes, former chaplain at Harvard, notes in his work *The Good Book:*

One of the greatest ironies available to people who take the Bible seriously is they may be tempted to take it, and themselves, so seriously that God and the truths of God to which the Bible points may be obscured, perverted or lost entirely.[6]

Similar license was taken by the Dutch Reformed Church in South Africa to justify the immoral practice of apartheid.

To right the accumulated wrongs against black Americans since 1864, organic suasion was set in motion when conscience, social activism, and politics combined to force American society to live up to its own ideals. The civil rights movement invoked the Declaration of Independence and Christian first principles to remind Americans that everyone is made in the image of God and deserves to be treated with dignity. Martin Luther King inspired and was admired because he refused to succumb to anger and hatred, despite the many personal grievances that he suffered. While most of his grief was caused by whites, he deeply believed in the white man's better nature. Should not America have a similar confidence in the ability of Muslims to conquer the evils that exist within their own community? Recent experience in Algeria suggests that it should.

The Case of Algeria (the Qur'an vs. the Extremists)

In the Algeria of the 1990s, there were at least three conflicts taking place (see Figure 13.1): a domestic rebellion by a fractionated Islamist opposition against the Algerian government, which had refused to honor the democratic victory of an Islamist party in the 1992 general elections; internecine conflicts among government factions and among the insurgent factions within the guerilla movement; and an international conflict in which France was discretely assisting the Algerian government while outside elements, mainly of Saudi origin, were fueling the Islamist opposition both with money and narrow religious ideology. Yet, in the end, it was respected Saudi *Salafi* clerics who dampened the terrorist zeal.

Figure 13.1
Algerian Civil War (1999–2002) Major Players

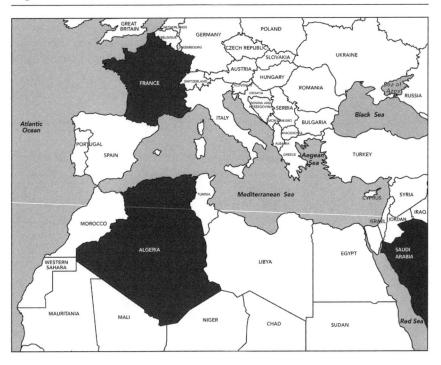

Aided by the views of highly respected conservative (*Salafi*) Islamic scholars who denounced the un-Islamic conduct of the insurgents, the Algerian
government eventually won control of an insurgency that gave the name
Black Years to the mid-1990s. Although the Algerian army grew better over
time at understanding and fighting the opposition, the tide turned only
after the so-called Islamic terrorists lost the support of an initially sympathetic urban populace that, like the Awakening movement in Iraq,[7] was
tired of bloodshed in the name of Islam and the dirtying of their faith by
Muslims who didn't deserve the name. Slaughtering innocents was not Islamic. It is important to note, however, that throughout the insurgency, the
Algerian government played on western fears of Islamist extremism and
was not shy about labeling all terrorists as "Islamic." Yet more than 50 Algerian imams were murdered for denouncing the insurgency as un-Islamic,
killings that were little reported in the Algerian press and which received
almost no attention from anyone in the West.[8]

Nuanced military tactics, intelligence penetration, a reinsertion of
"turned" prisoners into the terrorist ranks, and, importantly, condemnation
by leading *Salafi* clerics in Saudi Arabia led to a virtual halt to the violence

in 1999. During an interview on Algerian television in 1998 with a former terrorist, when asked why he had laid down his arms, he replied, "The Saudis told us."[9] "Scholars," explained Algerian Col. Fouad Gouni, "have an obligation to take the initiative."[10] And this was what happened during the 1990s. "They were motivated by an obligation to protect the faith from those who were defaming it. Ordinary Muslims in Algeria began to say that if what the terrorists were doing was Islam, they wanted out."[11]

Is it possible to equate those who are knowledgeable with those who are not?

—*Sura 39:9*

The denunciation of Armed Islamic Group (GIA) tactics during the Algerian insurgency by *Salafi* religious authorities points to the role that organic suasion played then and can play in the future. The contribution of three prestigious *Salafi* clerics to bringing an end to the violence cannot be defined with precision. Yet, it was clearly significant and dovetailed with the revulsion of the general population over the terrorists' indiscriminate tactics. Sheik Abdul Aziz bin Baz, Sheikh Mohammed bin Salih bin Othaimeen, and Mohammed Nasser Eddin al-Albani independently came to the same conclusion that Islam was being denigrated by the terrorism being conducted in its name. Accordingly, they issued fatwas in the mid-1990s denouncing as un-Islamic the conduct of the GIA. Collectively, these fatwas declared the following

- Rebellion against constituted authority is not permitted, unless the *ulama* (a body of recognized religious scholars) itself judges that it is in the public interest to engage in open rebellion.
- Only the *ulama* can determine who is an apostate;[12] otherwise killing other Muslims is strictly forbidden.
- Killing foreigners and non-Muslims who live in the country, whom Muslims are obliged to protect, is prohibited. Such acts violate the covenant of hospitality.
- Sit-ins and political demonstrations in mosques are not permissible.
- The killing of innocents, especially women and children and the elderly, is not permitted.[13]

Sheiks bin Baz and bin Othaimeen were both Saudis. Bin Baz was the widely respected Grand Mufti of Saudi Arabia, and bin Othaimeen was a member of the Saudi Council of Senior Ulama. Sheik al-Albani, on the other hand, was a follower of the conservative 13th-century Muslim scholar Ibn Taymiyya (who is often invoked carelessly by Islamist militants). Although Taymiyya himself advocated the *takfiri* practice of declaring others apostate, Taymiyya, as well as al-Albani, argued that disobeying apostates or non-Muslims is not permitted according to the *Sunna*, for even the Prophet Muhammad lived under unjust rulers and did not disobey. Rather, the Prophet gave them advice and called them to Islam. They chased him out of town.[14]

Al-Albani, another Saudi scholar, strongly disapproved of misappropriation of the word *Salafi* by the terrorists, because they adhered neither to the teachings of the Qur'an nor to the traditional scholars of Islam. He doubted that these people even deserved to call themselves Muslims. The jihad that al-Albani advocated was a "jihad for knowledge" and ridding Islam of non-Islamic cultural influences.

The pronouncements of these clerics caused some of the terrorists in the bush to question the righteousness of their cause.[15] From their hideaways in the mountains, terrorists used cell phones to call the clerics to verify that they had, in fact, issued such fatwas. During these conversations, Sheikh bin Othaimeen was recorded as having urged the foot soldiers of the GIA to lay down their arms should their emirs ignore the fatwas.[16] Furthermore, he told those who repented to return any property they had taken. Bin Othaimeen declared that women who had been raped were permitted to have an abortion up to the fourth month of pregnancy. He also urged the broader Algerian community to accept those who repented and accepted amnesty.

A fourth Saudi scholar, Sheikh bin Hadi al-Madakheely, also pronounced that these fighters could not be considered *Salafists* because they did not seek the advice of the *ulama* before embarking on their campaign of violence. He includes Osama bin Laden in this same category and condemns them all as the worst people imaginable for their killing of women and children.

Men never do evil so completely and cheerfully as when they do it from a religious conviction.

—*Blaise Pascal*

Judging the impact of these sheikhs on the terrorists' morale in Algeria during the 1990s must take into consideration a campaign that was simultaneously being waged by Algerian counterterrorism specialists among the prisoners. Those who were won over were filtered back into insurgent groups to sow doubt among the misguided *mufsiduun* (sinners) who believed they were doing God's work. "If you have doubts, questions and no answers, consult the scholars," Gouni said. He went on to explain that scholars are considered by many Muslims to be those that love God the most and have the religious, historical and civic responsibility to protect the faith from defamation.[17]

Algerian intelligence officers, working with prisoners, saw the war as having three fronts:

1. *Ideological*—combating corrupted or bastardized *Salafi* teachings that were being used to convince uneducated or illiterate followers that they were doing God's work.[18]

2. *Military*—Under Prime Minister Redha Malek, Algeria adopted a "terrorize the terrorists" approach, using highly specialized counterterrorist units drawn from some of the best people that the army, police, and gendarmerie had to offer. Selected military personnel also used higher knowledge of the Qur'an as a weapon in verbal exchanges with terrorists.

3. *Social/economic*—Improving economic and social conditions is a front where a great deal of effort is still needed. For now, the popular revulsion against the terrorists and their besmirching of Islam is still fresh, although other issues, such as Berber cultural rights, continued high unemployment, and housing shortages have become more recent flash points.

The highly delicate task of convincing prisoners to work as agents of demoralization within the ranks of the insurgents required a sophisticated multilevel interaction with the prisoners. This involved close observation of the prisoner, discerning the prisoner's motivation for fighting, assessing the prisoner's intelligence and his family situation, and introducing doubts about the Islamic correctness of the means that were being used to fight for justice.

ORGANIC SUASION AT THE COMMUNITY LEVEL

The Case of Iraq

Methods used by the Algerians in working with prisoners in the 1990s have been used more recently in Yemen,[19] Saudi Arabia, Singapore, and Indonesia. The United States has used them as well, thanks to the efforts of Marine Gen. Douglas Stone, former commander of the U.S. detention facilities in Iraq, who oversaw some 20,000 prisoners at Camp Bucca and another 3,000 at Camp Cropper (see Figure 13.2). The Algerians were interested in rehabilitation both for its own sake (as part of an amnesty approach to reclaim "lost sheep") and as a weapon to sow doubt among the insurgents. In similar fashion, General Stone's goal was to create a new environment that would deradicalize the detainees and separate the hard-core extremists from those judged not to be "enduring threats" (a term of art used by Iraqi counselors as a more accurate description than subjective labels like "radicals" or "irreconcilables"). As of March 2008, more than 6,000 prisoners had been released under this program, of whom only 21 had been recaptured because of suspected insurgent activity, an unprecedented recidivism rate of .35 percent.

Like the Algerian effort and efforts in Saudi Arabia and elsewhere, Stone's success rested on a multipronged approach to rehabilitation. Dismantling

Figure 13.2
Location of Camp Bucca and Camp Cropper

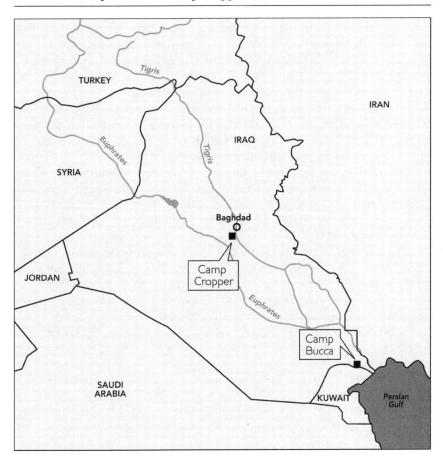

wrongly justified martyr ideologies through religious discussion groups with imams and others having a deep knowledge of divine law was one important component. As expressed by Sheikh Ali, a Sunni counselor at Camp Bucca, "I've seen detainees break down and cry when they realize that the conduct they thought was sanctioned by God is actually sin."[20] This program, in turn, allows for the release of those who agree to change their ways and whose families pledge to support their rehabilitation.

As occurred in Algeria with the population at large, Stone saw a clear turning point in the culture of the camps when a majority of the detainees turned against those regarded as "enduring threats." These hard-core extremists were re-creating al Qaeda cells in prison and threatening to break the legs of anyone who participated in the religious education programs. The detainees soon became irritated with them (particularly the foreigners) and began pointing them out to the prison guards. At Camp Bucca, about 1,000 extremists were so identified and isolated from the general prison population.

Of the 23,000 prisoners in detention as of May 2008, Stone estimates that about 10 percent were hard-core extremists who were determined to intimidate detainees from participating in the religious literacy program—one of the most popular, and, like all the others, voluntary. It is noteworthy that these extremists—the intellectual leadership of the radical Islamists—were drawn not from a formally trained pool of religious scholars but from self-taught, politically motivated individuals who were, for the most part, trained in technology. While their knowledge of their religion may be highly convoluted, if not virtually nonexistent, it is not easily challenged by followers who are either illiterate or uninstructed in Islamic law. About 10 percent of the extremists, in turn, were foreign fighters from more than 20 countries. Eighty-one percent of all detainees were Iraqi Sunni males.

The only common thread Stone found among the foreign fighters was a seven-minute film produced by al Qaeda on the abuses at Abu Ghraib. They had all seen it. If a film about the misdeeds of Americans toward prisoners could have such a powerful impact, reasoned Stone, might not a different prison experience have a different impact? "If it was so effective in getting so many to come over and kill thousands," Stone reflected, "could a different prison culture communicate a different view of the United States to the broader *umma*?" Stone went on to explain that the foreigners fight to die and will not quit, which is why there are so few of them standing around in prisons.[21]

Radical ideologies are often born in prisons. The Muslim Brotherhood, for example, acquired its violent edge in the torture chambers of Egyptian jails in the 1930s and 1940s, while still indirectly under British rule. Stone wonders whether prisons might also be vehicles for reversing the process. He believes that the way Americans treat detainees, more than anything else, will determine the outcome on the battlefield. His is a reasonable proposition, since every Iraqi or Afghan is part of an extended family of hundreds, if not thousands. Thus every abused or unjustly held prisoner/detainee becomes a reason for some percentage of that family to become an active or passive supporter of anti-American activity. Americans should ask themselves how they would react to the same situation. What is the legacy of bitterness going to produce for the thousands who haven't benefited from Stone's more enlightened approach?

Stone interviewed more than 2,000 detainees one-on-one, including many al Qaeda fighters. He distinguished "war fighting" versus "war winning"; how "war fighting" in the wrong way and against wrongly defined enemies can prevent "war winning." The greatest roadblock to success, Stone believes, "is our ethnocentric perspective."[22] The "American way" mentality makes it difficult, if not totally impossible, to engage successfully with the people, the society, and a faith-based culture that values collective identity over individual identity.[23]

Building trust and relationships that work require "doing," not saying. Says Stone, "Only the things we *do* really matter." Stone's "doing" involved questioning everything that was being done previously—policies that, at the time of his arrival in May 2007, had produced rioting by 10,000 detainees at one time, cost the lives of 78 Marine guards, caused the firing of 17,000 nonlethal rounds, and had created a climate of fear and loathing in the camps. In the first six months of 2008 under Stone's command, there was no detainee violence, no tunneling out. There were more than 70,000 family member visits, 10,000 detainees were enrolled in educational programs, and there had been nine public release ceremonies. Reporters who collectively spoke with some 3,000 of those released did not hear stories about torture but about how detainees learned to read, write, and acquire job skills. According to Stone, reporters grew sick of hearing prisoners praise the educational opportunities they had in prison.

Because about 68 percent of all detainees are illiterate, Stone's program taught reading and writing, in addition to civics and citizenship, Iraqi history, human rights in Islam, the rights of parents, manners, the rule of law, and democracy as well as courses in honesty, truth, and women's rights. The camps offered 21 different kinds of job training, all on a voluntary basis. Families were viewed as an essential pillar of the reintegration process, and family visits were actively encouraged.[24]

In Stone's view, Camp Bucca became a microcosm of a new society in the making. The intractable hard-core detainees, once identified by inmates, were physically isolated. The radical *irhabist* ideology was countered by the teaching of 120 imams who knew all of the relevant verses in the Qur'an and Hadith that were being exploited by the militants. These scholars were able to place them in a proper context for those who wanted to be good Muslims, without following the teachings of al Qaeda or *takfiri* (those who unilaterally declare other Muslims to be apostates). "War winning" for Stone was when his community of 400 imams, counselors, teachers, and psychiatrists felt empowered to confront the extremists with their faces fully exposed, knowing the risks. "They don't have passports to leave Iraq. Their risk is much greater than mine. I just redeploy. In a sense, the war is over when the moderate *umma* marginalizes the extremist," said Stone.[25]

Stone read the Qur'an, prayed with Muslims, and asserted "that nobody here has a greater regard for Islam than I do." "Ignorance of Islam is massive," says Stone, "and the 'fundamentalist' classification of violent Islam is wrong." Stone has many fundamentalist friends. Organic suasion works, even when it's stimulated from the outside, in this case by a culturally engaged Marine general.

Stone succeeded so well in establishing a respectful, family-friendly environment that he created another problem. Not only did many detainees not want to leave, they wanted their siblings and friends to join them in this new world of education, relative comfort, and respectful treatment. As Iraqi Vice President Tariq al-Hashimi is reported to have said to Stone, "America could win the war if they just applied the exact process that you're putting into detention to the rest of the nation."[26] The contrast between the effectiveness of this approach and those taken at Abu Ghraib and Guantanamo Bay could not be greater.

The previous leadership didn't assess the problem correctly. The camps were run by a manual, not adaptively. They were found to be "compliant" with Army regulations when inspected by the Army Inspector General. Stone attributes his success to one person—Gen. David Petraeus. Petraeus, like Stone, understands that there are many different insurgencies and many different enemies, all intermixed. Few of the "enemies" have to be permanent. Distinguishing one from the other and determining the different level of threat that each represents is the greatest challenge. In the end, it is a matter of judgment, and critics will simply have to understand that sometimes those judgments will be wrong. Meanwhile, a steady stream of rehabilitated detainees has been sent back into society with a mandate to help build a unified Iraq, as opposed to tearing it down.

Stone encountered "no's" everywhere he turned when he began to make changes in the camps. He was investigated, criticized, and even demonized by some. Only Petraeus said yes. Stone is absolutely convinced he was on the right course. "If there is one thing we must do, it is to ignore everyone else and go forward." On that score he was irreconcilable.

After Stone's departure from Iraq in July 2008, Rear Adm. Garland Wright and later Brig. Gen. David Quantock, at the order of General Petraeus,[27] continued Stone's reforms, focusing on vocational training, literacy education, increased family visitations, and mainstream Islamic study groups. The reforms lasted until the closure of Camp Bucca in September 2009[28] and the transfer to Iraqi control of Camp Cropper in July 2010.[29] In light of his success in Iraq, General Stone was assigned to review all detention issues in Afghanistan. He quickly separated extremist militants from the more moderate inmates detained for common crimes and, as in Iraq, established vocational courses, mainstream Islamic study groups, and other rehabilitation programs for moderate inmates.[30]

In addition to deradicalization programs in the prisons, selected Muslim countries are pursuing a range of other measures as well to counter the militancy and terrorism that are as threatening to their own regimes as they are to others. Saudi Arabia, for example, has purged more than 1,000 imams for inciting global jihad and is retraining 40,000 other imams to promote more tolerant interpretations of Islam.[31] It has also

1. issued an announcement prohibiting Saudi youth from waging jihad abroad;
2. engaged senior clerics in this same campaign, including (1) the issuance of a fatwa by the Saudi Grand Mufti, outlawing the waging of jihad abroad with-

out authorization from the king and (2) a statement by a member of the Senior Shura (advisory) Council condemning perpetrators of suicide operations to eternal suffering in hell;

3. developed a program to fight terrorist ideology in the schools, including the alteration of textbooks as appropriate;

4. initiated a dialogue campaign with extremists over the Internet and outlawed the establishment of Web sites that support terrorism, imposing a penalty of 10 years in prison.[32]

The government of Yemen has engaged a corps of "religious guides" to teach "the noble values of Islam" and to establish "principles of moderation and tolerance" in areas where a lack of religious knowledge is being exploited by extremists. The President of Yemen has also challenged the country's scholars and preachers to clarify Islamic teachings to the Muslim community in order to eradicate sedition, among other failings.[33] Indonesia, Egypt, and others are pursuing similar programs as well.

More broadly, in 2005, under the leadership of King Abdullah II of Jordan, a process was initiated to address three questions: (1) Who is a Muslim? (2) Is it permissible to declare someone an apostate (*takfir*)? and (3) Who has the right to issue fatwas? This process, which culminated in what is called the Amman Message,[34] initially involved 24 senior Islamic religious scholars from around the world, including the late Shaykh Tantawi, Ayatollah Sistani, and Sheikh Qaradawi.[35] It then brought the questions before a gathering of 200 leading scholars from 50 countries, with eventual sharing and adoption of the message by a universe of more than 500 scholars—representing the orthodox leadership of the Muslim world.

The message served three purposes: (1) it acknowledged the validity of eight legal schools of Islamic thought, including traditional Islamic theology (*Ash'arism*), Islamic mysticism (Sufism), and true *Salafi* thought; (2) it forbade the practice of *takfir* between Muslims; and (3) it established the preconditions for the legitimate issuance of fatwas, with the intent of exposing "ignorant and illegitimate edicts in the name of Islam." As expressed by one commentator:

This amounts to a historical, universal and unanimous religious and political consensus (*ijma'*) of the *Ummah* (nation) of Islam in our day, and a consolidation of traditional, orthodox Islam. The significance of this is: (1) that it is the first time in over a thousand years that the *Ummah* has formally and specifically come to such a pluralistic mutual inter-recognition; and (2) that such a recognition is religiously legally binding on Muslims since the Prophet (may peace and blessings be upon him) said: *My Ummah will not agree upon an error* (Ibn Majah, Sunan, Kitab al-Fitan, Hadith no. 4085).[36]

This combination of edicts issued by religious leaders and scholars who command respect and credibility in the eyes of most Muslims and recantations by extremist thinkers who have "street credibility" appears to already be having an effect. According to anecdotal evidence, *takfir*—once lauded by certain Muslim Brotherhood factions—is no longer considered acceptable practice among a growing number of the Brotherhood's members.[37]

The general sense of concern underlying these initiatives is that so long as a violent, individualist, total-war form of jihad can be considered justifiable, there will be those who will argue that it is precisely under the current conditions that it is warranted. Initiatives like the Amman Message would place the theological justification for such decisions in the hands of legitimate orthodox leaders, but the likelihood that this will influence those who are already politically radicalized does not seem high. Such pronouncements will probably have a better chance of influencing the overall population from which the extremists hope to draw their support, thus weakening the extremist base.

Also of note is the powerful statement released by respected scholars at the Darul-Uloom Deoband school in India, decrying terrorism as being un-Islamic.[38] The Deoband tradition is often linked to the more extreme forms of Islamic theology, and such a statement may well carry weight with the radicals. Another more recent edict that could also have an impact is an April 12, 2010, fatwa issued by the Saudi Council of Senior Ulama, which unambiguously denounces terrorism and its financial backers. The significance of this pronouncement lies in the fact that this council is the guardian of the conservative Wahhabi school of Islam, which had previously been seen as sympathetic to the extremists.[39]

Perhaps most significant of all, is a recent and direct repudiation of al Qaeda's ideology from within the ranks of the *irhabists* themselves in which the Libyan Islamic Fighting Group (LIFG), a militant body once close to bin Laden, issued a 417-page religious document that sets forth a new code for jihad. Prominent in its challenge to al Qaeda is the following:

Jihad has ethics and morals because it is for God. That means it is forbidden to kill women, children, elderly people, priests, messengers, traders and the like. Betrayal is prohibited and it is vital to keep promises and treat prisoners of war in a good way. Standing by those ethics is what distinguishes Muslims' jihad from the wars of other nations.[40]

In short, this "code" effectively delegitimizes the use of terrorism and violence.

An ongoing project in Turkey is taking aim at some of the traditionally more confrontational teachings by reexamining the reliability of Hadith-related sources through the application of modern scholarship and technology. Finally, there is an encouraging initiative under way at the International Islamic University in Islamabad in which PhD students in comparative religion are attempting to combine 1,000 years of Islamic learning with the latest developments in American and European humanities and social studies scholarship in order to integrate western and Islamic methodologies for studying history and religion. Their goal is to build a better future.[41]

It is too soon to know the ultimate impact of any of the above initiatives, but they all represent varying forms of organic suasion. As summarized a bit differently by Jamal Khashoggi, editor-in-chief of *Al-Watan*, a daily Saudi newspaper:

Our struggle against terrorism is primarily an ideological one. The position of a religious scholar takes precedence over that of a soldier, a journalist, a teacher, or an economist. We must re-erect the religious barriers that the extremists have torn down. . . . By [creating] loopholes in religious law, they have undermined the basic tenets [of Islam] and have permitted the forbidden.[42]

Exporting Organic Suasion to Afghanistan

Organic suasion at the community level also played a role in the summer of 2007 when 23 South Korean Presbyterian missionaries were captured by the Taliban and subsequently held hostage (see Figure 13.3). The Taliban initially demanded that all South Korean forces withdraw from Afghanistan within 24 hours and that the government of Afghanistan release all Taliban prisoners. A few days later, they demanded a sum of $100,000 in exchange for the right to contact the hostages via telephone. When the Afghan government refused their demands, the Taliban killed 2 of the male hostages. At this point, the International Center for Religion and Diplomacy (ICRD) received a call from the Korean Ambassador to the United States, asking if the Center could work through religious channels to help secure the release of the remaining hostages.

In response, the ICRD called upon one of its indigenous partners in Pakistan to take the lead in mounting a rescue effort. The partner agreed to help and contacted 15 religious leaders from Pakistan and Afghanistan who were known to have had some acquaintance with the spokesmen for the captors. He formed them into a makeshift *jirga* (council of respected elders), which then traveled to Afghanistan's Ghazni Province to negotiate with the captors.

With open Qur'ans, the *jirga* challenged the captors to provide Islamic justification for the kidnapping of innocent victims and within the first hour asked when they were going to release the women (not an inconsequential question in light of the fact that 18 of the remaining 21 hostages were women). After a week of exerting such pressure, the *jirga* returned home. Not only had they said all that they came to say, but they were violently ill from the local drinking water. Before leaving, however, they extracted three concessions from the captors: (1) that no further harm would come to the hostages while negotiations were taking place, (2) that they would release several female hostages as a sign of "good intent," and (3) that they would

Figure 13.3
Afghanistan and Pakistan

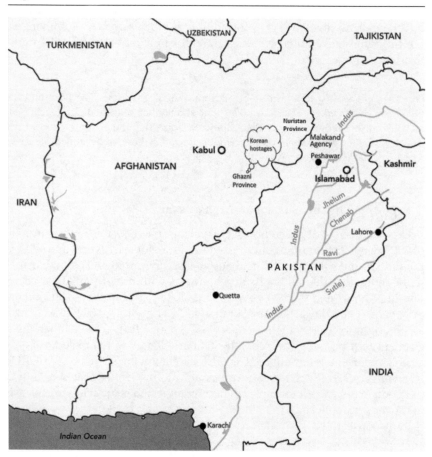

meet with the Korean delegation, which had been on scene for some time to negotiate the release of the hostages.

The captors then engaged the Korean delegates, with the Red Cross serving as intermediaries. Although the captors released two women who were sick, the negotiations soon broke down. At this point, the ICRD, capitalizing on its earlier networking with the Taliban commanders and working through the Afghan Minister of Religious Affairs, was able to secure the support of three ex–cabinet ministers of the former Taliban government. A reconstituted *jirga* was then formed consisting of these three ministers and four members of the earlier group. The *jirga* engaged the captors once again; and after another week of negotiations, the hostages were released.

There was considerable speculation after the fact as to whether the Korean government had paid a ransom to facilitate the release. One of the

Taliban negotiators mentioned to the ICRD's team leader that a sizable sum had been offered to free the hostages but that it had been turned down as a matter of religious principle. Because later evidence suggests that a modest sum may, in fact, have been paid, it appears that there were competing views on the matter among the captors. Either way, the Taliban negotiators later indicated that had it not been for the religious intervention, they would never have let the hostages go until all of their demands had been fully met. The complete truth may never be known, but the idea of intervening on religious grounds appears to have been sound.

The Madrasas of Pakistan: Teaching Different Ideas Differently

For the past six years, the ICRD has been using organic suasion to enhance the madrasas of Pakistan, including those that gave birth to the Taliban. Here, the organic suasion not only draws on the precepts of Islam but on the past accomplishments of the madrasas themselves.

Few in the West are mindful of the glorious history of these religious schools; but from the Middle Ages extending through the 16th century, they were without peer as institutions of higher learning. Indeed, it was European exposure to them that led to the creation of our own university system in the West.[43] In a later reaction to British colonialism, however, and out of a fear of losing their Islamic identity, the madrasas purged their curriculums of all disciplines that they considered to be either secular or western in nature—to the point where the majority of them today focus solely on rote memorization of the Qur'an and the study of Islamic principles.

The ICRD's principal goals in this project have been twofold: (1) to expand the curriculums to include the physical and social sciences, with a strong emphasis on religious tolerance and human rights (especially women's rights),[44] and (2) to transform the pedagogy in order to develop critical thinking skills among the students. The latter is particularly important because as things currently stand, these students, who do not really understand what they have memorized of the Qur'an (they are required to memorize it in its original Arabic, while their native tongue is Urdu), have no ability to question or challenge militants who misappropriate scripture to recruit them to their cause.

The success of this effort is exceeding expectations and stands in stark contrast to the failure of past attempts by the government of Pakistan to control these schools. With their independent funding base (most from local sources, some from the Gulf states), madrasa leaders have resisted government reforms for fear that their curriculums will be secularized and that they will lose their independence in the process. The ICRD's success, on the other hand, has been a function of (1) conducting the initiative in such a way that the madrasas feel it is their own reform effort and not something imposed from the outside (which means they have significant ownership in the change process); (2) inspiring them with their own heritage through periodic references not only to their past institutional history but also going back further in time to the pioneering breakthroughs in the arts and sciences—including religious tolerance—that took place under Islam a thousand years ago; and (3) grounding all proposed changes in Islamic principles so that participants can legitimately feel that they are becoming better Muslims in the process.

As its first step in taking the project to scale on a nationwide basis, the ICRD has engaged selected Pakistani universities to provide certification training for madrasa faculty. As of this writing, five such training programs have taken place, with encouraging results. These programs are important because they are providing quality control where none has previously existed. They are also bridging the social gap between the madrasas, which feel isolated and looked down upon, and the Pakistani elite, including the universities, that do, in fact, look down upon them. Once madrasa faculty walk through the university gates, the psychological implications are enormous in terms of their increased feelings of acceptance. More than any other initiative, this university training appears to offer the greatest potential for "mainstreaming" the madrasas into the Pakistani educational system.

The following examples are indicative of how the madrasa enhancement initiative is dealing with the ideas behind the guns:

1. At a January 2009 workshop involving leaders from 16 madrasas surrounding the Swat Valley, one madrasa leader, who also happened to be a commander in Lashkar-e-Taiba (the terrorist group associated with the attack on Mumbai), declared at the end that he had attended solely for the purpose of discrediting all that the workshop was teaching. But he now felt a strong sense of rage because for the past 26 years he had been studying and teaching the Holy Qur'an the way it had been taught to him. Now, as a result of his participation, he felt that for the first time in his life, he had experienced the soul of the Qur'an and its peaceful intent. He vowed to change what he had been teaching. ICRD's project director returned a month later to find him teaching these new ideas to his students and telling them why. Moreover, in a setting where one could lose his head for a lot less, he repeated his earlier statement to a CNN crew that had accompanied the ICRD on the trip to document the process of change. One cannot help but admire the courage of those madrasa leaders who undergo such change. Once the veneer of rage and hostility has been penetrated and they become open to hearing new ideas, a number become strong champions of change, often at great personal risk to themselves.

2. During an earlier workshop at a madrasa in the Punjab that was known to be a major al Qaeda feeder, one participant asked if waging jihad in Kashmir was sanctioned by Islam. The workshop moderator indicated that it was not and said that jihad was only justified when defending the faith, never for acquiring territory. This led to a major debate among the madrasa leaders and a consensus conclusion that the fighting in Kashmir is politically motivated but not religiously sanctioned. These madrasa leaders are now taking steps to tone down

the militancy of their graduates. A description of this episode was later carried in a newspaper in Balochistan, halfway across the country.

An intangible that has undoubtedly contributed to the success of the project is the posture of humility from which the ICRD has operated, driven by the Center's awareness that the United States was complicit in planting the seeds of jihad in the madrasas in the first instance in order to grow holy warriors to evict the godless Soviets from Afghanistan. Indicative of this is the following excerpt from a fourth-grade mathematics textbook for madrasa students that was underwritten by the U.S. government:

The speed of a Kalashnikov bullet is 800 meters per second. If a Russian is at the distance of 3,200 meters from a mujahid [fighter], and the mujahid aims at the Russian's head, calculate how many seconds it will take for the bullet to strike the Russian.[45]

Once the Russians left, so did we; and the madrasas are continuing to do what we encouraged them to do. Only now, it is an American standing at a distance of 3,200 meters. Yet another chapter in the book of unintended consequences.

ORGANIC SUASION AT A PERSONAL LEVEL

An example of organic suasion on a more personal level is that provided by U.S. Army Lt. Col. Alan King in Iraq, whose life was being threatened by a local sheik. King arranged to meet with the sheik and pointed out the inconsistency between his threat and the teachings of the Qur'an. The sheik backed down, and King proceeded to establish friendly relations with him and a number of other Muslim religious leaders. This episode was made possible by King's commitment to memorizing much of the Qur'an well before his arrival in Iraq in April 2003. During his 15 months in Baghdad with the 422nd Civil Affairs Battalion, King's ability to quote freely from the Qur'an became an effective tool for countering hostility as well as exposing to many Iraqis their ignorance of their own religion.

As with General Stone, King's respectful attitude toward Iraqis and his commitment to cultural engagement paid huge dividends. These dividends, including his successful encounter with the sheik, are highlighted in a 2003 *Christian Science Monitor* piece about King and excerpts from his Colby Prize–winning book, *Twice Armed: An American Soldier's Battle for Hearts and Minds in Iraq.*[46] Together, they show the potential for organic suasion to be exercised by knowledgeable American soldiers. Early on, the Virginia-born, Lutheran-raised King understood the importance of learning about Iraqi tribal culture and learning about their religion. "They are Muslim, I'm Christian," King explained to the *Monitor*, "so I try to explain to them that we are both believers and I can go into specific verses in the Bible and Koran."

As for the tribes, one of the first things King did in Iraq was to obtain a copy of an old British guide to Iraqi tribes, *Baghdad Wilayat*, and to begin learning the history of the different tribes. Within months, he had inventoried the 150 tribes and more than 2,000 clans in Iraq. King continually added to his Palm Pilot index of tribes and subtribes, clans and subclans, branches and families—a work that was largely the result of his regular meetings with tribal leaders and scholars. This knowledge enabled him to reverse a poor decision made by American military commanders in 2003.

Shortly after the U.S. invasion of Iraq, Sheik Hussein Ali al-Shaalan of the Khazzal clan offered his counsel and the loyalty of his 200,000-member clan to the American military. Al-Shaalan was a Shiite from Diwaniya who had fled Iraq after the 1991 uprising against Saddam Hussein. He had taken asylum in the United Kingdom where he studied law and political science and also managed to develop good relations with the U.S. State Department. The American military, however, did not take him seriously and rejected his offer. Al-Shaalan later said to the *Christian Science Monitor*, "The American officers have this arrogance and it really hurts them. Everyone, even the lowest ranking officer thinks he is a big shot and doesn't want advice. They just do what they please. This antagonized many people." Except Lieutenant Colonel King. After they met, Al-Shaalan said, "I noticed that he had done his homework. He told me complicated tribal tales. He was not arrogant and was doing his duty to his country by studying our culture."

Later, as Special Assistant for Tribal Affairs of the 352nd Civil Affairs Command, King was able to reverse the earlier decision and by December 2003, a council of tribal sheiks began meeting and advising the Coalition Provisional Authority (CPA) on a regular basis. Because Al-Shaalan's clan had branches in Syria, Jordan, southern Iran, Yemen, Palestine, and Egypt and included Shiites and Sunnis, they were able to hunt down foreign fighters filtering across these borders. Their tips helped King capture 6 of the 100 terrorists on the most wanted list. But as Shaalan said back in December 2003, "If the Americans had listened to our advice from the beginning, our *repeated* advice, all this chaos wouldn't be happening now."

King's obvious abilities to connect with Iraqis on their terms led to his later appointment as Deputy Director of the CPA's Office of Provincial Outreach. In that capacity, he eventually met with some 3,500 sheiks and Muslim clerics. Among his many honors, he was made an honorary sheik of the Janabi tribe, one of Iraq's largest.

CONCLUSION

Like General Stone, Colonel King went to Iraq armed with a respectful attitude and a desire to learn the culture. His experience in transforming individual attitudes and behavior among Iraqis was rooted in large measure in his study of tribal culture and of the Qur'an, from which he could quote chapter and verse. Imagine the difference in attitude that an American would have toward a foreigner who could quote from the U.S. Constitution and Declaration of Independence when trying to sort out differences on issues relating to American first principles versus a foreigner who was ignorant of such things. Cultural knowledge and respect are the twin pillars of influence in many situations, especially when one is an outsider in a potentially hostile setting.

It is clear that organic approaches rooted in knowledge of religious scripture such as that ultimately taken in Algeria and those taken by Gen. Douglas Stone and Col. Alan King in Iraq and the ICRD in Afghanistan and Pakistan have the potential to change hearts as well as minds. In short, organic suasion provides far greater leverage for moderating or marginalizing religious extremism than do policies based on isolation and demonization. In this context, Islam is not the problem. It is the solution.

The fact that groups like al Qaeda have no compelling vision to offer their prospective followers suggests that their brand of terrorism is inherently self-limiting and will fade over time, if allowed to run its course.[47] Thus, the overriding challenge becomes one of letting it implode from within, while containing it through organic suasion wherever possible, much as we did with the former Soviet Union. Beyond that, the overriding considerations should be to (1) exercise restraint by taking every measure possible to minimize civilian casualties during military operations and (2) mitigate the appeal of the terrorists by treating them as *irhabis* rather than jihadists and by fully exposing their narrative of death and destruction (and the horrific toll it is taking on fellow Muslims). Indicative of this toll is the following testimony of Ali Dayan Hussain, senior South Asia researcher with Human Rights Watch, before the U.S. Commission on International Religious Freedom on March 17, 2009.

In Dera Ismail Khan, which is the frontier town bordering the tribal areas and the Northwest Frontier Province proper, since 2006, 551 people have died in violence that can be construed to be religious or sectarian or, sometimes, is often reported as al-Qaeda and terrorism-related. Now, if you break down these figures, of these 551 people, there has been one Christian, one Hindu, nine Sunni and 540 individuals from the Shi'a minority who have been killed.

This is from one small town out of many. "Horrific" is an understatement.

V

Moving Beyond

CHAPTER 14

The Ideas behind Our Own Guns

> Observe good faith and justice toward all nations. Cultivate peace and harmony with all. Religion and morality enjoin this conduct. And can it be that good policy does not equally enjoin it? It will be worthy of a free, enlightened, and at no distant period a great nation to give mankind the magnanimous and too novel example of a people always guided by an exalted justice and benevolence.
>
> —George Washington in his Farewell Address

A month after the fall of Baghdad in April 2003, Iran reportedly approached the United States to open a dialogue on the key outstanding points of contention between the two countries, offering as an incentive possible concessions relating to full transparency in its nuclear program, aid in stabilizing Iraq, cooperation against al Qaeda, the termination of material support to Palestinian opposition groups, and acceptance of the Saudi-sponsored two-state solution to the Israeli-Palestinian conflict. The Iranians saw that the United States had taken just three weeks to vanquish an army they had been unable to defeat in eight years of fighting (during the 1980–88 Iran-Iraq War) and were anxious to avoid a similar fate.

This initiative allegedly took the form of a proposal transmitted to the State Department and the White House, which was preceded by a paraphrased version faxed to the State Department through the Swiss Ambassador in Tehran (see appendix C). There has been a great deal of debate surrounding the authority and authenticity of the offer (particularly as conveyed through the Swiss Ambassador), but suffice it to say that an offer was made; and there was no response from the United States. Unsurprisingly, the Iranian proposal also laid out a number of quid pro quo concessions that it wanted in return, including, among others, "mutual respect," the lifting of economic sanctions, recognition of Iran's "legitimate security interests," and full access to peaceful nuclear technology.[1]

This overture was not a one-time happenstance. Only the year before, at a conference in Tokyo to raise international support for the reconstruction of Afghanistan, Iranian diplomats approached Ambassador James Dobbins, then U.S. Envoy to the Afghan resistance, indicating their country's desire to open a dialogue with the United States on all of the issues standing in the way of a cooperative relationship.[2] Having both helped facilitate the American military victory in Afghanistan and supported American diplomacy in the aftermath,[3] Iran had every reason to hope for a positive response. Instead, one week later, it was elected to membership in the "axis of evil" set forth in President George W. Bush's January 2002 State of the Union address.

U.S. victories in Afghanistan and Iraq had enhanced Iran's security, but they had also positioned American troops near Iran's borders. Thus, there was significant incentive to repair relations with Washington. Washington, however, was feeling invincible. Having replaced the Taliban and Saddam Hussein in a little over a year, why negotiate with Iran's revolutionary theocracy when, as Ambassador Dobbins recounts, "an opportunity to replace it might be just around the corner"?[4]

Ignored in such a stance were the negative long-term consequences of America's earlier role in overthrowing the democratically elected regime of Mohammad Mosaddeq in 1953. Among the reasons behind that overthrow were concerns relating to the future disposition of Iran's oil resources and a fear among U.S. and British policymakers that Iran might fall into the Soviet camp under Mosaddeq's leadership. However compelling these reasons may have seemed at the time, it is clear that the bitterness resulting from that "regime change" was a major contributor to the later overthrow of the U.S.-backed Shah of Iran and the seizure of U.S. Embassy personnel.

Whether the outstanding issues between our two countries could have been successfully negotiated on either occasion remains an open question, but the absence of any response at all to either overture effectively closed the door to improved relations for some time to come and, in the process, undermined the reformist regime under President Khatami that had made the overtures in the first instance.[5]

If you want to make peace, you don't talk to your friends. You talk to your enemies.

—*Moshe Dayan*

Whatever opportunity may have been lost by ignoring Iran's proposals, it is clear that U.S. policymakers have an unsettling tendency to overlook how they themselves would react if they were on the receiving end of some of their own policies. (Instilling this kind of awareness in future deliberations would be consistent with Sun Tzu's admonition to "know others and know yourself.") It is also easy to understand why a desire for "mutual respect" would rank so high on the list of concessions sought by the Iranians. In today's evolving multipolar world, respectful engagement will be an inescapable prerequisite for successful international relations in the future. Indeed, one can easily argue that its absence was a key factor in the global loss of respect that America has suffered in recent years.

Foreign policy leadership in the future will thus place a higher premium on one's ability to develop common ideas and approaches in partnership with other nations. Even today, one is hard-pressed to think of any serious international challenge that can be fully met on a unilateral basis. Moreover, with the relentless march of technology, today's interdependence is but a faint shadow of that which is to come. Despite whatever distrust U.S. policymakers may have had toward multilateral approaches to problem solving in recent years, coalition leadership will clearly be the sine qua non of successful foreign policy in the years ahead. And here, we have a problem.

As the wars in Iraq and Afghanistan have clearly demonstrated, we have been experiencing increasing difficulty in finding partners to support our positions in international crises. In understanding why, it may be useful to go back to first principles as conveyed in the epigraph at the beginning of this chapter. The wisdom of George Washington's admonition to the first generation of Americans about observing "good faith and justice toward all nations" and cultivating "peace and harmony with all" holds even greater relevance today than it did then. The nation's evolution from isolationism and avoidance of "foreign entanglements" contrasts sharply with today's reality of total engagement and extensive global commitments, a reality that only makes more imperative the need to project an image of "exalted justice and benevolence."

In some ways we do project such an image; in others, not at all. In recent years, one read with depressing regularity references in overseas accounts to "American arrogance." While some of this may have been attributable to the normal slings and arrows elicited by unrivaled power, there is ample evidence to suggest that a disquieting proportion had to do with our unilateral, heavy-handed behavior toward others. One must always be prepared to go it alone when vital interests are at stake; but resorting to conflict when it is clearly not a measure of last resort will inevitably be difficult to sell to potential partners.

While excessive self-centered behavior has undermined our international credibility and moral authority over the last decade, the list of global imperatives awaiting a proportional international response continues to grow. Among these are the well-recognized needs to (1) combat *irhab* and organized crime, (2) prevent weapons of mass destruction from falling into the wrong hands, while at the same time eliminating existing global stockpiles of these weapons,[6] and (3) reduce the negative effects of globalization, rampant industrialization, and overpopulation on the global environment. One obvious way to address the latter need would be through a strong commitment to sustainable development. Not only would this require a focus on causes rather than symptoms, but it would also force those involved to frame difficult issues in terms of shared concerns rather than differences. As Teddy Roosevelt remarked at the beginning of the last century, "Nine-tenths of wisdom consists of being wise in time."[7]

SERVANT-LEADERSHIP

The early vision of America as an exemplary "city upon a hill"[8]—a recurring theme in U.S. politics—was merely a first hint of how America could serve beyond itself. It has been left to subsequent generations of Americans to determine how best to pursue this concept on a broader scale.

The appeal in Washington's Farewell Address, however, suggests a need for a different kind of leadership than that which America has been accustomed to providing. What will be required in tomorrow's multipolar world is not a single-minded pursuit of narrow national interests but a dose of what one might call "servant-leadership."[9] The principle of organization upon which servant-leadership is based—*primus inter pares*, or "first among equals"—if wisely pursued, can provide an effective basis for retaining America's leadership role.

This innovative approach to personal and organizational leadership, which was developed as a business management technique by Robert K. Greenleaf in the 1960s and 1970s, is a remarkably flexible yet morally-grounded formula for leadership. If adapted for international applications, it could go far toward enhancing America's influence and moral authority over the longer-term.

An early practitioner of this concept was George Washington himself, who regularly signed his personal correspondence "your humble and obedient servant" and who infused his approach to governing with this same spirit. In an open letter to the Cherokee nation in 1796, for example, he suggested ways in which the United States and the Indian nations on its borders could peacefully coexist and offered friendly advice on how the Cherokee nation in particular might benefit from colonial agricultural techniques.[10]

A new American president committed to the concept of servant-leadership might begin by categorizing and giving precedence to the nation's vital interests, that is, those interests that one is prepared to promote unilaterally by whatever means necessary. Beyond this, however, further prioritization could take place by broadening the scope of our decision making, with an eye toward doing the most good for the most people. Harvard professor Joseph Nye and former Deputy Secretary of State Richard Armitage, two of the country's leading advocates of smart power, expressed it a bit differently, "In a changing world, the United States should become a smarter power by once again investing in the global good—by providing things that people and governments want but cannot attain without U.S. leadership."[11] In short, what's right for the world *is* in the national interest.

RESPECTFUL ENGAGEMENT

The second requirement of a servant-leader president would be to pursue a strategy of respectful engagement based on (1) a genuine desire to understand other points of view, (2) a keen sensitivity to the legitimate rights of others, (3) an openness to changing our own perspective, and (4) a willingness to engage in joint problem solving. This sounds like a reasonably straightforward proposition, but Khalid Masud, who chairs the Islamic Council of Pakistan, provided several observations during a presentation at the Washington-based Center for Strategic and International Studies on July 21, 2009, that should give us cause to reflect and perhaps go deeper in our thinking:

- The British taught us how to debate but not how to engage in give-and-take dialogue that is open to change.
- Democracy, as it is practiced today, is a young system that should not be judged too soon.
- Reinterpretation and change should not be limited solely to Muslim societies.
- Americans have to learn to deal with others who do not accept their system.

Foremost among legitimate rights, of course, are territorial integrity and the inviolability of one's borders, including the right to be free from foreign occupation. However, because the sanctity of existing borders is becoming increasingly porous as the global community has acted to assist citizens in countries like Kosovo, Rwanda, and Sudan where individual human rights have been egregiously violated through acts of genocide and the like, it becomes helpful to take our analysis to an even deeper level by examining the legitimate rights of minority groups within nation-states. Here, the standards that have been established under international law provide an excellent starting point. Among these standards are the rights of groups to:

- "establish and maintain their own associations" and "to establish and maintain, without any discrimination, free and peaceful contacts with other members of their group . . . as well as contacts across frontiers with citizens of other States to whom they are related by national or ethnic, religious or linguistic ties" (*Declaration on the Rights of Persons Belonging to National or Ethnic, Religious, and Linguistic Minorities*, 1992; henceforth referred to as *Declaration*);

- "enjoy their own culture, to profess and practice their own religion, and to use their own language, in private and in public, freely and without interference or any form of discrimination" (*Declaration*, article 2 and *International Covenant on Civil and Political Rights [ICCPR]*, article 27, 1966);

- "participate effectively in decisions on the national and, where appropriate, regional level concerning the [group] to which they belong or the regions in which they live, in a manner not incompatible with national legislation" (*Declaration*, article 2);

- "promote their identity, express their characteristics, and develop their culture, language, religion, traditions and customs, except where specific practices are in violation of national law and contrary to international standards" (*Declaration*, article 4);

- "participate fully in the economic progress and development in their country" (*Declaration*, article 4).

SELF-DETERMINATION

Unmentioned above is the right to self-determination, which is also enshrined in international law,[12] although its precise meaning is controversial and open to varying interpretations. This right has been defined through various declarations and treaties as the "right by which peoples freely determine their political status and freely pursue their economic, social and cultural development." However, what constitutes a "people" has never been defined, and the concept has been considered problematic, particularly by states that are worried about maintaining their sovereignty and territorial integrity. Since the central governments of most states do not want to see their countries broken up by groups of secessionists (as our own history also makes clear), there has been an effort to balance the right of self-determination with that of territorial integrity and the "inviolability of frontiers." However, the Friendly Relations Declaration (General Assembly Resolution 2625, 1970) implies that this territorial integrity might not be protected if the central government is not representative of the entire population "without distinction as to race, creed or color."[13]

Muslim separatist groups are operating in Thailand, the Philippines, China, the Caucasus, Iraq (Kurdistan), and Kashmir. And there are non-Muslim separatist movements ranging from Taiwan to Quebec to Scotland and at least 15 other countries, in addition to five states of the United States.[14] By the right of self-determination, do all of these groups have the right to form their own country? And does this desire to be independent constitute a "legitimate aspiration"? Probably not, if the human rights of these groups are respected and if they enjoy political participation and representation in their respective governments. In such a case, they could already be said to enjoy self-determination; and their case for secession would weaken accordingly. Conversely, if the people desiring independence were oppressed in a major way, the case for secession would strengthen. The bottom line is that, under international law, having an independent state should not be seen as absolutely requisite to self-determination, although some of the above groups might argue otherwise.

FREEDOM FROM OCCUPATION

An Israeli arrived at Heathrow Airport. When he came to the passport control desk, the official asked, "Occupation?"

"No, just visiting," the Israeli replied.

The joke made its rounds in the cyber world in 2009, but as both Israel and the United States can attest, the forceful occupation of another country, or state, however seemingly justified, is no joking matter. The right "not to be occupied" does not exist in international law, since there is such a thing as a legal occupation. Thus, while few reasonable people would doubt that freedom from occupation is a legitimate aspiration, one should keep in mind that it is currently not an absolute right granted under international law.

The international law of occupation is based primarily on two pieces of legislation: the 1907 Hague Regulations and the Fourth Geneva Convention of 1949. The Hague Regulations delineate what constitutes a legal occupation and the responsibilities of the occupying power, while the Fourth Geneva Convention outlines further responsibilities and makes clear that the protections of international humanitarian law are extended to persons under occupation.

International legal scholar Eyal Benvenisti suggests that a foreign occupier has only temporary managerial powers until a peaceful solution is reached. In other words, the role of the occupant is very close to that of a "trustee."[15] This reading is also consistent with the *Oxford Manual on the Laws of War on Land*, which states:

No invaded territory is regarded as conquered until the end of the war; until that time the occupant exercises, in such territory, only a de facto power, essentially provisional in character.[16]

The occupying power is thus prohibited from annexing the territory and is "bound to respect and maintain the political and other institutions that exist in that territory." It is also responsible for maintaining public order and "civil life." Toward this end, Article 43 of the Hague Regulations states:

The authority of the legitimate power having in fact passed into the hands of the occupant, the latter shall take all the measures in his power to restore, and ensure, as far as possible, public order and [civil life], while respecting, unless absolutely prevented, the laws in force in the country.

This implies that the occupant has the right not to respect some of the local laws, although Benvenisti observes that "it seems the drafters of this phrase ["unless absolutely prevented"] viewed military necessity as the sole relevant consideration that could 'absolutely prevent' an occupant from maintaining the old order."[17]

Benvenisti also notes that UN Security Council Resolution 1483, which recognized U.S. and British forces as occupying powers in Iraq, seems to further enshrine the "neutral connotation" of occupation into international law. In this view, occupation is "a temporary measure for reestablishing order and civil life after the end of active hostilities, benefiting also, if not primarily, the civilian population. As such, occupation does not amount to unlawful alien domination that entitles the local population to struggle against it." He also contends that, while in the past, sovereignty of the territory would have passed to the occupant under the old doctrine of *debellatio*,[18] the resolution seems to put this notion to rest once and for all by suggesting that "sovereignty inheres in the people" and that the collapse of whatever regime happened to be governing them would not "extinguish [that] sovereignty."[19]

Thus, while Article 43 of the Hague Regulations requires the occupant to respect the laws of the country that existed prior to occupation, UNSC Resolution 1483 implies that the previous legal system could be transformed to the extent to which it would allow the Iraqi people to, in the words of the resolution, "freely determine their own political future," "control their own natural resources," and "form a representative government based on the rule of law that affords equal rights and justice to all Iraqi citizens without regard to ethnicity, religion, or gender."[20]

Ultimately, based on the provisional and temporary nature of legal occupation, the idea that sovereignty belongs to the people (which stems from the idea of self-determination), along with the inadmissibility of the acquisition of territory by the real or threatened use of force, one can safely conclude that freedom from occupation is indeed a legitimate aspiration under international law, despite the fact that there can be, at least in theory, occupations that are perfectly legal.

THE QUESTION OF INTERVENTION

The foregoing discussion leads, in turn, to the difficult question of when one should intervene militarily in response to challenges beyond one's borders. A useful starting point might be to develop a predetermined set of considerations that must be taken into account whenever the question of intervention arises. Such a set, among other possibilities, might include (1) whether or not the proposed intervention represents a measure of last resort, (2) the scale of the crisis, (3) our capacity to make a difference, (4) the relative effectiveness of unilateral action versus acting in partnership with others, (5) the probable costs in both lives and money, (6) the likelihood

of success, and (7) the impact of our intervention on the interests and attitudes of other nations and people in the region. This particular set would
also fit comfortably within the servant-leader paradigm. It would be up
to the President to apply these criteria on a situational basis and to rally
the support of the American public whenever a decision is made to go forward. In this regard, any foreign policy, to be sustainable, will have to play
to the nature of the American public as a people—combining realism with
idealism—and, wherever possible, be based on cost-benefit arguments
that demonstrate how the policy in question will serve the interests of the
United States over the long-term (even while serving the greater good).[21]

Rather than continuing our current counterproductive, knee-jerk response to disruptive and rogue regimes, a servant-leader President would
seek to capitalize on the new dependencies and sources of influence that
are being created by today's increasing interdependence. He or she would
also recognize that resorting to coercion after events have turned against
us is a poor recipe for effective leadership. Instead, fresh ways should be
sought for influencing behavior, starting first with an attempt to expand the
friendly options, whether they be political, economic, or cultural in nature.
The President should operate on the premise that engagement is always
preferable to isolation and that inducements for good behavior should
normally enjoy preference over punishments for bad.

If we are to have partners for peace, then we must first be partners in
sympathetic recognition that all mankind possesses in common like aspirations and hungers, like ideals and appetites, like purposes and frail-
ties, a like demand for economic advancement. The divisions between
us are artificial and transient. Our common humanity is God-made
and enduring.

—Dwight Eisenhower

DEALING WITH ROGUE STATES

A strategy of engagement becomes most challenging when one is dealing with a so-called rogue or pariah state. Indeed, the recent tendency in
these situations has been to avoid engaging at all on the premise that doing
so will bestow an undeserved legitimacy on the rogue regime and morally taint our reputation in the process. While it is true that meeting with
pariah states might enhance their credibility, that possibility should only
rule out meeting if it is clear that the potential negative consequences are
disproportionately greater than the possible benefits.

On numerous occasions (and most often in response to domestic political pressures), the United States has imposed comprehensive *unilateral*

sanctions against other countries in an attempt to change unwanted behavior. As of this writing, at least 35 such sanctions are in place for one reason or another.[22] Not only do unilateral sanctions almost never achieve their intended purpose, they often exacerbate the problem by enabling the offending regime's leadership to tighten its grip on the population, as they point to the United States as the source of their country's problems. In other words, unilateral sanctions and the refusal to engage tend to strengthen the radicals, while weakening the moderates, thus making bad situations even worse.

Yet another negative effect of ostracizing foreign leaders is the incentive it provides for violating accepted norms of behavior. It is akin to the International Criminal Court indicting a leader for crimes against humanity while the conflict in which those crimes are being committed is still under way. The indictment only provides added incentive for the leader in question to continue fighting and, in some situations, to misbehave even more, as President Bashir of Sudan did when he terminated humanitarian aid to a suffering population in the wake of his indictment.

The undue preoccupation with "imparting legitimacy" has to some extent become a simplistic mantra for inhibiting constructive political thinking. When one decides to engage questionable political leaders, steps can be taken to minimize the downside potential by either (1) meeting with them privately, (2) meeting with them in the company of opposition leaders, or (3) sending a respected third party to convey the message and receive a response. Theoretically, the factors (both positive and negative) to inspire changed behavior are only limited by one's imagination, so long as one remains engaged with the target country in question. Finally, in his servant-leader capacity, the President would actively consult with key members of Congress and with interested foreign governments as he seeks to orchestrate a coordinated response to an offending country's behavior.

A DISQUIETING CHALLENGE

In summing up, we would do well to consider the fact that America's sacrilization of democracy bears little resemblance to the spirit that George Washington expressed in his Farewell Address to the nation in 1797 or to the admonitions of Thomas Jefferson who called for "peace, commerce and honest friendship with all—entangling alliances with none"[23] or of John Q. Adams who warned against America ever donning "an imperial diadem, flashing in false and tarnished luster the murky radiance of dominion and power."[24]

Thus, one sees a divergence of viewpoints between that of our early statesmen, who felt the United States would be best served by confining itself to peaceful commerce and serving as a beacon for others versus the posture of proselytization (of democracy and free markets) that currently prevails. To be sure, that was a different time, with different challenges. However, experience suggests the Founding Fathers may have been on to something. In the course of fighting illiberal tyranny abroad, it has become increasingly clear that force-fitting democracy in foreign cultures that are not ready for it—or our particular brand of it—can be a self-defeating exercise. In short, if the United States is to stay ahead of the curve that lies ahead, it must become a "beacon" of respectful engagement and an artful practitioner of servant-leadership.

> Whoever undertakes to set himself up as a judge of truth and knowledge is shipwrecked by the laughter of the gods.
>
> —*Albert Einstein*

Finally, the late George Kennan, chief architect of America's cold war strategy to contain the Soviet Union, echoed in his memoirs similar sentiments as Washington. "As befits a country of its size and importance," Kennan suggested the United States should:

- show patience, generosity, and a uniformly accommodating spirit in dealing with small countries and small matters;
- observe reasonableness, consistency, and steady adherence to principle in dealing with large countries and large matters;
- observe in all official exchanges with other governments a high tone of dignity, courtesy, and moderation of expression;
- while always bearing in mind that its first duty is to the national interest, never lose sight of the principle that the greatest service this country could render to the rest of the world would be to put its own house in order and to make of American civilization an example of decency, humanity, and societal success from which others could derive whatever they might find useful to their own purposes.[25]

CHAPTER 15

Toward a New Paradigm

The greatest obstacles are less in the country than in ourselves.
Let us change our methods and we will change our fortune.
—Alexis de Tocqueville

The broad Muslim critique and perception of western culture as too materialistic, too individualistic, too self-indulgent, and too devoid of moral guidelines, restraint, and spiritual sensibility is part of a larger, worldwide resistance to the dominant secular western view that religious-based morality should be kept private and, in any event, constitutes an irrelevant authority for guiding and disciplining community life. Taken to its deepest level, this critique is about the nature of people and finding the right balance between a person's needs as a social animal who requires for his or her well-being community, cooperation, and justice versus a person's need for individualism, competition, and self-expression as the more appropriate basis for promoting the greater good. Clearly these dualities provoke cultural tensions that will be resolved differently in China, Iran, Hungary, and America.

Scholars such as Mark Juergensmeyer, President of the American Academy of Religion, and French specialist on Islam, Olivier Roy, see the challenge of Islam (which Roy and others believe must be disaggregated to the country level) as part of a disparate, transnational form of religious activism that includes Christians, Buddhists, Orthodox Jews, Sikhs, and others who are questioning the moral authority of the western concept of nation-state as the supreme claimant of its citizens' loyalty. "While these movements vary greatly in their values, goals, methods, and political context," says

Juergensmeyer, "they are united by a common enemy—secular nationalism."[1]

Juergensmeyer reminds us that the western notion that there should be a clear distinction between religion and politics is a recent one, associated with post-Enlightenment thinking and the French Revolution. The word *religion* only became widely used in America and Europe in the 19th century. Previously, and still in most parts of the world today, words that translate as "tradition," "community," and "faith" are used instead of religion. "It was unthinkable," says Juergensmeyer, "that *religion* in this sense might be separate from other parts of life."[2]

This cultural critique of an overcompartmentalized, oversystematized, overoptimized, overanalyzed, and desacralized western world connects four emblematic spiritual figures of this century—Thomas Merton, Alexander Solzhenitsyn, Joel Salatin, and Sayyid Qutb—from very different backgrounds and disciplines whose views are holistic and assume that humankind has a source outside itself (and is therefore *not* the sole measure of all things).

The four share an ontological view of nature and humankind as grounded in a Creator or a Supreme Power. They share a belief in divine revelation, a Judgment Day, and a moral order that sees our brief temporal existence as prologue to another, eternal realm. They all believe in the sovereignty of God, who invokes His believers to do His will. They all share the belief that ultimate freedom comes with service to God. By serving God, one is liberated from slavery to ego and the vanities of this world. Reflective of this difference are the varying translations of the motto of the Groton School in Groton, Massachusetts, *Qui Servire est Regnare,* which was freely translated in the beginning as "To serve is perfect freedom." This Episcopal boarding school founded by Rev. Endicott Peabody in 1883 educated Dean Acheson, Franklin Roosevelt, McGeorge Bundy, and other public servants. But by their day, the school motto had been interpreted to mean "Service to others."[3] The four also share a similar attitude toward our post-Enlightenment western culture.

THE MONK

With Thomas Merton, a Trappist monk of Gethsemane, Kentucky, whose writings have been read by millions around the world and whose influence continues to grow 40 years after his death,[4] one finds a spiritual being who wanted to distance himself from the mental geography of "impatient men of the West." He saw them as thinking in terms of "money, power, publicity, machines, business, political advantage, military strategy—who seek, in a word, the triumphant affirmation of their own will, their own power, considered as the end for which they exist."[5] In the 1950s and 1960s, Merton had harsh things to say about America—that behind the patina of innocence and idealism was "a hard reality of national greed, pride and misdirected lust to be first in everything." In keeping with the original intent of the Groton School motto, he preached that "the only true liberty is in the service of that which is beyond all limits, beyond all definitions."[6]

Like Boyd, Merton distrusted all "obligatory" answers, formulas, and theories. "True solutions are not those we force upon life in accordance with our theories, but which life itself provides for those who dispose themselves to receive the truth."[7] Merton believed the world itself is not a problem but that we are a problem to ourselves because we are alienated from ourselves by the habit of breaking reality into pieces and then wondering why, after we have manipulated all the pieces until they fall apart, we find ourselves out of touch with life, with reality, with the world, and, most of all, with ourselves. "What can we gain by sailing to the moon," says Merton, "if we cannot cross the abyss that separates us from ourselves?"[8]

The sacred attitude is, then, one of deep and fundamental respect for the real in whatever new form it may present itself.

—Thomas Merton

Merton was also politically minded and deeply concerned about issues of peace and racial equality. Pushing the envelope of Catholic dogma, Merton saw value in ideas from the East, particularly Zen Buddhism, and accordingly advocated dialogue between these usually polar schools of thought. Merton's ideas were not always accepted by the church and are not totally devoid of controversy even today. Nevertheless, Merton has gone down as a preeminent Christian thinker who tackled head-on the excesses of materialism, modernism, and other ideas that ran counter to his beliefs.[9]

THE DISSIDENT

Intelligence, said Goethe, a prominent 19th-century German intellectual, finds differences, but genius finds similarities. It was the similarities between American (western) and communist societies that Alexander Solzhenitsyn expounded upon in his commencement address at Harvard University in 1978. East and West were both places where the spirit was suffocated, in America by consumerism and commercial interests, which are endlessly generating new material wants, and in the East it was destroyed by the "dealings and machinations of the ruling party . . . the split in the world is less terrible than the similarity."[10] Both societies suffered from a loss of spirituality.

The Renaissance was a turning point—one that has run its course today. "The Middle Ages had come to a natural end" by virtue of the "despotic repression of man's physical nature" in favor of a spiritual one.[11] Now we have "turned our backs upon the spirit and embraced all that is material with excessive and unwarranted zeal."[12] This new way of thinking does not admit the existence of man's intrinsic capacity for evil stemming from his innate pride, envy, lust, and greed, nor does it see any goal higher than the attainment of happiness on earth. The path from the Renaissance to the present day, Solzhenitsyn readily admitted, has "enriched our experience, but we have lost the concept of a Supreme Complete Entity which used to restrain our passions and irresponsibility."[13]

In Solzhenitsyn's view of the world, another turning point is in the making. Like Merton, Solzhenitsyn saw a disaster looming, arising from this despiritualized and irreligious human consciousness that makes people and their terrestrial happiness the sole touchstone for judging everything on earth. "We have placed too much hope in political and social reforms, only to find we were being deprived of our most precious possession—our spiritual life."[14] In this way, Solzhenitsyn argued, communism and capitalism were the same; they both used the same yardstick for progress—material well-being. While the West was better at producing economic wealth and technological invention, wrapped in its wealth, comfort, and self-satisfied sense of "superiority," it didn't even know it was sick. In speaking to a further manifestation of this superiority:

How short a time ago, relatively, the small, new European world was easily seizing colonies everywhere, not only without anticipating any real resistance, but also usually despising any possible values in the conquered people's approach to life. . . . There is this belief that all those other worlds are only being temporarily prevented (by wicked governments or by heavy crises or by their own barbarity and incomprehension) from taking the way of Western pluralistic democracy and from adopting the Western way of life. Countries are judged on the merit of their progress in this direction.[15]

One pill for all diseases doesn't work for the human body, nor will it likely work for the human family.

THE FARMER

The emerging concerns over agricultural monoculture resulting from a fixation on technical and economic efficiency have given rise to the worldwide ecology-minded sustainability movement. The movement's concerns parallel those of Solzhenitsyn. Joel Salatin of Swoop, Virginia, is a modern-day prophet whose methods and philosophy were highlighted in Michael Pollen's best-selling book *The Omnivore's Dilemma*.

Salatin is a maverick farmer who has become an icon of the farm-friendly food and sustainable farming movement. When his father moved to Virginia in the 1950s from Venezuela, his family bought a run-down farm with 200 acres of exhausted soil and brought it back to life. Against the advice of the experts that his family consulted, they did not industrialize their new operation in order to grow unbroken fields of corn for beef cattle. Instead they re-created the biologically diverse family farm. Today, they raise free-range broiler chickens, layer chickens, beef cattle, and pigs.

The methods used at Polyface Farm hearken back to native practices. Salatin raises herbivores and other animals in the old-fashioned natural way: eating grass—the ultimate solar energy converter, unconfined, un-corn fed—using their excrement as fertilizer, moving them constantly, and spending no money for the past 15 years on fertilizer, pesticides, or growth hormones. A chapter in *The Omnivore's Dilemma* featured Polyface Farm as the anti-industrial, farm-friendly model of food production. Salatin is a Christian who wears his faith lightly but is filled with a sense of the sacredness of God's creation. He believes that nature, which is God's way, is the only sensible, rational template for thinking about how one should treat animals, plants, and the earth itself.

In his own context, Salatin is making the same argument as Solzhenitsyn about the need for moral restraints on how we raise food and treat animals and to provide a habitat for each plant and animal that allows it to fully express its distinctive nature. "It asks the question: is the pig happy?" The pig is a part of God's work, like everything else out there. "When we respect nature or The Creator's design enough to reverence the plow on the end of a pig's nose, the graceful beak on the front of a chicken, the earthworms gamboling around in the soil underneath the cabbages, then we have a moral framework in which to contain our human cleverness."[16]

Extending this idea, Salatin proposes that our ability to coexist with people who are different from us is directly related to how we respect the differences in the plants and animals. Indeed, what would happen if western governments took the same approach by respecting the distinctive features of different human cultures, helping them to evolve according to their own respective timetables? Studying the sense of what they do and not imposing a western template—usually one that involves buying U.S. corporate products?

Fast growth, profit margins, and economic efficiencies, Salatin says, are only noble goals so long as the larger reverence for life is maintained. Happy pigs provide the most nutritious food with the least amount of pharmaceutical intervention. Industrial agriculture and farming policy that promote monoculture and "unnatural" and "anti-nature" policies will only lead to a bad end. He is not anti-technology, yet he understands that all new technologies have a downside. Salatin sees western culture as unbalanced:

The United States is a culture predicated on a decidedly western interpretation of the world . . . this worldview essentially looks at pieces as the key to the whole. Its key words are compartmentalized, disconnected, fragmented, reductionist, linear and it glorifies the individual. . . . It studies parts rather than wholes. . . . It also gave us the Renaissance, front-end loaders, electric lights and the Age of Discovery. It gave us electric fences, plastic wrap and manure spreaders. . . . An equally valid worldview comes from the east. It studies the whole rather than the parts. Key words are interrelated, holism, community, we instead of I. It tends to give human characteristics to the natural world, like Mother Earth. . . . It spawned deep ecology, the environmental movement and a reverence for nature. The clean food movement, wellness centers, and Yoga sprang out of eastern thought. Native Americans were eastern. . . . Taking the best of both worlds provides balance. . . . Eastern thought provides the moral boundary around the cleverness of western discovery. . . .

True progress comes when we marry eastern indigenous heritage wisdom with appropriate western techno-glitzy discoveries to create synergism and symbiosis.[17]

In some respects, the nonindustrial food movement could be viewed as a direct response to over-industrialization and its "mechanistic view" toward everything living.[18] This search for meaning, for the soul of food, says Salatin, is driving everything that is alternative.[19]

The search for meaning beyond consumerism, materialism, and "economic efficiency" in the narrow sense, is also driving much of the global rebellion described in Juergensmeyer's 30 years of research—a rebellion with political dimensions that are more obvious in the developing world where there is an ambivalence toward western "technological cleverness" and material riches.

THE MILITANT

Sayyid Qutb is widely regarded as the father of modern jihadism, or aggressive "militant" Islam. Yet in important ways, he is on the same wavelength as the other 20th-century spiritual rebels mentioned above. His writings have a different edge while still sharing the same underlying complaint of spiritual deprivation and destruction of the soul found among western critics. In *Milestones,* Qutb's 1964 book on the malaise affecting the Muslim world, he provided the intellectual underpinnings of aggressive *irhab* today. By manipulating the meaning and interpretation of Islamic scripture in response to modern times, *Milestones* provided the foundation for pitting Islam against nonbelievers in a millennial confrontation, not only on a collective basis, but as an individual religious duty as well. He was not only an observer, commentator, and polemicist, but a victim of the values he saw contaminating Islam. His work bears the anger and scars of a man who spent 10 years in Egyptian prisons where he was tortured and finally executed in 1966.

Somewhat prudish, of literary sensibility and scholarly bent, Qutb was already unhappy with the vulgarity of western culture that he saw penetrating the Egypt of King Faruq. His later years of study and travel in the

United States (1948–1950) left him convinced that racist, materialistic America was sinking into depravity and debauchery. Dark-skinned, he was frequently denied entrance to restaurants and hotels. His stay coincided with the release of the Kinsey Report that portrayed a society in which adultery was common, prostitution virtually normal, and homosexuality not uncommon. Attending a college in Colorado, he was scandalized by the overt sexuality and forwardness of the coeds. America, he decided, was a land of spiritual emptiness where the dollar was the only real God. He returned to Egypt convinced America and the West had nothing to offer the Arab world.[20]

Qutb's immediate preoccupation upon returning to Egypt, however, was not America but corrupt Arab rulers who were embracing democracy and secularization. The only people who seemed to care about the impoverished masses were the members of the outlawed Muslim Brotherhood, which had even then established an entire counterculture of schools, mosques, hospitals, and charities. He joined and became a shaper of the Brotherhood's vision to dismantle the corrupt, secular government and impose Islamic law on all aspects of life.

Smuggled out of prison, *Milestones* became and still remains the basic text of the jihadi movement. Qutb's solution to the contemporary situation of Muslims was to establish a vanguard whose role would be to fight the present-day *jahiliyyah* (time of darkness) of materialism and self-centeredness. He begins with an apocalyptic vision: "Mankind today is on the brink of a precipice, not because of the danger of complete annihilation which is hanging over its head—this being just a symptom and not the real disease—but because humanity is devoid of those vital values which are necessary not only for its healthy development but also for its real progress,"[21] or what Solzhenitsyn called at Harvard "moral progress."

Thus Qutb signals that Islam is at war with the West over values and what gives life meaning. The modern western idea that he most wanted to replace was the separation of church and state mentality, which confines religion to a personal sphere of influence. The first principle of his Islamic revolution would be the undoing of religion's separation from other aspects of culture. Such an ideal Islamic community existed once in the golden age of the Prophet and the rightly guided caliphs. The first milestone therefore on the way to an Islamic revolution must be a return to the past—to Islamic practice in its golden age. As was the culture of European Christendom in the Middle Ages, Qutb asserts that every aspect of life should be under the sovereignty of God. Since Islam means "submission to God," Islam can have no other meaning.

For Qutb the battle was between asserting the truth of God's way and the pagan falseness of western culture, which worships the idols of physical beauty, money, power, technology, and democracy. Both the means and the ends need to be defined by divine principles. By returning to the past to go forward into a more virtuous and humane future, Qutb was saying globally what Joel Salatin and certain Christian evangelicals are saying about stewardship of the earth and respect for God's creation. Let us rediscover the ways and wisdom of the primitive natives who were not driven by the desire to dominate nature but to live in harmony with it. Qutb was asking simple questions: What is a better guide for society—man's law or God's law? Who are the best interpreters of God's law? Who has the authority to decide? Who has the authority to enforce? Is God's law so clear cut that there is no room for latitude? These questions are at the heart of what is not only an intra-Muslim conflict that has spilled over into the West but that is echoed within America itself.

The current influence of Qutb's *Milestones* demonstrates what Solzhenitsyn warned would happen. The formerly despised victims of colonialism are pushing back, but they are no longer alone. Globalization and its offspring—the anti-globalization forces—may ultimately join and even embrace the Islamic critique of western secularism for some of the same reasons that Merton, Solzhenitsyn, Salatin, and others are arguing for a new paradigm to replace the vacuous cult of materialism—one that produced American leaders whose best advice, the day after the worst attack on America since Pearl Harbor, was to urge its citizens to keep shopping.

Echoing but predating Qutb is an observation by Basil Mathews, Literature Secretary in the World's Alliance of YMCAs, in a 1926 book titled *Young Islam on Trek: A Study in the Clash of Civilizations:*

Obsessed by material wealth, obese with an industrial plethora, drunk with the miracles of its scientific advance, blind to the riches of the world of the spirit, and deafened to the inner voice by the outer clamor, Western civilization may destroy the old in Islam, but it cannot fill the new.[22]

A disturbing trend that counterterrorism authorities in Europe and the United States are observing is the growing number of American and European al Qaeda sympathizers who are making their way to camps in Afghanistan and Pakistan.[23] What is drawing them? That is a question that can have many answers, from a desire for adventure to pulling Uncle Sam's nose, or (as Mathews implies) from cultural discontent to lofty spiritual aspirations.

INTO THE FUTURE

When paradigms change, there are usually significant shifts in the criteria determining the legitimacy both of problems and of proposed solutions.

—Thomas Kuhn

In 1987, John Boyd was assigned by Marine Corps Commandant Al Gray to rewrite the Marine Corps war-fighting manual. Re-baptized "FM-1War-Fighting," Boyd insisted that it not be written as a formula but as a guide for teaching officers to think in new ways about war. "War is ever-changing, and men are ever-fallible. Rigid rules simply won't work.... And keep the goddamn thing simple so generals can understand it."[24] The new manual stressed the importance of professional education, of instilling a stronger sense of ethics, and of promoting unit cohesion, all of which serve the end-goal of developing maneuver warfare. The fundamental tenant of maneuver warfare is to give the officer on the spot the authority to make tactical decisions, and this requires trust.

History is replete with inspiring examples of maneuver warfare. One that stands out is General Patton's race across Europe following the invasion of Normandy. Another, which perhaps speaks even more poignantly to the elements of trust and unit cohesion, was Adm. Horatio Nelson's victory in the Battle of the Nile on August 1, 1798, which gave Britain uncontested command of the Mediterranean in its long-running war with France:

This month-long search [for Napoleon's fleet], while trying Nelson's nerves to the utmost, was by no means wasted time. Unlike many naval commanders of his day, he refused to hold himself aloof. Scarcely a calm day passed that he did not have one or more of his captains aboard the Vanguard to share his meals and, more important, his views. Every conceivable circumstance was reviewed—combats at sea and at anchor, by day or by night. Nelson never relinquished his command or his responsibilities, but his leadership and his professional judgment so unified his captains that their minds became extensions of his own, his decisions theirs. "I had the happiness," Nelson later wrote ... "to command a Band of Brothers."[25]

Nelson's approach yielded quick dividends. Soon after engaging the French at the mouth of the Nile, he was knocked unconscious for a number of hours while his "Band of Brothers" carried on with flawless execution.[26]

Boyd's theories of maneuver warfare owed their origin to his introduction to thermodynamics at Georgia Tech as a young officer on academic leave, a subject that transformed him from a simple fighter jock to an intellectual fighter jock and a thinking soldier's soldier. Thermodynamics, simply stated, can be defined as the study of energy. For a pilot in air-to-air combat—perhaps the ultimate in maneuver warfare—the most important information he wants is to know how much energy he has with which to maneuver and how many "g-forces" that will produce.[27]

Thermodynamics may also help us understand in the broadest of terms what may be happening in the world, not physically, but culturally. The key to thermodynamics is understanding the mathematical relationship between the amount of energy that goes into a substance and the resulting change that takes place in the properties of that substance. The first law is well-known as the Law of Conservation of Energy. Energy does not disappear, it is merely transformed. It is the second law that can help us think differently about the process of globalization and what it is doing to low-energy cultures. The second law puts a limit on what is physically possible in energy conservation. It is the Law of Entropy and applies to all systems. It states that in a closed system, the expenditure of energy does not ebb and flow, like money in a bank account, but rather goes in only one direction—from high temperature to low temperature. If a small amount of water and an ice cube are put in a sealed enclosure that is above freezing, heat will transfer to the ice from the surrounding water until the ice melts and the water is all the same temperature. Energy transfer ends and the system is stable, homogeneous, and uniform. But it is considered to be in a greater state of disorder than before the ice melted.

This second law is the first nonreversible law in physics. It says the universe is going from order to disorder, which suggests there had to be something to establish order in the first place. If there is no first cause, then the universe itself must be self-ordering, something that has mathematically been proven to be impossible.[28] The Law of Entropy seems counterintuitive since in human activity many associate "order" with making things uniform. Yet complete uniformity, in reality, is associated with death. A healthy, orderly heart produces an electrocardiogram with peaks and valleys. A flat, uniform line is a dead heart. Nature that is uniform, with few distinctions, has the smell of death, whether deserts of sand or sheets of ice. Unhealthy environments are measured by the loss of their natural diversity. Salatin and the agro-sustainability movement is about moving away from an ultimately unhealthy—physically and economically—monoculture.

Thus, if separate cold and warm bodies represent a higher state of order than a uniform one, then by analogy, "modern" western societies are "hot." Globalization is seen by more and more scientists as destructive to the world of food production, as well as to animal and human health. It is creating a westernized monoculture. While many of the benefits of western culture are welcomed, the benefits often come at the cost of destroying local traditions, art forms, languages, and lifestyles. And the United States is the leading force in the world for producing this monoculture of secular liberal democracy. America and its western partners are the water in the system. Our societies are literally and figuratively hot. They consume a lot of energy and produce a lot of heat. Being more energetic, their natural tendency is to melt down the glacially slow, less technologically developed, less heat-emitting tradition-bound cultures. As a result, the world is losing its healthy human diversity and knowledge of old ways that may hold valuable solutions for the present as well as the future. In other words, many view globalization as Americanization ("the West over the rest"), and are concerned that diversity is falling victim to intimate interdependence.

Perhaps the new paradigm to support the concept of leading by example rather than force can thus be found in a combination of physics and the wisdom of our 20th-century prophets.[29] The Islamic challenge has many levels and many different faces. As a country that ostensibly believes in diversity and competition, America should want for the rest of the world what it celebrates for itself. The threat is not Islam's challenge to the West to rebalance itself—that is a plus. Qutb, Merton, Solzhenitsyn, and Salatin are voices and virtual representatives for the thousands, perhaps millions who share their sensibilities but who haven't articulated their own unease with a pervasive culture that seemingly equates happiness and human welfare almost exclusively with the acquisition of material things and physical attractiveness.

The threat is from a very narrow spectrum of modern *irhabis* who are a threat to Muslims and non-Muslims alike. They believe they are divinely ordained agents to establish the dictatorship of God (as they interpret divine guidance) and that blood and martyrdom sanctify their calling. They also exaggerate the pervasiveness of moral depravity among westerners— a weak point in their worldview that spiritual engagement can address. To meet this threat, American policy needs to begin doing what Boyd and other experienced military practitioners have done for years: trust our allies and treat them as equals.

Trust is the glue and moral force that ties people together, wrote Boyd.[30] The United States will not find true allies among the Muslims, without whom we cannot prevail, until we are willing to weigh seriously their advice and assume they are willing to do the same with us. Meanwhile, we would do well to heed another insight of U.S. Secretary of Defense Robert Gates:

Where possible, what the military calls kinetic [violent, or force-on-force] operations should be subordinated to measures aimed at promoting better governance, economic programs that spur development, and efforts to address the grievances among the discontented, from whom the terrorists recruit. It will take the patient accumulation of quiet successes over a long time to discredit and defeat extremist movements and their ideologies.[31]

CHAPTER 16

Meeting the Challenge of Spiritual Engagement

Secularism is not the future; it is yesterday's incorrect vision of the future.

—David Brooks

Virtually every culture and every person is "spiritual" on some level, although not every individual is religious or accepts the idea of a creator, a first cause, or believes in the divine revelation of scripture, or even the sacredness of nature. If, as it says in the New Testament, "God is love. Whoever lives in love lives in God, and God in him,"[1] then there are many millions of loving people in the world who love God, perhaps unwittingly, when they display respect, empathy, goodwill, fairness, and compassion toward others. These different expressions of "love" in the Christian sense can be simply summed up as "decency." It is what Jesus means in the parable of how the sheep are separated from the goats: those who will enter the Kingdom are those who feed the hungry, clothe the naked, welcome the stranger, and visit the sick.

It is this sense of decency that unites each of the Abrahamic faiths and which holds all God's creatures worthy of such love, even those we don't like or understand. "For if you love those who love you, what reward will you get?" asked that famous rabbi, prophet, or Son of God. Even the tax collector, that most reviled of creatures in those days, was capable of that. If we only respect people and cultures "like us," then nationalism is merely tribalism writ large. It translates into the belief that American and white European lives are worth more than others outside the tribe, be they from a different race, nation, or religion. The renowned Austrian philosopher Karl Popper equated nationalism with racism. My country, or my race, is the best. Religion, however, if twisted by hatred, anger, ignorance, or political agendas into a species of celestial nationalism, becomes the most dangerous of all exclusionary ideologies. For people who are absolutely convinced they are doing God's work, with paradise as their reward, cautionary self-interest has died. There is no limit to their spirit of sacrifice, delusional or not.

When religion goes wrong, it goes very wrong.

—*Archbishop William Temple*

The Abrahamic faiths declare that God is in all things and all things are in God. Nature and all nature's creatures deserve to be treated as holy, not as instruments for gratifying human ego and the will to dominate over fellow man and beast. This belief in a divinely created world is the unifying element in each of the Abrahamic faiths. It produces good conduct and wisdom, qualities that are all too often overwhelmed by the more visible bad news of religious fanaticism.

"Without respect, there can be no love,"[2] was the late Cardinal Leon Etienne Duval's Golden Rule. Brotherly love was the essence of his faith. While serving as French bishop in Algiers during the Algerian War of Independence (1954–1962), he reminded his parishioners that a Catholic bishop is a bishop for all people, Arabs included; otherwise he is only the head of a sect. To love God is to love all His children as brothers or sisters. Love of neighbor leads to love of God. His reward for insisting that his ministry was also for Arabs was vilification, death threats, and having excrement smeared on his churches by irate French nationalists. After Algerian independence, Duval was given Algerian citizenship and was (and still remains) one of the most respected men in the country.

Duval himself never read the Qur'an, didn't speak Arabic, and wasn't particularly interested in Islam. However, he was very interested in living by the Gospels. For that, he won the deep admiration of Muslims and even many Christians at the time. Being ecumenical in a time of sectarian conflict invites wrath in the short term but usually wins honor and respect over the long run. In 1979, Duval held a Christmas Mass in Tehran and played a role in getting the Algerian government to negotiate the release of the American diplomats held hostage there.

Christian love is not a sentiment. It is about respect, empathy, patience, good will, justice, and generosity of spirit—qualities one can profitably apply in any environment. What lesson does Duval's behavior toward Muslims hold? First, it shows that not all Muslims hate Christians, as many westerners believe. Many may hate Christian hypocrites, but Muslims are hardly alone in that. Indeed, monks and priests are called out in the Qur'an for special respect and protection. Yet in times of conflict, Christians have been, or can become, symbols of an unwanted foreign presence that is associated with colonialism and past indignities.

Hopelessly idealistic; utopian, you say? No. The Golden Rule, with or without the Spirit, is simply practical and smart (perhaps this is why Boyd emphasized "ethical" education for Marines). In the film *The Fog of War*, Robert McNamara, the hard-headed, Ford Motor–trained Secretary of Defense who bedazzled Washington during the Vietnam years with his crisp analyses and quantitative presentations was asked to give his most important lessons learned from that debacle. Lesson number one was "empathize with the enemy." He could not imagine the North Vietnamese will to resist and readiness to absorb pain in order to achieve their goal of unification. As for our allies, he wrote in his book *In Retrospect:*

We viewed the people and leaders of South Vietnam in terms of our own experience. We saw in them a thirst for—and a determination to fight for—freedom and democracy. We totally misjudged the political forces within the country. . . . Our misjudgment of friend and foe alike reflected our profound ignorance of the history, culture and politics of the people in the area, and the personalities and habits of their leaders.[3]

Empathy can be a tool either to win wars or to prevent wars. How often do Americans ask themselves, before criticizing Russia, how would we react to having foreign-controlled missiles on our borders? (Perhaps the Cuban Missile Crisis provides a clue.) Any human capacity can be used as a weapon or as a means to solve problems and settle differences. True empathy requires knowledge, study, and the ability to put one's self in the shoes of others to view the world from their cultural and historical perspectives. The more familiar the context, the easier it is to empathize. The best teachers, generals, police officers, welfare workers, employers, and parents have this ability. Atheists and those who are instinctively contemptuous of religion and religious people will have difficulty empathizing with those whose faith gives ultimate meaning to their lives. They will ignore or give short shrift to people who could be most important to achieving certain goals.

The more unfamiliar the context—the language, the culture—the more dangerous it is to simply project one's own mental framework. As an occupying power or a foreign presence trying to win goodwill from the local population, such projection can be a costly and deadly mistake. How people in a town in Vermont react to a prospective Walmart invasion, refusing to let it in for fear of transforming the local mom-and-pop culture, provides a simple clue to how conservative cultures might react to an American infiltration of customs, values, and symbols at odds with local values. American business has long since learned that the American way of selling and merchandizing has to be acculturated, modified, or scrapped to succeed in foreign markets. The American military is now realizing that cultural awareness and sensitivity are crucial to succeeding in this new and unfamiliar form of globalized, cyber guerilla warfare in which the United States and its allies find themselves.

PRACTICAL IMPLICATIONS

What then does "spiritual engagement" mean as a practical guide to U.S. interaction with the world and specifically with Muslims, whether they be American or foreign?

Attitude

First, it is about attitude. Is the "spirit" that will implicitly infuse American diplomacy going to continue to be the self-gratifying belief expressed by the Marine officer in Stanley Kubric's film *Full Metal Jacket* that "inside every Gook is an American struggling to be liberated"? An updated version of that marine's view of the world was provided by Condoleezza Rice when she opined in 2000 that "American values are universal."[4] Up to a point, perhaps; but certainly in different proportions. Proportions matter and differ according to circumstances: liberty vs. authority, security vs. insecurity, individual vs. collective good, freedom vs. equality, material vs. spiritual values, tight moral boundaries vs. loose boundaries—the list goes on. Rice's was a statement that echoed General Motors' Charles Wilson who once declared to Congress that "what's good for GM is good for America" (little did he dream). In its extreme nationalistic form, though, it boils down to an America über alles (over all) attitude.

True spiritual engagement means looking for the best in the "other." It means looking at the stranger as a potential friend. It means going back to the spirit of America's Founding Fathers, specifically Washington, Jefferson, and John Quincy Adams, who urged their new country to be friends with all nations, not simply those like ourselves. They did not divide the world into "good" republics and "bad" everything else. A spiritual attitude is about healing, reconciling, and getting along with different forms of governance, not simply dominating and getting our way (and growing angry when others don't agree). It is about a spirit of generosity rather than of compulsion, of humility not arrogance. It is about servant-leadership that empowers and trusts others.

People across the globe do share certain common values and needs, but they share them in different ways and different proportions according to their different histories and circumstances. We are all human, yet each of us expresses our humanity differently. Likewise, all cultures bring gifts to the world, as do all individuals. A spiritual attitude recognizes that there is richness in diversity and that all the cultures of the world are products of a mixture of influences that reflect geography, genetics, and history. These attitudes were present in some of the most successful and enduring achievements of statesmanship in the 20th century, the Marshall Plan and General MacArthur's culturally attuned approach to rebuilding Japan representing two of the better examples.

The success of the Marshall Plan can be attributed to its transparency and to the spirit of respect shown the recipient countries in looking to them to initiate and coordinate their own recovery and reconstruction policies rather than forcing them to accept imposed conditions. Further, the support it offered extended to all European nations, excluding and punishing no one.[5]

Our policy is directed not against any country or doctrine, but against hunger, poverty, desperation and chaos. Its purpose should be the revival of a working economy in the world so as to permit the emergence of political and social conditions in which free institutions can exist.

—*George C. Marshall, Harvard Commencement, 1947*

In Japan, although conditions were imposed, they were enlightened and amazingly far-sighted conditions that reflected MacArthur's keen sensitivity to Japanese culture, thought, and tradition. The process of reconstruction that he facilitated took into full account the country's sense of national dignity and provided a basis for broadscale reconciliation in the course of rebuilding the country's infrastructure and industry on the one hand and its social, political, and moral order on the other. Remarkably, the constitution that MacArthur spearheaded in six days has yet to be amended.[6] Both East and West owe much to these gifted American generals.

Virtue

Second, spiritual engagement is about virtue. What is virtue for a government? "American power must be matched by American virtue," reflects Hank Crumpton, the CIA's architect of our initial success in Afghanistan in 2002.[7] Virtue needs to be a quality associated with American power, otherwise countries will not trust us. As David Kilcullen has noted, to prevent an adversarial "balance-of-power" response to the current unprecedented scale of American military power, other nations will need to be assured that "the United States will exercise its power responsibly, sparingly, virtuously, and in accordance with international norms."[8]

Saint Thomas Aquinas gave 13th-century Christendom and the entire world enduring guidelines for virtuous behavior. He knew what all good monks knew in the Middle Ages, that virtue requires four qualities: prudence, moral courage, justice, and self-restraint. Aquinas developed eight criteria relating to virtue that should constitute a decision checklist for foreign policy deliberations of serious consequence:

1. Humility, which is necessary for learning, seeking advice, and finding new teachers
2. Insight, which comes from having an informed conscience
3. Honest, long-term memory to learn correct lessons from the past in order to inform the present
4. An intuitive ability to find balance between extremes
5. Practical reasoning skills
6. Foresight, or the ability to evaluate the future and anticipate the consequences of different choices
7. Circumspection, or the ability to consider all of the facts surrounding one's choices
8. Precaution, or an awareness that even seemingly good choices have a hidden potential for evil

In short, virtue, says Aquinas, exists not only in intellect (prudence) but in will (courage) and emotion (self-control).[9]

Never fight evil as if it were something that arose totally outside of yourself.

—Saint Augustine

Understanding

Religious leaders have consistently been excluded from past Middle East negotiations on the assumption that the absolutism which often accompanies religious convictions is ill-suited to negotiating the kind of compromise that would be required to reach an agreeable settlement. Yet, unless religious leaders feel some ownership in whatever political agreement emerges, they have the power to make it or break it owing to their unrivaled influence at the grassroots level.

An additional attribute that religious leaders can bring to such a process is their moral authority. When questioning Sudanese elder statesmen, who were present during the signing of the 1972 Addis Arabia Accords (which brought a halt to Sudan's first civil war between the Islamic north and the Christian/African Traditionalist south), as to why they let two Christian organizations negotiate the settlement, their response was, "Because of the moral authority that they brought." Then, as now, the Muslims had far greater political, economic, and military power than the Christians, yet they engaged the World Council of Churches and the All-African Council of Churches to mediate their differences.

Finally, and perhaps most important, religious leaders bring an informed ability to deal with religious issues based on a level of understanding that is seldom present among the political negotiators. Indicative of this ability are three historical elements that are often forgotten, overlooked, or ignored in the political posturing that surrounds the Israeli-Arab conflict: historical Jewish-Muslim theological fraternity, Christian Zionism, and modern western barbarism, usually associated with Nazism. For the majority of Jews, certain Orthodox sects excepted, the conflict is not about religion but about real estate. For American evangelicals, who fervently support the State of Israel, it is about religion. For them the State of Israel and especially the restoration of Jerusalem is a precondition to the second coming of Christ. This helps explain why religious Christians, not religious Jews, are the principal demonizers of Islam. Indeed, Jewish scholars have been among the greatest admirers of Islamic monotheism.

Jewish-Muslim Fraternity

In April 2009 at Princeton University, two leading Jewish scholars of Islam presented lectures sponsored by the Perelman Institute of Judaic Studies. Rabbi Isma Schorsch spoke of how 19th-century Jewish scholars helped shape the study of Islam in the West, and Susannah Heschel reflected on how Islam shaped Jewish self-understanding. Heschel said that scholars such as Goldzieher, Geiger, Palgrave, and others viewed Islam as a "handmaiden" of Judaism that demonstrated the power of Jewish monotheism. Unlike the vast majority of Christian scholars, "Jews brought empathy to the study of Islam," Schorsch noted. "Jews loved Islam for what it offered them in the Middle Ages when the vast majority of learned Jews spoke and wrote Arabic." Jewish admirers of Islam brought Islam out of the shadows of departments of pagan and heretical studies where Christian academe had relegated "Mohammedanism," which was widely dismissed as a religion created by a man and sustained only by the passing enthusiasm of a nomadic people.[10]

One scholar who particularly stood out in this regard was Ignaz Goldzieher, a Hungarian Jew trained in the new German school of biblical criticism. For him, Judaism was the "pulse beat of his life." Goldzieher possessed a deep knowledge of Hebrew and the Talmud and was concerned about the future of Judaism in the secularizing years of the late 19th century. For him, authentic Judaism was the monotheism of the prophets who were, in turn, channels of the moral and ethical imperatives of a divine creator, imperatives that were fixed in holy writ. Law and ritual came later. They were the product of particular times, places, and interpretations of scholars. To Goldzieher, these aspects of religion should be studied in their historical context to throw light on the age in which they were produced. He considered Islam also to be an authentic prophetic faith, a close cousin of Judaism that should be studied in the same manner.

Goldzieher may have been the first European to study at Al-Azhar University in Cairo where he learned the importance of jurisprudence and law in Islam. Islam was for him the only religion in which superstition and pagan elements were forbidden, not by rationalistic thinking, but by orthodox teaching (for example, the divination of entrails and astrology are strictly forbidden in the Qur'an). Islam provided him a touchstone for judging other monotheistic religions. Goldzieher wrote, "A life lived in the spirit of Islam—which is submission to the will of God, can be an ethically impeccable life demanding compassion for God's creation, honesty in one's dealings, love, loyalty, and the suppression of selfish impulses."[11]

Goldzieher's immense scholarship and empathetic understanding of Islam (which he saw as having absorbed elements from Christianity, Judaism, Zoroastrianism, and the Greco-Roman tradition) was echoed in the scholarship and writings of numerous Jewish scholars and writers, including Jewish converts to Islam such as Leopold Weiss and Margaret Marcus who became important Islamic thinkers. British Prime Minister Benjamin Disraeli, whose Jewish parents converted to Christianity, often called the Arabs "Jews on horseback." More recently, former U.S. Ambassador to Saudi Arabia, Chas Freeman, tells the story of his encounter with a prominent Saudi who told him that the best Muslim he knew was a Jew.

Regarded by many as the founder of modern Islamic studies, Goldzieher also became a defender of Islam and Judaism against the anti-Semitic theories of the French Catholic philosopher Ernst Renan. Unfortunately, this history of generally respectful engagement between the two faiths has largely faded into the ether in the midst of today's conflict. However, on October 6, 2010, the Center for Jewish, Christian, and Muslim Studies at Merrimack College in North Andover, Massachusetts, presented its first annual Goldzieher Prize to Dr. Mark Cohen of Princeton. The prize of $25,000 from this Augustinian institution recognizes outstanding contributions to works of both an academic and more popular nature that celebrate the co-fraternity of Islam and Judaism. A more comprehensive description of the poignant similarities between Judaism and Islam can be found in appendix D.

Christian Zionism

The role of Christian Zionism is another under-studied and under-reported aspect of the Middle East quagmire, one that is rooted in a Protestant brand of Christianity known as "premillenial dispensationalism." This is a branch of Christian thinking that emphasizes biblical eschatology (the theology of the end-times). While there is diversity of opinion within the evangelical community as to whether or not Jews will be saved on the Day of Judgment (based on their adherence to their original covenant), a fundamental tenet of dispensationalism is that Jews must first return to the land of their Old Testament ancestors before the Messiah will return.

Unconditional American support for Israel is often justified as support for democracy, or at least the only democracy in the Middle East that reflects American values. However, as James Skillen, Senior Fellow at the Center for Public Justice, implies, democracy has become a form of secular religious save-the-world ideology.[12]

The seeds for such thinking were planted early by the 17th-century Puritan settlers of New England. These straitlaced dissidents were fleeing the moral corruption of the Church of England, intending to establish themselves in the New World as a new Israel. Following principles based on Christian love, they would create a promised land and a shining city on a hill, a new Zion. "The fortunate must practice love, mercy and gentleness" to produce a caring community, knit together as one, and to "delight in each other, make others' condition our own."[13] By the time of the American Revolution, that self-image had spread throughout the colonies, giving rise to a sentiment of American exceptionalism, even as its Christian basis was being eroded.

This Puritan notion of itself as representing a collective agent of Providence, a re-embodied Israel, was not understood as a mission for the sake of the Jews but for the Puritans' own sake. Israel no longer existed, and the Puritans who came to America took upon themselves the identity of Israel. They alone represented God's recovery of true Christianity. They were a covenanted people who would serve as a model for all nations. Today, the distinctive Puritan elements have disappeared, reduced to a "God Bless America" bumper sticker and the residual belief that what is good for America must be good for the world.

As early as 1810, the New England Church established the American Board of Commissioners for Foreign Missions. The Middle East was prominent in its thinking. As Skillen notes, "All too often, historians and political commentators start with the mistaken notion that the separation of church and state is America's distinctive mark and they presume thereby that the republic became something *nonreligious* as it made room for the religious freedom of different churches."[14] But as George McKenna, a professor of political history, has noted, "That presumption misses the all-embracing sense of the 'American way of life,' a way that was nothing if not religious, albeit in a profoundly nationalistic sense."[15]

Michael Oren's *Power, Faith, and Fantasy: America in the Middle East* recounts the long love affair that American Christians, especially Protestants, have had with the Holy Land. The earliest members of the "Israeli lobby" were Puritan settlers, who even before they reached America had petitioned the Dutch government to "transport Izraell's sons and daughters . . . to the land promised their forefathers."[16] Among the political heirs of the Puritans were John Adams, Lincoln's Secretary of State William Seward, and later Woodrow Wilson, who took delight in the thought that he might help restore the Holy Land to its people. When President Truman recognized the new State of Israel in 1948, he exclaimed "I am Cyrus," comparing himself to the ancient Persian king who repatriated the Jewish exiles.

Skillen's analysis presents us with an historical irony. The first modern Zionists were highly religious Christians, not Jews; while the leading 19th-century Jewish Zionists were not particularly religious, at least not in the traditional sense. Among Jews, Zionism was not a movement to restore a Torah-keeping, temple-oriented way of life. Rather, it arose as a secular reaction to modern European nationalism and the festering legacy of Christian anti-Semitism that blended with "modern" racial theories. For many Christian Zionists of the 19th century, prominently the seventh Earl of Shaftsbury (1801–1885), Jews were not a people, but a mass error "that must be brought to a belief in Christ in order that the whole chain reaction leading to the Second Coming and redemption of mankind might be set in motion."[17]

Western Barbarism

The event that overcame the various sources of resistance to the creation of a Jewish state was provided by European barbarism. Germany, defeated and humiliated by the Treaty of Versailles, still remained a powerhouse of scientific and technological achievement—especially in physics and chemistry. Yet it was this highly "civilized" and cultured society of Beethoven and Bach, Goethe and Schiller, Heisenberg and Hahn that ultimately bred the horrors of Nazism. An advanced, modern European democracy burdened with overwhelming feelings of defeat, humiliation, and a deep sense of injustice bore its rotten fruit: technology and learning were transformed by the politics of paganism, anger, and revenge into a malignancy that destroyed millions of Jews, Slavs, and Gypsies. To the Arab bystanders of this European genocide, a guilt-ridden Europe and America committed another injustice as compensation for a persecuted "people without a land, in a land without people."[18]

Religious issues underlying a conflict can come back to haunt a peace process if not adequately addressed. By the same token, they can also provide added opportunities for coming together by virtue of past precedent. As noted by Jewish scholar Yehezkel Landau, "The Oslo Accords failed, in part, because they were a secular framework imposed by secular leaders on a Holy Land, where large and influential minorities of both Jews and Palestinians are motivated by deeply held religious convictions."[19] The same will hold true for the "road map" initiative, unless negotiators can find a way to capitalize on the insights of recognized religious authorities, both to enhance their own understanding of (and ability to deal with) the highly sensitive religious issues and to provide the religious legitimacy that will be required for widespread acceptance of whatever settlement emerges.

Proactive Engagement

Finally, spiritual engagement is about taking a proactive posture in the religious sphere, as opposed to merely reacting to the initiatives of others or, alternatively, not acting at all. To illustrate this aspect, we turn again to the country of Iran.

As the slings and arrows darken the sky over Iran's perceived march toward nuclear weapons, lost in the darkness is any mention of the opportunity costs associated with the adversarial contest of wills between that country and the United States. Indeed, the case for developing a cooperative relationship is strong and should be taken into account in the policymakers' calculus. Although both nations share strategic interests that would be best served through active collaboration, they are today working at cross-purposes, thwarting each other's aims, even if it means thwarting their own in the process. Were it possible to develop a new, more hospitable relationship—cooperating in some areas, while compromising in others—both sides could reap important gains.

A RELIGIOUS OPENING

In May 2006, President Ahmadinejad of Iran broke 27 years of official silence when he sent an 18-page letter to then-President George W. Bush.[20] The letter, which used religious principles to argue against American foreign policy, was quickly dismissed, probably because of its rambling and somewhat incoherent nature, its numerous references to God, and its repeated use of the teachings of Christ as a standard for evaluating U.S. foreign policy.

However, instead of ceding the religious high ground to Ahmadinejad by not responding, consideration should have been given to crafting a response that could have conceivably turned the tables politically, while laying down a marker that the United States is as capable as anyone of playing in the religious arena. Although it may have transcended the comfort zone of the U.S. foreign policy community, a religious response along the following lines would have enabled the United States to lay a credible claim to the spiritual high ground[21]:

Dear Ayatollah Khamenei:

In response to President Ahmadinejad's letter to me of May 9, 2006, I have spent the intervening period comparing his words with the actions of your government to determine how best to respond.

In the President's letter, he raised many questions, some touching on issues that are very important to the American people and some that highlight the differences between our two countries. What is clear to me, however, is the deeply religious nature of our respective societies as reflected in the different faith traditions that contribute to our national well-being.

In looking to the Qur'an to find a basis for peace founded on the Abrahamic principles that Islam and Christianity share in common, the first passage that caught my attention was sura 8:61, which I am sure you know well: "For if the enemy inclines toward peace, do thou also incline toward peace, and trust in God: for He is the one who heareth and knoweth all things." It is in this same spirit of peace that I write this letter.

The revered prophets of both Islam and Christianity told of the special regard that God held for the leaders of ancient Persia. Indeed, it was because Cyrus the Great showed such kindness to the Children of Jacob that God looked upon Persians with favor and granted peace to their land. Today, those same Children of Jacob live in fear that their country will be destroyed by their neighbors, including that same land of Persia.

The United States is not in search of war with the Iranian people. But just as President Ahmadinejad has said that Iran will not bow down to the West, neither can the United States bow to Iran. We must work together to avoid war at all costs and to look beyond the past in a spirit of charity and forgiveness. We must give new meaning to the Abrahamic ethic of love for God and neighbor by providing security for the Children of Jacob and by honoring the legitimate rights of the Palestinian people. I recall the promise God gave to Abraham: "I will bless those who bless you, and I will curse those who curse you, and in you, Abraham, all the families of the earth shall be blessed."

In the Holy Qur'an, God extols the virtues of understanding between nations: "O Mankind! . . . we made you into separate nations and tribes that you may know one another and cooperate with one another (49:13). In yet another passage (5:48), we are enjoined to "compete with one another in good works." Let us put our injured history behind us and begin that competition. It is God's command.

With my regards,
GWB

Although the nonresponse to Ahmadinejad's letter represented yet another lost opportunity, there is reason to hope that in light of President Obama's June 2009 Cairo speech to the Muslim world, opportunities to engage in the future will be treated more seriously. In many respects, that speech was all about respectful engagement (as have been some of his other speeches); and it certainly opened the door to spiritual engagement at some future date. However, opening the door is one thing, having the capability to follow through is quite another. Before reviewing what such a capability might require, it is important to understand that spiritual engagement can derive either from the authority of a religious institution or from the faith commitment of individuals acting independently of organized religion.[22]

Developing a capability to understand and deal with religious considerations in the practice of U.S. foreign policy would first require moving to the new paradigm and giving high priority to a previously all but totally neglected area of inquiry—difficult under the best of circumstances.

Understanding and dealing with religious imperatives will not only require major changes in organizational structure and personnel training programs; but, even more challenging, it will require changing the mind-sets of those who remain captive to the old ways of thinking. While the challenges are formidable, so too are the opportunities—especially if one's engagement is informed by the OODA Loop.

IRAN REVISITED

It is sadly ironic that the one Muslim country the United States appears most likely to bomb next is the one Muslim country in the world where there is widespread affection for Americans,[23] notwithstanding the steady, 30-year drumbeat of castigating the "Great Satan." It is also a country in which the potential for spiritual engagement to lead to better understanding and possibly improved relations appears quite high. The following provides the basis for such an assessment.

Observation

In 2002, Marshall Breger, a professor of law at Catholic University in Washington, D.C., was invited to Iran to lecture at universities in Tehran, Qom, and Isfahan. An American Jew who had served as President Reagan's liaison with the Jewish community, Breger was more than a little apprehensive about what might await him. As it turned out, however, he was met at the airport in Tehran by his government-assigned guide and several members of the local Jewish community bearing a large sign saying "welcome" in Hebrew. Moreover, during the three days that he lectured in Qom (Iran's spiritual capital), arrangements were made by the government to bring him kosher food from Tehran (some 90 miles away) each day.

Throughout the 20 days of his lecture tour, Breger felt nothing but positive feelings toward him as an American and as a Jew. Once, when he lectured at the Islamic Academy of Sciences on the U.S. Constitution and the First Amendment, he received a standing ovation—as he says, "for the First Amendment, not for me." Upon his return to the United States, Breger met with Cardinal Theodore McCarrick, then Archbishop of Washington, suggesting that "what I learned from my trip is that if you want to talk with the Iranians, you have to enter through the portal of religion. If you start with a conversation about religious faith you can talk about anything."[24]

The insights gleaned from his lecture tour prompted a later visit to Iran in 2003 of a nine-member Abrahamic delegation, including Jews, Christians, and Muslims, under the leadership of Cardinal McCarrick. At each of the delegation's many meetings with top religious and political figures, McCarrick suggested that they open with prayer. This simple but important gesture was interpreted as showing respect toward Islam and effectively placed the delegation beyond the bounds of the "Great Satan."

After prayer, the members of the delegation found that, based on the moral grounding of their respective religious faiths, they could hold discussions on any topic, ranging from weapons of mass destruction, to terrorism, to the end of days—to mention only a few of the more telling.

Subsequent to the Abrahamic visit, Catholic University convened a meeting on family law in Bellagio, Italy, which included six-member delegations from Iran, Israel, and America. At the opening dinner, the delegations were reluctant to sit down to eat for fear of who they would be sitting next to; but by the end, they were going for walks in the woods together. Although Iranians can no longer meet with Israelis as they were able to do under President Khatami, the chemistry achieved in Bellagio is indicative of the art of the possible when spiritual engagement can be brought to bear.

In 2005, the ICRD, which had participated in the 2003 trip to Iran, raised the funds to cosponsor with Catholic University a reciprocal visit by a high-level Abrahamic delegation from Iran. Although the Iranians came with deep reservations, they left with newfound respect for America as a religious country. They were particularly impressed with the idea of churches being built from private donations, which they saw as a testament to people's faith. In Iran, the government builds the mosques.

A highlight of the Iranian visit took place one morning in a town house close to the Capital where the delegation sat down with eight U.S. Congressmen who were well versed on the Middle East. The meeting began with a religious discussion and then segued to the various hot-button issues. At one point, one of the Congressmen pointed at the Ayatollah in charge of the delegation and said, "Tell me, do you think Israel has a right to exist?" To which the Ayatollah replied with a slight chuckle and said, "Of course Israel has a right to exist—just as we have a right not to recognize it."[25]

Although the Congressmen gave a good account of themselves, the Iranians probably earned the higher marks, if only because of the inherent difficulty of defending America's double standards in the region—putting extreme pressure on Iran over the nuclear question, while turning a blind eye to Israel (this meeting predated by four months President Ahmadinejad's election and his later bellicose statements regarding Israel), or criticizing Iran for its treatment of religious minorities, while giving Saudi Arabia a free ride, where the treatment of minorities has been far worse. As the Iranians pointed out, their country is the only one in the region that protects the rights of minority religions in its constitution, specifically Jews, Christians, and Zoroastrians. (That same protection does not extend to Baha'is, however, who are treated as a heretical sect of Islam.) Following the meeting, the Jewish member of Parliament and a Christian Archbishop who were part of the delegation said that their religious communities had been given one million dollars by the Iranian government that year to repair their synagogues, churches, and hospitals and that it would be increased to two million dollars the following year.[26]

Indeed, the actual plight of the Jews in Iran may not be as onerous as some would think, in spite of the strident threats to Israel. Aside from the special treatment that Breger personally received during his visit in 2003, while he was there, he found that the Jewish community did not consider itself in peril; those who wanted to emigrate could do so (although they could not take their money with them). The government generally turned a blind eye to travel to Israel to visit relatives. Jewish institutions—synagogues, old age homes, the community center, and the kosher restaurant—were protected. The Jewish Community's impact on Iranian culture and society runs deep; and while Iranians often employed Jewish stereotypes such as "being good with money and taking care of their brethren" in popular speech, they did so as models to emulate, not as terms of derision.

Breger was in Iran in 2003 before the election of Ahmadinejad. Since then, the situation has deteriorated, as the lines have blurred between Zionism, Judaism, and Israel. There are indications that popular anti-Semitism (as opposed to anti-Zionism) has increased.[27] Still, the fact that there are far more Jews in Iran than in any other Muslim country in the region suggests a degree of welcome that is not prevalent elsewhere. Thus one is left to ponder the contrast between the relatively benign treatment of Jews within its borders and the rabid anti-Zionism that dominates its foreign policy.

The latter is all the more puzzling in light of the early cordial relations between Israel and Iran. At that time, it was for both a matter of hedging their respective bets against perceived threats from the Arab states. This was manifested most graphically in Israel's support for Iran during the Iran-Iraq war despite Iran's hostile rhetoric toward Israel at the time. The collective impact of the end of the cold war and Iraq's defeat in 1991, however, effectively removed any geopolitical incentive for further cooperation. With the resulting erosion of Israel's strategic significance to the United States, concern arose that improved relations between the United States and Iran could come at the expense of Israeli security interests, thus contributing to the polarized relationship that exists today.[28]

As for Iran's stance, Breger offers four possibilities. First, Israel was close to the Shah, which may have impacted Khomeini, whose legacy continues, in his view of Israel. Second, Iranians don't subscribe to the theological connection between Judaism and the land of Israel. They see this linkage as having been concocted for political and imperialistic reasons; and by opposing it, they gain added credibility in the Arab world. Third, while the Iranian Revolution has had to make a number of compromises since 1979, helping the Palestinians is a way of retaining, at little cost, their sense of revolutionary purity. And finally, anti-Israeli ideas have become so engrained in their revolutionary doctrine that they have taken on a life of their own. Whichever of these possibilities is dominant at any particular point in time, Israel is right to be concerned, as is everyone else, until a more effective process can be put in place to resolve the impasse.

Orientation

Additional Track Two meetings with Iranians have subsequently taken place in different European locations. Among other things, these interactions have helped to clarify the Iranian perspective on a range of issues:

What Iranians Want Americans to Know about Iran

September 11, 2001

1. There were no Iranians or Shiite Muslims among the attackers on 9/11.
2. Iran was the first Islamic country to condemn the 9/11 attacks.
3. Iran cooperated with United States and coalition forces to defeat the Taliban in Afghanistan.
4. Al Qaeda and the Taliban have never been friends of Iran, and Iran has never funded or supported either group. Arab countries supposedly friendly to the United States have provided major sources of funding for both.

Regional Context

1. Iran is a Shia Persian country in a hostile Sunni Arab neighborhood.
2. Iran has been a victim of Arab extremism. More than 250,000 Iranians died in the Iran-Iraq War when the United States and other western countries were supportive of Saddam Hussein. Nearly every family in Iran lost someone in the war. In proportion to the population, Iranian casualties exceeded U.S. casualties in World War II. The West, including America, did nothing to prevent Saddam from using weapons of mass destruction against Iran. In fact, many Iranians believe, and there is evidence to suggest, that western nations helped Iraq obtain the chemical weapons that were used against them.
3. The Wahhabis, a radical Sunni Muslim sect that works closely with the Saudis, hate Persian Shia Muslims more than they hate Americans or Jews. Wahhabis, who are funded by the Saudis, are exporting their radical brand of Islam throughout the Muslim world even to the Balkans and the United States.

Security Concerns

1. Iran's neighbors, including Russia, China, India, Pakistan, and Israel, all have nuclear weapons and effective delivery systems.
2. Israel is estimated to have between 100 and 200 nuclear weapons and has not signed the Nuclear Non-Proliferation Treaty that Iran is criticized for violating.

U.S.-Iranian Relations

1. The majority of Iranians living today do not remember the Shah.
2. The Iranian people do not hate the United States. The large majority, especially the young, want a better relationship with America, but Iranians will unite to defend their country against any foreign attack, just as they did during the Iran-Iraq War.

3. The United States may have felt humiliated when the U.S. Embassy was seized in 1979, but all Americans were released unharmed by their Iranian captors.

4. Democracy in Iran is far from perfect, but Iranians do have competitive elections for their president and for the 290 seat Unicameral Islamic Consultative Assembly (or *Majlis*). President Ahmadinejad's controversial reelection notwithstanding, in the past there has been more democracy in Iran than in Saudi Arabia, Kuwait, or Egypt—all staunch U.S. allies.

5. The United States and Iran want stability in Iraq and Afghanistan.

6. America needs Iran to assist in the Middle East with Iraq, Afghanistan, and Lebanon. Iran needs America but has lived without it for more than 30 years.[29]

These are the kinds of insights that one would expect to flow from interactions based on respectful engagement in which one attempts to look at the world through the other's side of the prism. In contrast, spiritual engagement takes into account the deeper realities that flow from religious convictions and the higher level of accountability (to God) that comes with them. In dealing with the highly charged topic of Iran's pursuit of nuclear weapons, for example, it becomes useful to contemplate the significance of the fatwas issued by both of Iran's Supreme Leaders, Ayatollah Khamenei and, before him, Ayatollah Khomeini, against weapons of mass destruction on the basis that such weapons are inherently un-Islamic, because they cannot be used without killing innocents in the process. Buttressing this line of thinking is Iran's claim that it consciously chose not to respond in kind when attacked with chemical weapons by Iraq during the first five years of the Iran-Iraq War. Also of note is the fact that in a poll taken of Iranian attitudes toward nuclear weapons at the beginning of 2008, more than 70 percent were opposed to developing them, regardless of whether the respondents were conservatives, moderates, or reformists.[30]

Commentary by UK correspondent Robert Fisk in remarks to a Washington audience in 2008 provides added perspective:

What is the real story of Iranian nuclear power? It starts with the Shah of Iran, our friend, the policeman of the Gulf, the King of Kings. He wanted nuclear facilities in Iran, and the Europeans stood on each other's shoulders to bid on contracts for nuclear facilities. The big nuclear station at Bushehr, such a big threat to us now apparently, was built by Siemans, a German company. And when the Shah came to New York on his way for a big bear hug from Carter on the White House lawn, he gave an interview on TV in New York in which he said, "I'd like to have the atom bomb for Iran." And when asked why, "Not in any hostile way, of course," he said, "Well, the soviets have got one, the Americans have one, why shouldn't Iran?"

I was present after the Islamic revolution when Khomeini . . . spoke in Tehran . . . and I hear him say . . . nuclear facilities are the work of the devil and we should close them down. And the Iranians closed them down. Then came the Iran-Iraq war, and by 1984, Saddam, who had invaded, of course, with our encouragement and military systems began to soak the Iranian front lines in gas . . . some of the components came from the United States of course and from Germany. At which point, the Iranian military went to Khomeini and said Saddam is using weapons of mass destruction. He'll use nuclear weapons next. We've got to reopen the facilities and Khomeini reluctantly did so.[31]

Later in 2004, Hossein Mousavian, then Secretary of Iran's Foreign Policy Committee of the Supreme Council for National Security, explained in an interview, "The religious verdict of our leader [Ayatollah Ali Khamenei] is that using weapons of mass destruction is forbidden, is *haram* ["unlawful" in Islam]. For Iranians, this verdict is much more important than the NPT."[32] Even more recently, in 2006, Javad Zarif, then Iranian ambassador to the United Nations, wrote in the *New York Times*, "Ayatollah Ali Khamenei, the leader of the Islamic Republic, has issued a decree against the development, production, stockpiling and use of nuclear weapons."[33] HRH Prince Turki al-Faisal, former head of Saudi intelligence, has confirmed the existence of the fatwas. While he thinks that Khomeini's dictum was genuine, he suspects that Khamenei's may be disingenuous.[34]

From a realpolitik standpoint, it stands to reason that Iran would want a nuclear weapons capability, if only to deter its neighbors who already have them (see Figure 16.1). In view of the fatwas, however, and the fact that such edicts are taken seriously in a country where religion allegedly trumps all else and constitutes the very glue that holds the theocracy together, it seems entirely plausible that Iran might want to acquire such weapons without any intention of using them, quite apart from Ahmadinejad's pronouncements. Iran is a highly advanced culture that probably has more philosophers per square hectare than any other country in the world. Although Iranians live in a tough neighborhood and are walking a very fine line, such people do not value life lightly.

In view of the fact that Pakistan's and North Korea's nuclear tests came as a total surprise to the West, one might be tempted to ask if in the final analysis, the West would prefer to have a friendly or an unfriendly nuclear-armed Iran. President Ahmadinejad's gratuitous but seemingly serious threats against Israel, however, effectively preclude asking such a question.

Decision

Out of the observation phase, an important insight emerges relating to Iran: religious intercourse can be an important trust builder for engaging in meaningful dialogue about challenging issues. Politically, Iranians don't trust the United States because of its recent fixation on regime change and their perception that America speaks out of both sides of its mouth politically. Religion, on the other hand, is very important to them and something they inherently trust. How then might this insight be brought to bear in practical terms?

In the wake of the devastating earthquake that hit Iran in late 2003, the United States offered to send a team under the leadership of Senator Elizabeth

Figure 16.1
Countries with Nuclear Weapons

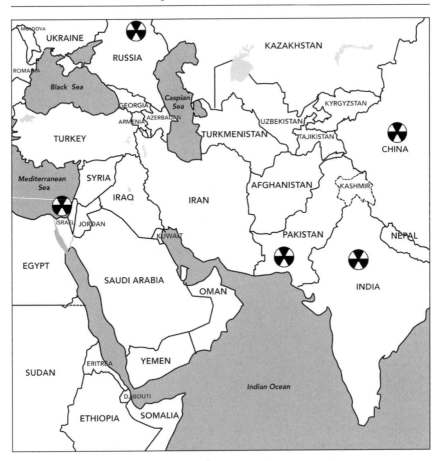

Dole to assess the situation as a precursor to providing humanitarian assistance. On the face of it, Dole seemed the perfect choice—politically influential and eminently well qualified as a former head of the American Red Cross. The offer was rejected by Iran. Had Cardinal McCarrick (who already commanded deep respect in Iran) been chosen to head such a delegation, however, the chances of Iranian acceptance would have been commensurately higher.

Because of existing church/state legal ambiguities and the problems they create for U.S. government officials, our government would do well to glean as many insights as possible about Iranian behavior and intentions from NGOs and other unofficial parties that travel to Iran. The 2003 student riots in Iran, for example, which took place during the U.S. Abrahamic delegation's visit and that were interpreted in the United States as a protest for democratic reform, were actually about something entirely different (as the delegation can readily attest). The government of Iran had decided as a matter of national policy to privatize a number of government-sponsored activities, including education. This meant that students who up until then had received free education were now going to have to pay tuition, which some students could afford and others could not. Their protest was not about initiating another revolution but rather to honor the one they already had.

Based on the insights gleaned from the above observation and orientation phases, what decision consistent with the OODA Loop might one then contemplate? In light of the strained relations that continue to exist at the official level in Iranian-American relations, logic would suggest that formulating a potentially helpful Track Two initiative around Iran's openness to religion could make some sense. Here, one possibility that comes to mind is what one might call a "peace game." Since Iran has been the focus of any number of war games, this would represent a peacemaking counterpart. However, rather than a scenario-driven exercise as most war games tend to be, a peace game would be more akin to facilitated brainstorming.

The basic concept would call for bringing participants from Iran and the United States together for a week to discuss how the obstacles that stand in the way of a cooperative relationship might be overcome. Among the reasons for pursuing such a relationship are our overlapping interests in Iraq, Afghanistan, and Lebanon and our mutual aversion to Wahhabism. U.S. policy options for facilitating peace in the region would also be considerably enhanced if existing differences could be overcome.

Participants for the game would be chosen from the ranks of respected religious, political, academic, and professional figures who (1) are not in government, (2) are known to be spiritually minded, and (3) have views that would command serious consideration by their respective governments. A religious framework for the discussions would be established at the outset, a world-class expert on negotiations would facilitate the "game," and the final recommendations would be presented to both governments for appropriate consideration. Taking this out of the realm of the theoretical, it is worth noting that when President Ahmadinejad was approached with the "peace game" idea during his September 2009 visit to the United Nations, he indicated that he would support it.[35] It is also worth noting that on the other side of the impasse, the U.S. President's National Security Strategy for 2010 specifically calls for engaging Iran "without illusion."[36]

Action

Assuming that the political planets of both countries achieve sufficient alignment to permit conducting such a game, the action phase would consist of implementing whatever recommendations emerge (either from that encounter or succeeding encounters) that are deemed acceptable to both governments. While it seems highly unlikely that mutually acceptable recommendations can be reached on all of the salient issues, agreement on any one of them would constitute a major step forward in establishing a helpful momentum for the future.

The relationship between Iran and the United States is complex and multifaceted. In contrast to this inherent complexity, the above application of the OODA Loop process appears quite simple; and so it is, if only to illustrate the process. Loop applications can be as complex as they need to be. However, even one as simple as this can lead to new beginnings.

CONCLUSION

This book is about change—a change in paradigm, a change in how we deal with religion, a change in how we make decisions. Quite apart from the compelling or unconvincing nature of the supporting arguments for said change, one thing is crystal clear: it will not come easy. As Niccolo Machiavelli aptly noted in *The Prince* almost five centuries ago:

It ought to be remembered that there is nothing more difficult to take in hand, more perilous to conduct, or more uncertain in its success, than to take the lead in the introduction of a new order of things. Because the innovator has for enemies all those who have done well under the old conditions, and lukewarm defenders in those who may do well under the new. This coolness arises partly from fear of the opponents, who have the laws on their side, and partly from the incredulity of men, who do not readily believe in new things until they have had a long experience of them.[37]

Confirming the above and indicative of the inertia to be overcome is the following observation by a conservative commentator in response to recent attempts by the United States to reach out to regimes that were previously deemed off-limits:

The world is in fact a dangerous place, inhabited by fundamentalist regimes, crusading radicals, and amoral power seekers. Realism would dictate that we be pessimists and cynics, never trusting until verified, basing our foreign policy on the past actions of our opponents and not on their sweet words or our even sweeter hopes.[38]

History suggests the need to heed such advice and, above all, to proceed with our eyes open. It does not, however, negate the fact that the world is changing and that we need to anticipate that change by making the necessary adjustments to our prospective role and leadership style. Our customary assertiveness and de facto role as global policeman will no longer suffice in tomorrow's multipolar world, where the opportunities for going it alone will soon disappear. Leading more by example than force and, to the extent possible, facilitating better governance and improved stability in sensitive areas will likely yield far better results in dealing with "irregular actors" over the long term.[39] Despite the daunting nature of this challenge, we have every reason to feel confident. As the late Rabbi Abraham Joshua Heschel, former Professor of Ethics and Mysticism at the Jewish Theological Seminary of America, reminds us:

The greatest sin of man is to forget that he is a prince—that he has royal power. All worlds are in need of exaltation, and everyone is charged to lift what is low, to unite what lies apart, to advance what is left behind. It is as if all worlds . . . are full of expectancy, of sacred goals to be reached, so that consummation can come to pass. And man is called upon to bring about the climax slowly but decisively.[40]

For a new paradigm to be accepted, it needs only to be provably better than its predecessor. There is no requirement that it explain all of the facts or situations with which it is confronted, only that it does a better job of predicting and responding to them than any of its competitors. Crisis often proliferates new discovery, and it is typically the failure of existing rules (think rational actor) that leads to a search for new ones.[41] Because the stakes are so extraordinarily high in today's interconnected world, we can neither afford the "crisis" nor the "failure of rules" as a prerequisite to making the necessary change. The future is now.

APPENDIX A

CC CPSU Letter on Afghanistan, May 10, 1988

From a May 10, 1988, letter from the Central Committee of the Communist Party of the Soviet Union to all Party members. The withdrawal of Soviet troops from Afghanistan began on May 15 and was completed February 15, 1989. The letter is among documents related to the Soviet occupation of Afghanistan published in February [2009] by the National Security Archive. Translated from Russian by Svetlana Savranskaya.

The decision to invade was made when there was a lot of uncertainty in the balance of forces within Afghan society. Our picture of the real social and economic situation in the country was also insufficiently clear. We do not want to say it, but we should: at that time, we did not even have a correct assessment of the unique geographical features of that hard-to-enter country. This was reflected in the operations of our troops against small, highly mobile units, where very little could be accomplished with the help of modern military technology.

In addition, we completely disregarded the most important national and historical factors, above all the fact that the appearance of armed foreigners in Afghanistan has always been met with arms in the hands of the population. This is how it was in the past, and this is how it happened when our troops entered Afghanistan, even though they came there with honest and noble goals.

Babrak Karmal became head of the Afghan government at the time. His first steps in that capacity gave us grounds to hope that he would be able to solve the problems facing his country. Nothing new emerged, however, in his policies that could have changed for the better the attitude of a

significant portion of the Afghan population toward the new regime. Moreover, the intensity of the internal Afghan conflict continued to grow, and
our military presence was associated with [the] forceful imposition of customs alien to the national characteristics and feelings of the Afghan people. Our approach did not take into account the country's multiple forms
of economic life and other characteristics, such as tribal and religious
customs.

One has to admit that we essentially put our bets on the military solution,
on suppressing the counterrevolution with force. We did not even make
full use of the existing opportunities to neutralize the hostile attitudes of
the local population toward us. Often our people, acting out of their best
intentions, tried to transplant the approach to which we are accustomed
onto Afghan soil, and encouraged the Afghans to copy our ways. All this
did not help our cause; it bred feelings of dependency on the part of the
Afghan leaders in regard to the Soviet Union, both in the sphere of military operations and in the economic sphere.

Meanwhile, the war in Afghanistan continued, and our troops were getting engaged in extensive combat actions. Finding any way out became
more and more difficult as time passed. Combat action is combat action.
Our losses in dead and wounded—and the Central Committee believes it
has no right to hide this—were growing heavier and heavier. Altogether,
by the beginning of this month, we had lost 13,310 dead in Afghanistan;
35,478 Soviet officers and soldiers were wounded, many of whom became
disabled; 301 people are missing in action. There is a reason people say that
each person is a unique world, and when a person dies that world disap-
pears forever. The loss of every individual is very hard and irreparable. It
is hard and sacred if one died carrying out one's duty.

The Afghan losses, naturally, were much heavier than ours, including
the losses among the civilian population.

One should not disregard the economic factor either. If the enemy in
Afghanistan received weapons and ammunition worth hundreds of millions and later even billions of dollars, the Soviet-Afghan side also had to
shoulder adequate expenditures. The war in Afghanistan has cost us 5 billion rubles a year.

Source: Alexander Lyakhovsky, *Tragedy and Valor of Afghan*, Iskon, Moscow 1995,
Appendix 8, (as carried in an article on why the Soviet Union gave up in Afghanistan in the June 2009 issue of *Harper's Magazine* entitled "Known Knowns").
Reprinted with the permission of the National Security Archive at George Washington University.

APPENDIX B

Department of State
Structural Alternatives

OPTION 1

Under this option, a Deputy Assistant Secretary for Religion (DASR) would be assigned to each of the six regional assistant secretaries serving under the Under Secretary for Political Affairs (whose title would be changed to "Under Secretary for Political and Religious Affairs"). The DASRs would be specialists in the major religions practiced in the regions of their assigned bureaus. At the same time, Religion Attachés (or their equivalent) would report to their corresponding regional DASR. To enhance coordination, these DASRs could have a "dotted-line" reporting relationship to the Under Secretary for Public Diplomacy and Public Affairs (USPD).[1] This would essentially parallel the approach taken with the public diplomacy officers posted overseas who currently report to their regional bureaus in Washington.

Religious reporting under this configuration would flow from the embassies (via the Religion Attaché or equivalent) to the deputy assistant secretaries and the USPD (in addition to the ambassadors and regional bureau chiefs). Thus, through the reporting of the regional DASRs, the USPD would be able to inform the direction of the bureaus under his or her immediate control with relevant religious considerations and perspectives. The information provided to the USPD would include indirect reporting from the Religion Attachés "on the ground," in addition to the expertise and analysis directly provided by the DASRs. This could help address the problem of "posts in the Muslim world [continuing] to generally employ the same exchange, cultural, and information programs used throughout the world" instead of tailoring their programs to fit Muslim audiences.[2]

Figure B.1
State Department Organizational Alternative 1

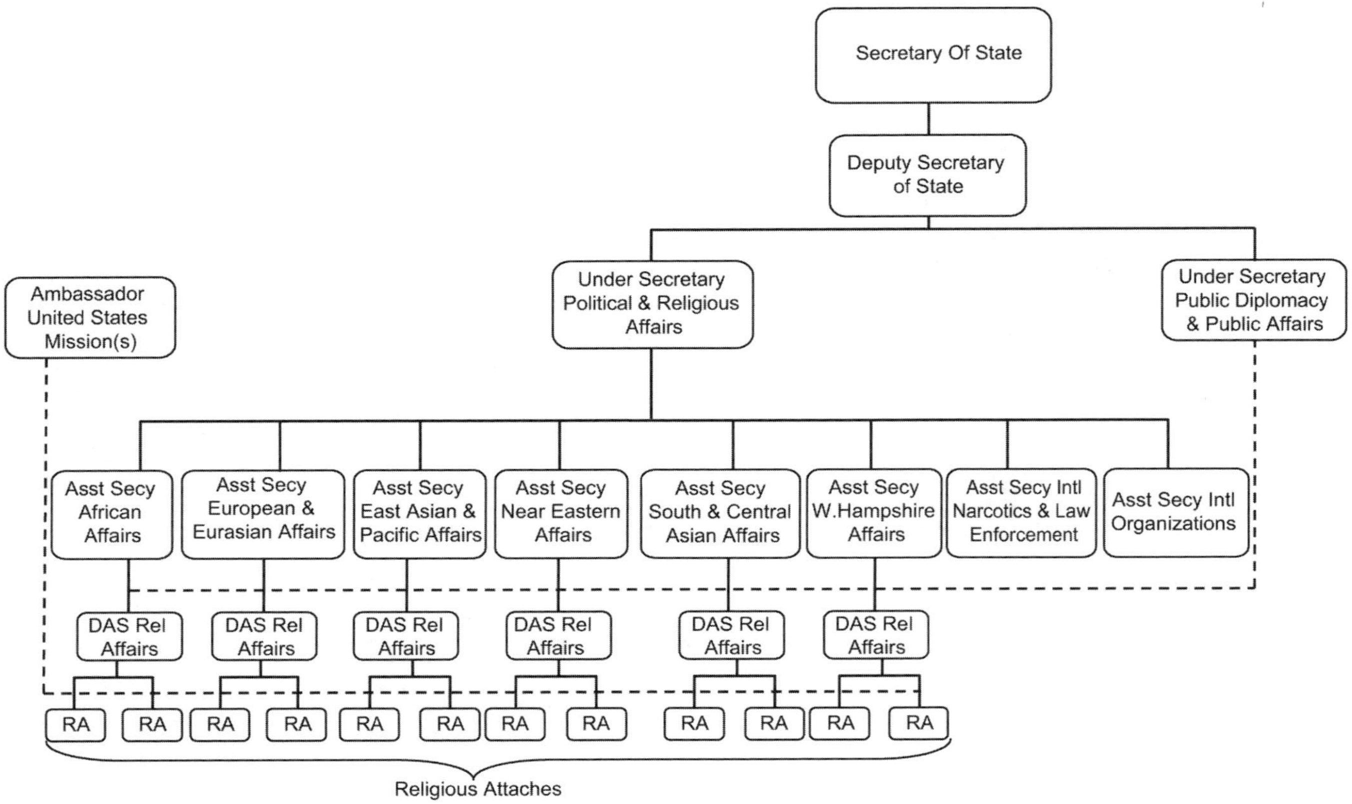

OPTION 2

Another alternative, one that would further enhance the consideration of religious imperatives in State Department calculations, would be to establish an Assistant Secretary for Religious Affairs (ASRA) under the Under Secretary for Political and Religious Affairs. Under this arrangement, the DASRs would report directly to the ASRA, while interacting directly with their respective regional bureaus. The ASRA would then have the dotted-line relationship with the USPD.

Further, to facilitate the Under Secretary for Political and Religious Affairs' focus on religion, one or both of the nonregional bureaus under his or her authority could be transferred to other under secretaries. For instance, the International Organizations Bureau could be transferred to the Under Secretary for Democracy and Global Affairs, while the International Narcotics and Law Enforcement Bureau could be transferred to either the Under Secretary for Economic, Business, and Agricultural Affairs or to the Under Secretary for Arms Control and International Security Affairs. At present, the overburdened Under Secretary for Political Affairs is responsible for more bureaus than any other under secretary (save for the Under Secretary for Management, who controls a like number), so why not redistribute some of these responsibilities and thereby enable him or her to focus more on regional issues pertaining strictly to political and religious affairs?

OPTION 3

A third alternative for incorporating religious considerations into DOS decision making would be to tie them specifically to the public diplomacy function.

A cursory overview of the way the State Department conducts public diplomacy, however, reveals a disjointed approach. Logically, one would assume that public diplomacy officers in U.S. embassies would be under the purview of the Under Secretary for Public Diplomacy and Public Affairs (USPD), but such is not the case. Instead, public diplomacy officers "operate under the authority of the Chiefs of Mission[3] and report to their regional bureau managers in Washington, D.C."[4] In addition, the regional bureaus in Washington have their own public diplomacy offices overseen by a deputy assistant secretary, but they report to the assistant secretaries of their bureaus, who are under the authority of the Under Secretary for Political Affairs. The USPD, on the other hand, has three bureaus under his or her purview: Educational and Cultural Affairs (which coordinates people-to-people exchanges), Public Affairs (which is geared toward domestic audiences), and International Information Programs (which project pro-American programs overseas).

Figure B.2
State Department Organizational Alternative 2

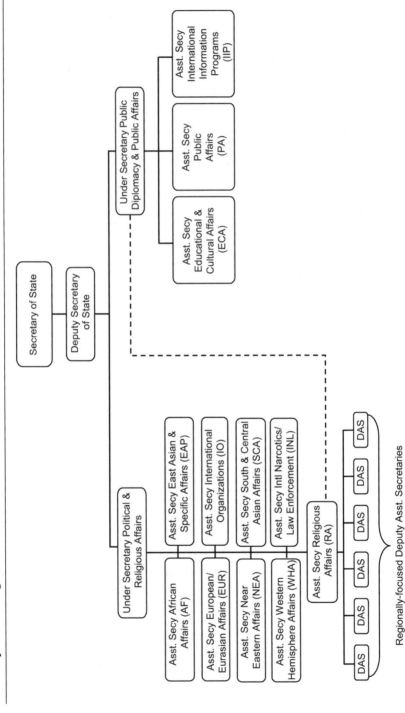

Figure B.3
State Department Organizational Alternative 3

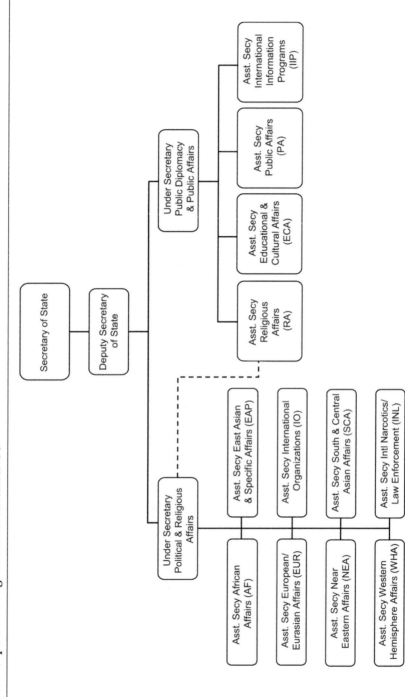

At first glance, the solution seems obvious: put all public diplomacy offices and officers under the authority of the USPD.[5] Indeed, the Advisory Group on Public Diplomacy for the Arab and Muslim World recommended moving in this direction by empowering the USPD with added responsibilities,[6] although they suggested that he or she act "in collaboration with missions abroad and in consultation with the geographic and functional Assistant Secretaries."[7] A number of noteworthy ideas emanated from the Advisory Group's report, including (1) the establishment of an Office of Policy Plans and Resources to coordinate strategy with the regional bureaus, produce country-specific plans, and allocate human and financial resources and (2) the establishment of an Arab and Muslim Countries Public Communications Unit, modeled in part after the highly effective Islamic Media Unit that the Foreign and Commonwealth Office of the United Kingdom established following the 9/11 attacks.[8]

In 2004, Congress approved establishment of the Office of Policy, Planning, and Resources (R/PPR) within USPD, which allocates financial resources to the regional bureaus. While the funds must be used for PD, the USPD does not control the specifics of how they are spent, and his or her influence in this regard is limited to "moral suasion" and the "honor system."[9] R/PPR also has authority over human resources and, as of September 2008, assigns all PD officers to the various embassies.[10] It does not require embassies to produce country-specific plans, but there have been "pilot country projects" where these plans have been drawn up for a few countries on an ad hoc basis.[11] Although there is no "Arab and Muslim Countries Public Communications Unit," media hubs have been established in Brussels, London, and Dubai (with the latter two focused on the Arab media). Most significant, it is still largely the case that public diplomacy officers at embassies operate independently of the USPD and report directly to the Chief of Mission and their regional bureaus. However, the USPD does issue guidance (in the form of cables) to ambassadors on key messages that they should be getting across to certain media outlets, such as Al-Jazeera.[12] In addition, the USPD can fund his or her own ideas for programs; and posts can approach the USPD with their own "extraordinary requests" for funding.

Based on the above, while some of the Advisory Group's recommendations have been adopted, there has not been the kind of comprehensive structural reform that would be required to ensure that public diplomacy is fully and effectively coordinated.[13] Indeed, a strong case can be made that such reform is long overdue, dating back to 1999 when the U.S. Information Agency was merged with the Department.[14] If the needed reform were to take place, however, it would probably make sense to have religion specialists working in the office of the USPD (or, more specifically, in the Office of Policy Planning and Resources). In addition, religion specialists at the embassies would report to the same office.

OPTION 4

Yet another structural arrangement that might have merit would be to elevate and expand the scope of the existing Office of International Religious Freedom (OIRF) within the Bureau of Democracy, Human Rights, and Labor to a stand-alone bureau responsible for the oversight of all aspects of religious influence in the conduct of U.S. foreign policy. Indeed, one could make the case that the marginalized existence of this office with its constricted mandate has actually become part of the larger problem. As things currently stand, there is a widespread tendency within the Department to defer religious matters of any kind to OIRF on the basis that it is responsible, which, of course, it is not (other than for matters dealing specifically with religious freedom).

Figure B.4
State Department Organizational Alternative 4

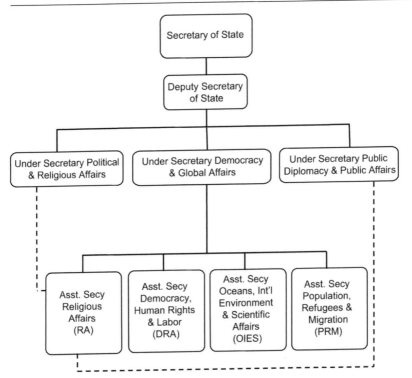

APPENDIX C

The Grand Bargain

The following documents from the Swiss ambassador to Iran, Tim Guldimann, were received by American officials on May 4, 2003, and subsequently rejected.[1]

May 4, 2003

1. On April 21, I had a longer discussion with Sadeq Kharrazi who came to see me (S. Kh. is the Iranian Ambassador in Paris, former Deputy FM and nephew of the Foreign Minister, his sister is married to the son of the Religious Leader Khamenei). During this discussion a first draft of the enclosed Roadmap was developed. He said that he would discuss this with the Leader and the Foreign Minister.

2. On May 2, I met him again for three hours. He told me that he had two long discussions with the Leader on the Roadmap. In these meetings, which both lasted almost two hours, only President Khatami and FM Kharazzi were present; "we went through every word of this paper." (He additionally had a series of separate meetings with both).—The question is dealt with in high secrecy, therefore no one else has been informed. (S. Kh. himself has become also very discreet in our last contacts.)—S. Kh, presented the paper to the Leader as a proposal which he had discussed with a friend in Europe who has close contacts with higher echelons in the DoS. The Leader explicitly had asked him whether this is a US-proposal and S. Kh. denied this, saying that, if it is accepted, this friend could convey it to Washington as the basis for opening the bilateral discussion.

3. Then S. Kh. told me that the Leader uttered some reservations as for some points; the President and the Foreign Minister were very positive, there was no problem from their side. Then he said: "They (meaning above all the Leader)

agree with 85%–90% of the paper. But everything can be negotiated." (By 'agree' he meant to agree with the points themselves referred to as 'US aims' in the Roadmap, and not only to agree that the US puts these points on the agenda.)—"There is a clear interest to tackle the problem of our relations with the US. I told them, this is a golden opportunity, one day we must find a solution."—Then S. Kh. asked me whether I could present the enclosed Roadmap very confidentially to someone very high in the DoS in order to get to know the US-reaction on it.—He asked me to make some minor changes in the Roadmap draft of our previous meeting, we re-wrote for instance the Iranian statement on the Middle East, and he said that he thinks that this statement would be acceptable—"the peace process is a reality."

4. Then he said: "If the Americans agree to have a discreet bilateral meeting on the basis of this Roadmap, then this meeting could be arranged very soon. In this meeting our remaining reservations could be discussed as well as the US would bring in their reservations on this paper. I am sure these differences can be eliminated. If we can agree on a Roadmap to clarify the procedure, as a next step it could already be decided in this first meeting that the two Foreign Ministers could meet for starting the process" along the lines of the Roadmap, "to decide on how to proceed to resolve everything from A till Z."—Asked whether the meeting between the two foreign ministers has been agreed by the Leader, he said: "Look, if we can agree on the procedure, I believe honestly that it is O.K. for the meeting of the foreign ministers in Paris or Geneva, there is soon an occasion."—Asked whom he thinks would participate in the first discreet meeting, he mentioned Armitage, referring to the positive positions of the latter on Iranian democracy.—I told him that I think that this is impossible, but then he mentioned a meeting these days between Khalilzad and Zarif (Ambassador to the UN) in Geneva on terrorism and said it could be a similar level from the DoS and on their side maybe him or Zarif or both.

5. When I tried to obtain from him a precise answer on what exactly the Leader explicitly has agreed, he said that the lack of trust in the US imposes them to proceed very carefully and very confidentially. After discussing this problem with him I understood that they want to be sure that if this initiative failed, and if anything about the new Iranian flexibility outlined in it became known, they would—also for internal reasons—not be bound to it.—However, I got the clear impression that there is a strong will of the regime to tackle the problem with the US now and to try it with this initiative.

ROADMAP

US Aims: (Iran agrees that the US puts the following aims on the agenda)

- WMD: full transparency for security that there are no Iranian endeavours to develop or possess WMD, full cooperation with IAEA based on Iranian adoption of all relevant instruments (93+2 and all further IAEA protocols)

- Terrorism: decisive action against any terrorists (above all Al Qaida) on Iranian territory, full cooperation and exchange of all relevant information

- Iraq: coordination of Iranian influence for actively supporting political stabilization and the establishment of democratic institutions and a democratic government representing all ethnic and religious groups in Iraq.
- Middle East:
  1. stop of any material support to Palestinian opposition groups (Hamas, Jihad, etc.) from Iranian territory, pressure on these organisations [sic] to stop violent action against civilians within borders of 1967
  2. action on Hisbollah to become an exclusively political and social organization within Lebanon
  3. acceptance of the two-state-approach

Iranian Aims: (the US accepts a dialogue "in mutual respect" and agrees that Iran puts the following aims on the agenda)

- US refrains from supporting change of the political system by direct interference from outside
- Abolishment of all sanctions: commercial sanctions, frozen assets, refusal of access to WTO
- Iraq: pursuit of MKO, support of the repatriation of MKO members, support of the Iranian claims for Iraqi reparation, no Turkish invasion in North Iraq, respect for the Iranian national interests in Iraq and religious links to Najaf/ Kerbala
- Access to peaceful nuclear technology, biotechnology and chemical technology
- Recognition of Iran's legitimate security interests in the region with the according defense capacity
- Terrorism: action against MKO and affiliated organizations in the US

Steps:

1. Communication of mutual agreement on the following procedure
2. Mutual simultaneous statements "we have always been ready for direct and authoritative talks with the US/with Iran with the aim of discussing—in mutual respect—our common interests and our mutual concerns, but we have always made it clear that such talks can only be held if genuine progress for a solution of our own concerns can be achieved"
3. A direct meeting on the appropriate level will be held with the previously agreed aims
   a) of a decision on the first mutual steps:
      - Iraq: establishment of a common working group on Iraq, active Iranian support for Iraqi stabilization, US commitment to resolve MKO problem in Iraq, US commitment to take Iranian reparations claims into the discussion on Iraq foreign debts
      - Terrorism: Iranian commitment for decisive action against Al Qaida [sic] members in Iran, agreement on cooperation and information exchange

- Iranian statement "that it supports a peaceful solution in the Middle East, that it accepts a solution which is accepted by the Palestinians and that it follows with interest the discussion on the Roadmap, presented by the Quartet"

- US acceptance of Iranian access to WTO-membership negotiations

b) of the establishment of three parallel working groups on disarmament, regional security and economic cooperation. Their aim is an agreement on three parallel road maps, for the discussions of these working groups each side accepts that the other side's aims (see above) are put on the agenda:

   1. Disarmament: road map, which combines the mutual aims of, on the one side, full transparency by international commitments and guarantees to abstain from WMD with, on the other side, access to western technology (in the three areas)

   2. Terrorism and regional security: road map for the above mentioned aims on Middle East and terrorism

   3. Economic cooperation: road map for the lifting of the sanctions and the solution of the frozen assets

c) and of a public statement after this first meeting on the achieved agreements

APPENDIX D

Recapturing the Spirit of Jewish-Muslim Dialogue

Rabbi David Rosen

Rabbi David Rosen is Chairman of the International Jewish Committee on Interreligious Consultations and the former Chief Rabbi of Ireland. In 2005 he was made a papal Knight Commander for his contributions to Catholic-Jewish reconciliation.

Few religions have as much in common as Islam and Judaism. Despite the exigencies of history, which took the majority of the Jewish People outside the Middle East, Judaism has historically remained overwhelmingly rooted in its Semitic worldview.

At the heart of the two faiths is an ethical-monotheistic vision that determinedly resists any compromise on the idea of the transcendence and unity of God, who is envisaged as just and merciful and who has revealed a way of life in accordance with these values for the benefit of human society. Much the same religious narrative and similar religious injunctions are found in the Hebrew Pentateuch (the Torah) and the Koran.

Common to the two traditions are central practices of prayer, fasting, almsgiving, dietary laws, and aspects of ritual purity. The two faiths have traditionally shared other fundamental religious concepts such as reward and punishment related to a Day of Divine Judgment and belief in the afterlife.

The structure and modus operandi of their respective religious jurisprudential codes of conduct—Sharia and Halachah—bear striking similarity and neither tradition has clergy who by virtue of sacrament are separate from the rest of the community. Religious authority is essentially a function of individual mastery of religious sources to be able to guide the community in accordance with their teachings.

Jews under Islam, in marked contrast to Christian rule, were free to practice their religion without interference, although a number of restrictive conditions applied ensuring their subordinate status that were codified in the Pact of 'Umar. Places and periods of positive interaction between the two communities are part of their heritage.

In addition, cultural advancement and productivity in Muslim society was mirrored in the respective Jewish communities—most notably in the Iberian peninsula in the region known in Arabic as al-Andalus.

The relatively open society of al-Andalus ended as North African armies came to help defend against the Spanish Christians. In other parts of the Islamic world, the open and humanistic qualities of Islamic society began to give way by the 13th century to more feudalistic mentalities of rigidity and control with negative impact upon Jewish communities.

However, we should note that even then there were Muslim societies in which Jews were welcomed and that despite periods of tension and even conflict, the heritage of positive Muslim-Jewish relations prevailed in different corners of the Muslim world.

Despite popular interpretations, modern nationalism did not make a conflict of Arab nationalism with Jewish nationalism inevitable. Indeed, the principal leaders on both sides in 1919 signed an historic document that presented the return of the Jewish people to its ancestral homeland as having potential blessing and benefit for Arab society as a whole.

Tragically that vision did not materialize and the Israel-Arab conflict—and now more specifically the Israeli-Palestinian conflict—became the focus of a sense of historical injury within the Arab world, and subsequently in the Muslim world beyond.

The resultant widespread misconception of some innate hostility between Judaism and Islam is a travesty of our respective heritages and denies the noblest periods of our mutual history. It transforms a territorial conflict, which can be resolved through territorial compromise, into an intractable religious conflict and has become a lightening [sic] rod for a plethora of historical and contemporary ill feeling.

Aside from political action that needs to be taken to resolve conflict, it is essential to recapture and develop the spirit of Jewish-Muslim dialogue and mutual respect. This should take place not only to be true to the most sublime teachings and historical experience of our respective faith traditions, but also to facilitate genuine reconciliation—both in the Holy Land itself and in terms of the relationship between the Muslim and the non-Muslim world at large.

Source: Islam and the West: Annual Report on the State of Dialogue, January 2008, Box 5.3, p. 63. Courtesy of the World Economic Forum.

Notes

CHAPTER 1

1. Douglas Johnston, "Why America Should 'Serve' as World Leader," *Brown Journal of World Affairs* 5, no. 2 (1998): 67–68.

2. For a detailed explanation of the rational actor model of decision making, see Graham Allison and Philip Zelikow, *Essence of Decision: Explaining the Cuban Missile Crisis*, 2nd ed. (New York: Addison-Wesley Educational Publishers, 1999), 23–33.

3. Maneuver warfare is as old as conflict itself and thus has many authors. Its greatest appeal is the fact that it offers the possibility of obtaining results disproportionately greater than the resources applied to the effort, thus providing a chance of victory for the materially weaker side. In its most recent manifestation, the U.S. Army played a leading role in its development under successive Chiefs of Staff Gen. Edward (Shy) Meyer and Gen. John Wickham based on the recommendations of a comprehensive study led by strategic analyst Edward Luttwak, who recommended a concerted emphasis on light infantry. In fact, an unstated purpose of the Army's advent to light infantry divisions was to "beat the Marines to the punch" in the rapid-deployment mission. Michael Mazarr, *Light Forces and the Future of U.S. Military Strategy* (Washington, DC: Brassey's, 1990), 31.

4. Upon first meeting the F111's designer, Harry Hillaker, Boyd told him it was a "piece of s—." Unlike many pilots who don't like the way a plane handles, Boyd knew exactly where all the problems were, and so did the designer. They eventually became close collaborators.

5. Robert Coram, *Boyd: The Fighter Pilot Who Changed the Art of War* (New York: Back Bay Books, 2002), 341.

6. Ibid., 424. Defense Secretary Cheney quietly applied some of Boyd's ideas in the run-up to Desert Storm.

7. Col. Stanton Coerr, "Fifth Generation War: Warfare versus the Non-State," *Marine Corps Gazette* 93, no. 1 (2009): 68. See also John Boyd, "Patterns of Conflict," ed. Chet Richards and Chuck Spinney (Defense and the National Interest, 2007), 111, www.d-n-i.net.

8. Coerr, "Fifth Generation War," 68.

9. As of June 29, 2010, more than $1.04 trillion had been spent by the United States for post-9/11 operations in Iraq, Afghanistan, and elsewhere. Stephen Daggett, *Costs of Major U.S. Wars* (Congressional Research Service, 2010), 2, www.fas.org.

10. Osama bin Laden, videotaped message aired on Al-Jazeera, quoted in "Transcript: Translation of Bin Laden's Videotaped Message," *Washington Post*, November 1, 2004, www.washingtonpost.com.

11. William S. Lind, *Maneuver Warfare Handbook* (Boulder, CO: Westview Press, 1985), 5.

12. Thomas Hammes, "Countering Evolved Insurgent Networks," *Marine Corps Gazette* 91, no. 10 (2007): 92.

13. Coram, *Boyd*, 326.

14. Ibid.

15. Since its inception in the 6th century C.E., the Rule of Saint Benedict has become the guideline for Benedictines, Cistercians, and numerous other monastic orders around the world. A practical and concise outline for the development of self-discipline, it played an instrumental role in shaping the European world artistically, literally, academically, spiritually, and even politically during the 10th–12th centuries, which are sometimes called "the Benedictine centuries."

16. Alexis de Tocqueville, *Writings on Empire and Slavery*, trans. and ed. Jennifer Pitts (Baltimore: John Hopkins University Press, 2001), 49.

CHAPTER 2

1. Reza Shah-Kazemi, *My Mercy Encompasses All: The Koran's Teachings on Compassion, Peace and Love* (Berkeley, CA: Shoemaker & Hoard, 2007).

2. Particularly renowned for preventing the massacre of foreign diplomats and thousands of local Christians in Damascus in 1860, el-Kader counted Pope Pius IX, President Lincoln, and Queen Victoria among his many admirers. Even in 1846, long before his intervention in Damascus, the town of Elkader, Iowa, was named after him. See John W. Kiser, *Commander of the Faithful* (Rhinebeck, NY: Monkfish, 2008).

3. Mustafa Ceric, "Islam Against Terrorism" (speech, Euro-Atlantic Partnership Council, Vienna, Austria, June 14, 2002).

4. David Kilcullen, introduction to *The Accidental Guerrilla: Fighting Small Wars in the Midst of a Big One* (New York: Oxford University Press, 2009), xviii.

5. These insights have benefitted from the good work of attorney and former U.S. government employee Jim Guirard as reflected on his TrueSpeak.org Web site.

6. Department of Homeland Security directives under the Bush 43 and Obama administrations, which have sought to bring semantic clarity to the U.S. government's references to terrorism by disassociating them from Islam, reflect an informed awareness of the consequences of carelessness in this area.

7. World Economic Forum, *Islam and the West: Annual Report on the State of Dialogue* (Geneva: World Economic Forum, 2008), 30.

8. Khaled Abou El Fadl, *The Great Theft: Wrestling Islam from the Extremists* (San Francisco: Harper Collins, 2005), 217.

9. Valentin Aksilenko (former KGB Colonel), *Let Us Settle Our Score with Osama Bin Laden* (n.p., 2009).

10. Ibid.

11. N. J. Dawood, ed., *The Koran: With a Parallel Arabic Text*, 5:32 (London: Penguin Classics, 1990), 112.

12. Graham Allison and Philip Zelikow, *Essence of Decision: Explaining the Cuban Missile Crisis*, 2nd ed. (New York: Addison-Wesley Educational Publishers, 1999), 23–33.

13. Data attained from the U.S. Census Bureau (April 19, 2010) and the CIA World Factbook (July 2009 estimate). See www.census.gov and www.cia.gov for details.

14. William F. Vendley, "The Recovery of Transcendence in Political Order: The Role of Multi-religious Cooperation" (address, UNESCO, Paris, France, June 1, 2005), www.futureislam.com. Or, as stated differently by another scholar, "Over 80% of all living people look to religion for purpose, meaning, spiritual guidance and a channel for good works." Grady E. Means, *The New Enlightenment* (Minneapolis, MN: Two Harbors Press, 2010), 9.

15. Findings in a study of all suicide attacks between 1980 and 2003 reveal that suicide attackers are usually not poor, uneducated, immature religious zealots or social outcasts. See Robert Pape, *Dying to Win: The Strategic Logic of Suicide Terrorism* (New York: Random House, 2005), 79–85, 210–16.

16. For more information, see Louis Savary, *Pierre Teilhard de Chardin: The Divine Milieu Explained; A Spirituality for the 21st Century* (New York: Paulist Press, 2007).

17. French aviation pioneer, inventor, and adventure writer, 1890–1944. *Le Petit Prince*, published in 1943, became his most widely read work. It sold 80 million copies and was translated into 180 languages.

18. Acts 5:29–39 (New American Standard Bible).

19. Robert Jastrow, *God and the Astronomers*, 2nd ed. (Toronto: George J. McLeod, 1992), 17, 106–7.

20. Peter Berger, "The Desecularization of the World: A Global Overview" in *The Desecularization of the World: Resurgent Religion in World Politics*, ed. Peter Berger (New York: Eerdmans, 1999), 13.

21. Qur'an 29:46.

22. Vali Nasr, *The Shia Revival: How Conflicts within Islam Will Shape the Future* (New York: W. W. Norton, 2006), 74.

23. During a standoff in 1992 at the Ruby Ridge complex in Idaho between the FBI and the Weaver family over illegal gun charges, the FBI "mistakenly" killed Mrs. Weaver and the Weavers' son during the resulting shoot-out. The incident was later cited by Timothy McVeigh as a motivation for the 1995 Oklahoma City bombing.

24. Marc Aronson, "The British Heaven," in *John Winthrop, Oliver Cromwell, and the Land of Promise* (New York: Clarion Books, 2004), 9–22.

25. For example, as the first college in the New World, Harvard was established to promote the doctrinal beliefs of the early Puritan leaders of Massachusetts.

In reaction to Harvard's later adoption of more secular ideas about philosophy, some leaders in the church established Yale in a renewed attempt to maintain Puritan orthodoxy. Shortly thereafter, the College of William and Mary was founded by the Anglican Commissary of Virginia; and Princeton was founded by Presbyterians, who faced opposition among their fellow Calvinists in New England. J. David Hoeveler, *Creating the American Mind: Intellect and Politics in the Colonial Colleges* (Lanham, MD: Rowman & Littlefield, 2002), 52, 54, 73, 85, 101, 113.

26. Is it mere coincidence that 15 of the 19 hijackers on 9/11 were Saudis—citizens of a country with a famously wide gulf between the strict official puritanical Wahhabism and the outrageous behavior of many in the royal circle and the privileged classes?

27. *Albion* is a literary name for England that was traditionally used for solemn occasions or in poetry.

28. As the apostle Paul said to the Corinthians, "But a natural man does not accept the things of the Spirit of God, for they are foolishness to him." 1 Cor. 2:14 (New American Standard Bible). Perhaps this explains a visit to Wesley Seminary by a CIA delegation to speak with President David McAllister-Wilson in the wake of 9/11. The gentlemen from the Agency were at a loss about their inability to foresee the role religious faith was playing in the world. Faith-based behavior was not part of their multivariable predictive models for anticipating regional instabilities. Faith may be an accelerator of violence or a brake, depending on how leaders preach and believers react.

29. John Cassian, *Conferences* (New York: Paulist Press, 1985), 62.

CHAPTER 3

1. John L. Esposito and Dalia Mogahed, *Who Speaks for Islam? What a Billion Muslims Really Think* (New York: Gallup Press, 2007), 58, 83–84, 92, 97, 98.

2. Ismael Hossein-Zadeh, "The Muslim World and the West: The Roots of Conflict," *Arab Studies Quarterly* 27, no.3 (2005): 10.

3. Shirin S. Deylami, "Cultures in Collision? Islamism, Westoxification, and the Possibility of Global Dialogue" (paper presented at the 2007 Annual Meeting of the American Political Science Association, St. Olaf College, Northfield, MN, August 30–September 2, 2007).

4. Ruhollah Khomeini, "Message to the Pilgrims," in *Islam and Revolution: Writings and Declarations of Imam Khomeini*, trans. Hamid Algar (Berkeley, CA: Mizan Press, 1981), 195.

5. Middle East Studies Association (MESA), "The Circle of Tradition and Progress: A Statement of Purpose," *MESA News Letter* (Herndon, VA: International Institute of Islamic Thought, 1997), http://iiit.org.

6. There were other contributors to this loss of self-confidence as well; among them, the inability of Muslim forces to breech the city walls of Constantinople from the seventh century onward at great expense in men and material (and an eroded conviction that Islam was superior to Christianity and thus due Allah's favors and victories). It wasn't until the Fourth Crusade (1202–1204), when Christian forces from Europe attacked their fellow Christians and sacked the city, that Muslim penetration into the Balkans became possible.

7. Nathan C. Funk and Abdul Aziz Said, *Islam and Peacemaking in the Middle East* (Boulder, CO: Lynne Rienner, 2009), 30.

8. Steven Kull et al., "Public Opinion in the Islamic World on Terrorism, Al Qaeda, and U.S. Policies," WorldPublicOpinion.org, www.worldpublicopinion. org (accessed May 26, 2009).

9. Esposito and Mogahed, *Who Speaks for Islam*, 39–40.

10. The six-year Gallup poll taken between 2001 and 2007 involved over 50,000 interviews conducted in more than 35 predominantly Muslim nations or nations with sizable Muslim populations. It represents more than 90 percent of the world's Muslim communities. This poll is the largest, most comprehensive study of its kind.

11. Esposito and Mogahed, *Who Speaks for Islam*, 62.

12. Hossein-Zadeh, "Muslim World and the West," 9–10.

13. Ibid., 10.

14. Mauri' Saalakhan, *Islam and Terrorism: Myth and Reality*, 2nd ed. (Silver Spring, MD: Awakening, 2007), 52–53.

15. Memri TV Project, *Wafa Sultan vs. Ahmad bin Muhammad*, Al-Jazeera TV (Qatar), July 26, 2005, www.youtube.com.

16. Esposito and Mogahed, *Who Speaks for Islam*, 88.

17. Ibid., 41–42.

18. Ibid., 84.

19. Ibid., 32.

20. Esposito and Mogahed base the distinction between moderates and the politically radicalized on the basis of whether or not they believed the 9/11 attacks were "completely justified." Some critics have pointed out that those who said the attacks were "mostly justified" might also be considered extremists.

21. Esposito and Mogahed, *Who Speaks for Islam*, 84.

22. Ayaz Amir, "Unintended Consequences," World Prout Assembly, August 11, 2006, www.worldproutassembly.org.

23. Saalakhan, *Islam and Terrorism*, 50.

24. Ibid., 22.

25. Ibid., 50.

26. Akbar S. Ahmed, *Journey into Islam: The Crisis of Globalization* (Washington, DC: Brookings Institution Press, 2007), 16–17.

27. Esposito and Mogahed, *Who Speaks for Islam*, 61.

28. Ibid., 87–88.

29. Ibid., 157.

30. Ibid., 165.

31. Quoted in Husain Haqqani, "The Ideologies of South Asian Jihadi Groups," *Current Trends in Islamist Ideology* 1 (May 19, 2005), www.futureofmuslimworld.com.

32. Osama bin Laden, "Letter to the American People," Observer World View, *Guardian* (Manchester), November 24, 2002, www.guardian.co.uk.

33. Ibid.

34. Ibid.

35. Ibid.

36. Bernard Lewis, *Islam in History: Ideas, People, and Events in the Middle East* (Peru, IL: Open Court, 1993), 292.

37. Edward N. Luttwak, *The Grand Strategy of the Byzantine Empire* (Cambridge, MA: Harvard University Press, 2009), 211.

38. Daveed Gartenstein-Ross, *My Year Inside Radical Islam* (New York: Tarcher/ Penguin, 2007), 278.

39. In Islam, the Hadith is the collection of the sayings of the Prophet Muhammad. It is held as a major source of religious law and moral guidance, second in authority only to the Qur'an.

40. Qur'an 9:29 (Al Madinah: King Fahd Holy Qur-an Printing Complex, 1989), 506–7.

41. Abdul Aziz Said, "Making Peace with Islam" (presentation delivered at Conflict Resolution Institute Gala, University of Denver, CO, April 28, 2007).

42. Ed Husain, author of *The Islamist: Why I joined Radical Islam in Britain, What I saw Inside, and Why I Left*, interview by Krista Tippett, "Reflections of a Former Islamist Extremist," *Speaking of Faith,* NPR, December 7, 2007, http://speakingof faith.publicradio.org.

43. Farid Esack, "Is the Face of Islam Changing? The Editors Interview Farid Esack," Tegenwicht, www.tegenwicht.org.

44. Chas W. Freeman Jr., "Diplomacy in the Age of Terror," (remarks to the Pacific Council on International Policy, American Academy of Diplomacy, Washington, DC, October 4, 2007), www.mepc.org.

CHAPTER 4

1. These incidents represent only some of the better known. See *The 9/11 Commission Report: Final Report of the National Commission on Terrorist Attacks upon the United States*, authorized ed. (New York: Norton, 2004), 59–73, 190–91.

2. Pew Global Attitudes Project, *The Great Divide: How Westerners and Muslims View Each Other* (Washington, DC: Pew Research Center, 2006), 1, http://pew global.org.

3. Ibid., 21.

4. Pew Forum on Religion and Public Life, *Public Expresses Mixed Views of Islam, Mormonism* (Washington, DC: Pew Research Center, 2007), 1–2, http://pew forum.org.

5. The poll data can be found at *"Washington Post*–ABC News Poll," *Washington Post*, conducted March 26–29, 2009, www.washingtonpost.com. Also see Jon Cohen and Jennifer Agiesta, "Most in Poll Back Outreach to Muslims," *Washington Post*, April 6, 2009, A10; Anthony H. Cordesman, "ABC News/*Washington Post* Poll on US Views of Islam: Key Trends," *Center for Strategic and International Studies*, April 22, 2009, http://csis.org.

6. Quoted in Mauri' Saalakhan, *Islam and Terrorism: Myth vs. Reality*, 2nd ed. (Silver Spring, MD: Awakening, 2007), 249.

7. Gustave LeBon in his book *La civilization des Arabes, Livres II: Origines de la puissance des Arabes* (Paris, 1884), 121, http://classiques.uqac.ca. Also cited by the Grand Mufti of Egypt, Shaykh Ali Gomaa, in an article titled "Questions from America" published in six installments in *Al Ahram*, an Arabic daily newspaper. Sheikh Ali Gomaa, "Questions from America Part 2," *Al-Ahram Arabic Daily*, April 3, 2006, 11. Also see Common Ground News Service, www.sfcg.org. More recently, in an article entitled "Why the West Craves Materialism & Why the East Sticks to Religion," Imran Khan, a well-known Pakistani politician, notes that "no Muslim missionaries or armies ever went to Malaysia or Indonesia. The people converted to Islam due to the high principles and impeccable character of the Muslim traders."

8. Indicative of this religious preference is the fact that non-Muslims generally do not enjoy full equality of rights with Muslims in Muslim-majority countries. Saudi Arabia offers one of the more glaring examples. See Bureau of Democracy, Human Rights, and Labor, *Annual Report on International Religious Freedom: Saudi Arabia* (Washington, DC: Government Printing Office, 2009), U.S. State Department, www.state.gov.

9. There have been a number of such declarations against terrorists dating from the 1999 Afghan clerics' fatwa against bin Laden to the present by clerics from North America and overseas. See Sheila Musaji, "Muslim Voices Against Extremism and Terrorism—Part 1—Fatwas," *American Muslim*, May 5, 2010, www.theamericanmuslim.org. Also see Islamic Society of North America (ISNA), "Against Terrorism and Religious Extremism: Muslim Position and Responsibilities," www.isna.net. A particularly important declaration was that of Tahir ul-Qadri, a Pakistani Sufi sheikh, who released a 600-page fatwa on March 2, 2010, that totally discredited the ideology of terrorist groups who refer back to the Qur'an and Sunnah. This fatwa is significant because of its comprehensive, in-depth approach to addressing the dictates and nuances of Islamic scripture in proving that suicide bombers are nothing more than common criminals. "Islam: A Fatwa Against Religious Justifications for Islamic Terrorism," *Asia News*, March 10, 2010, www.speroforum.com. For prominent Sunni and Shia religious leader fatwas, see The Amman Message, www.ammanmessage.com.

10. In Moorish Spain, the Muslim rulers applied the literal tolerance of the Qur'an toward Judaism and Christianity and created an environment for cooperation and creativity within which ancient knowledge was preserved and pioneering breakthroughs in the arts and sciences were facilitated. While Europe during that period generally embraced ignorance and superstition, the Moors promoted the scholarship that prepared the way for the Italian Renaissance.

11. Gracie Davie, *Religion in Britain since 1945: Believing Without Belonging* (Oxford: Blackwell, 1994).

12. Kirsten Verclas, *Religion and Its Impact on Foreign Policy in the United States and Germany: Similarities and Differences*, AICGS Issue Brief 20 (February 2008), www.aicgs.org.

13. Ibid.

14. Karin L. Johnston, *Religion and Politics: The European Debate*, AICGS Issue Brief 15 (May 2007), 1, www.aicgs.org.

15. Integration began early in the United States when Roger Williams founded the state of Rhode Island in 1636 to provide a home for people of all faiths to live in peace.

16. Johnston, *Religion and Politics*, 5.

17. Dalia Mogahed, "Muslim Americans: An In-Depth Analysis through Gallup Polling" (speech, Rumi Forum, Washington, DC, April 21, 2009), www.rumiforum.org.

18. Ed Husain, interview by Krista Tippett, "Reflections of a Former Islamist Extremist," *Speaking of Faith*, NPR, December 7, 2007, http://speakingoffaith.publicradio.org.

19. According to the CIA 2010 World Factbook, fertility rates are 1.97, 1.42, and 1.32 for France, Germany, and Spain respectively. The average fertility rate of all countries in the EU is 1.5.

20. Pew Forum on Religion and Public Life, *An Uncertain Road: Muslims and the Future of Europe* (Washington, DC: Pew Research Center, 2004), 1, http://pew forum.org.

21. Mark Steyn, *America Alone: The End of the World as We Know It* (Washington, DC: Regnery, 2008), ix.

22. Pew Forum on Religion and Public Life, *Mapping the Global Muslim Population* (Washington, DC: Pew Research Center, 2009), 6, 21, http://pew forum.org.

23. Ibid., 21.

24. Esther Pan, "Q&A: Islam and Europe," *New York Times,* July 14, 2005, http://www.nytimes.com.

25. Quoted in Steyn, *America Alone,* 35–36.

26. Quoted in ibid., 39–40.

27. Bruce Bawer, *While Europe Slept: How Radical Islam is Destroying the West from Within* (New York: Doubleday, 2006), 33.

28. Quoted in Oriana Fallaci, *The Force of Reason* (New York: Rizzoli International, 2005), 56.

29. World Economic Forum, *Islam and the West: Annual Report on the State of Dialogue* (Geneva: World Economic Forum, 2008), 25.

30. Dr. Rowan Williams, "Civil and Religious Law in England: A Religious Perspective" (lecture, Royal Courts of Justice, London, UK, February 7, 2008), www.archbishopofcanterbury.org.

31. Steyn, *America Alone,* 77.

32. Ibid., xvi.

33. Ibid., 16.

34. Ibid., 197.

35. Bawer, *While Europe Slept,* 33.

36. Ibid., 20.

37. Ibid., 19, 26, and 56.

38. Steyn, *America Alone,* 83.

39. Shenaz Ahmeda et al., "Thalassaemia Carrier Testing in Pakistani Adults: Behaviour, Knowledge and Attitudes," *Community Genetics* 5, no. 2 (2002): 121.

40. Bawer, *While Europe Slept,* 18.

41. Edward Cody, "Lawmakers in Belgium to Ban Full-Face Veils," *Washington Post,* April 30, 2010, A8.

42. World Economic Forum, *Islam and the West,* 47.

43. Chelsea J. Carter, "Air and Allah," *Times West Virginian,* July 7, 2007, http://timeswv.com.

44. Steyn, *America Alone,* 70.

45. Ibid., 82.

46. "Harvard Sets Women-Only Hours for Gym, Complying With Muslim Students' Request," *Fox News,* March 2, 2008, www.foxnews.com.

47. Robert Spencer, *Stealth Jihad: How Radical Islam is Subverting America without Guns or Bombs* (Washington, DC: Regnery, 2008), 168.

48. Steyn, *America Alone,* xxv.

49. Walter Clarke and Jeffrey Herbst, "Somalia and the Future of Humanitarian Intervention," *Foreign Affairs* 75, no. 2 (1996), www.foreignaffairs.com.

50. Charles Krauthammer, "Outreach, Yes. Apology, No.," *Washington Post,* January 30, 2009, A19.

51. John L. Esposito and Dalia Mogahed, *Who Speaks for Islam? What a Billion Muslims Really Think* (New York: Gallup Press, 2007), 158.

52. Ibid., 61.

53. Ibid., 87.

54. Ibid., 156.

55. Ibid., 89 (quote), 159 (concept).

56. WorldPublicOpinion.org, *Public Opinion in Iran and America on Key International Issues* (WorldPublicOpinion.org, April 2008), 9–10, www.sfcg.org.

57. Pew Research Center, *Muslim Americans: Middle Class and Mostly Mainstream* (Washington, DC: Pew Research Center, 1997), 2, http://pewresearch.org.

58. Esposito and Mogahed, *Who Speaks for Islam*, 155.

59. Gary Langer, "Most Back Outreach to Muslim Nations, but Suspicion and Unfamiliarity Persist," *ABC News*, April 5, 2009, http://abcnews.go.com.

60. Bobby Ghosh, "America's Islam Problem," *Time* 176, no. 9 (2010), 26.

61. Ibid., 23.

62. Barack Obama, "Inaugural Address" (speech, Capitol Building, Washington, DC, January 21, 2009), www.whitehouse.gov.

63. Barack Obama, interview by Hisham Melham, Al-Arabiya, January 29, 2009, www.alarabiya.net.

64. Matt Apuzzo, "Not All Terrorism: Obama Tries to Change Subject," Associated Press, April 7, 2010, www.google.com/hostednews/ap.

65. Esposito and Mogahed, *Who Speaks for Islam*, 154–55.

66. Leadership Group on U.S.-Muslim Engagement, *Changing Course: A New Direction for U.S. Relations with the Muslim World* (Washington DC: Search for Common Ground and the Consensus Building Institute, 2008), 85.

67. World Economic Forum, *Islam and the West*, 58.

68. Ibid.

CHAPTER 5

1. Samuel P. Huntington, *The Clash of Civilizations and the Remaking of World Order* (New York: Simon & Schuster, 2003), 20.

2. Ibid., 316–21.

3. Ibid., 320.

4. Ibid., 47.

5. Daniel Fickel, e-mail message to his uncle David Ard expressing his personal opinion, September 27, 2006.

6. Canon Andrew White, "Iraq Five Years On," e-mail message to Foundation for Relief and Reconciliation in the Middle East mailing list, March 19, 2008.

7. Lt. Col. Mike Bush, e-mail message to author, June 4, 2010.

8. Douglas Johnston and Brian Cox, "Faith-Based Diplomacy and Preventive Engagement," in *Faith-Based Diplomacy: Trumping Realpolitik*, ed. Douglas Johnston (New York: Oxford University Press, 2003), 15–16.

9. Alauddin Masood, "Sowing Intolerance, Reaping Violence," *Weekly Pulse* (Pakistan), September 10–16, 2010, 7.

10. John Lillywhite, "Cultural Diplomacy and the Religion Question," *Cultural Diplomacy News*, May 9, 2008, www.culturaldiplomacynews.org.

11. This conversation was related firsthand by a Pakistani American friend of the author who was working in the area at the time and who asked to remain

anonymous. His observations are consistent with a comment by a former U.S. senior career official responsible for U.S. economic assistance to Afghanistan: "The principal provider of U.S. economic assistance, the U.S. Agency for International Development, is severely constrained in Afghanistan by security rules that tolerate no risk for our Foreign Service officers. They are rarely allowed outside the fortress-like U.S. Embassy in Kabul. When they get out, to attend a meeting or visit the site of a project financed by USAID, they are often surrounded by heavily-armed security personnel who make it virtually impossible to interact with the Afghan people they are helping." Mark Ward, "An Afghan Aid Disconnect," *Washington Post*, December 26, 2008, www.washingtonpost.com.

12. Mohammed Abu-Nimer, *Nonviolence and Peace Building in Islam: Theory and Practice* (Gainesville: University Press of Florida, 2003), 93.

13. Ibid.

14. Ibid., 97.

15. Ibid., 100.

16. Qur'an 5:13, trans. Abdullah Yusuf Ali (Hertfordshire: Wordsworth Editions, 2000), 83.

17. Marc Gopin, *Holy War, Holy Peace: How Religion Can Bring Peace to the Middle East* (New York: Oxford University Press, 2005), 136.

18. Abu-Nimer, *Nonviolence and Peace Building*, 108.

19. Ibid., 94–95.

20. "Rwanda to Use Traditional Justice in '94 Killings," *New York Times*, October 7, 2001, www.nytimes.com.

21. Toran Hansen, *The Gacaca Tribunals in Post-Genocide Rwanda* (St. Paul, MN: Center for Restorative Justice and Peacemaking, 2005), 2, www.cehd.umn.edu.

22. National Security Archive, "CC CPSU Letter on Afghanistan," George Mason University, www.gdw.edu. Also see Svetlana Savranskaya, "Known Knowns," *Harper's Magazine*, June 2009, 24.

23. Adm. Charles Abbot (address, European Command Military Chiefs Chaplains Conference, Vienna, 1999).

24. Lt. Gen. Peter Chiarelli, quoted in "HTS Overview," U.S. Army, http://humanterrainsystem.army.mil.

25. The Defense Department's establishment of the Foreign Area Officers (FAO) Program in 2005 represents a major step forward, but it has thus far been a halting step, with only spotty coverage in those geographic areas of greatest importance to U.S. national security.

CHAPTER 6

1. John Keegan, *Intelligence in War: The Value and Limitations of What the Military Can Learn about the Enemy* (Toronto: Vintage Canada, 2004), 319.

2. *Elwell Evangelical Dictionary*, "Christian Fundamentalism—General Information" (by C. T. McIntire), http://mb-soft.com/believe/text/fundamen.htm. For more information, see Bradley Longfield, "For Church and Country: The Fundamentalist-Modernist Conflict in the Presbyterian Church," *Journal of Presbyterian History* 78, no. 1 (2000): 36–50.

3. Qur'an 3:84, trans. Mohammed Marmaduke Pickthall (New York: Mentor Books, 1955), 69.

4. According to the International Crisis Group, "Political Islamists criticize or at least dissociate themselves from Salafis primarily on the grounds that Salafis are excessively preoccupied with individual behavior and thus distract the attention of Muslims from more urgent issues." International Crisis Group, "Understanding Islamism," *Middle East/North Africa Report*, 37 (March 2005): 4, www.crisisgroup.org.

5. These disputes were ultimately resolved by the Supreme Court, which sided with the Amish on both counts.

6. "Admiral: Troops Alone Will Not Yield Victory in Afghanistan," *CNN.com*, September 10, 2008, www.cnn.com.

7. It was easier to offer objective evidence that capitalism provides a better life than communism than it will be to show that living peacefully will lead to a better afterlife.

8. "Editorial: A Road Safety Prayer for Yom Kippur," *Jerusalem Post*, September 16, 2010, www.jpost.com.

9. International Crisis Group, "Understanding Islam," i.

10. As stated in the National Defense Strategy for 2008, "Victory will include discrediting extremist ideology, creating fissures between and among extremists groups." Robert M. Gates, *National Defense Strategy* (Washington, DC: Department of Defense, 2008), 9.

11. "Views Improve Sharply in Afghanistan, Though Criticisms of the U.S. Stay High," ABC News/BBC/ARD Poll, *ABC News*, January 11, 2010, http://abcnews.go.com.

12. John W. McDonald, "Today's Conflicts Demand a Spiritual Approach," *For a Change* 7, no. 4 (1994): 18.

13. Country teams assist ambassadors in the coordination of U.S. foreign policy when engaging allies, partners, and competitor countries at state and local levels.

14. Joseph J. Collins and Gabrielle D. Bowdoin, *Beyond Unilateral Economic Sanctions: Better Alternatives for U.S. Foreign Policy* (Washington, DC: CSIS Press, 1999), 1, 6, 8. Also found in the CSIS Panel Report by Douglas Johnston and Sidney Weintraub, *Altering U.S. Sanctions Policy: Final Report of the CSIS Project on Unilateral Economic Sanctions* (Washington, DC: CSIS Press, 1999).

15. This will be even more true in the future as our military doctrine for guerrilla warfare shifts to a more restrained use of force to protect innocent civilians. The increased U.S. casualties that are likely to result could become increasingly unacceptable over time. See Greg Jaffe, "Joint Chiefs Chairman Mullen Outlines a More Restrained Art of War," *Washington Post*, March 5, 2010, A6.

CHAPTER 7

1. A well-known French author whose eight-part novel series, *Les Thibault*, earned him the 1937 Nobel Prize in Literature.

2. John W. McDonald, "Today's Conflicts Demand a Spiritual Approach," *For a Change* 7, no. 4 (1994): 18.

3. An excellent Muslim rationale and framework for interreligious dialogue developed by Qazi Abdul Qadeer Khamosh, Chairman of the Muslim Christian Federation International in Pakistan and indigenous Wahhabi partner of the

International Center for Religion and Diplomacy (ICRD) in its project to enhance Pakistan's madrasas, can be found at the following link: http://www.icrd.org/index.php?option=com_content&task=view&id=112&Itemid=123.

4. The Policy Coordinating Committee (PCC) is composed of representatives from the Departments of State, Defense, Homeland Security, and Treasury, in addition to the intelligence community, U.S. AID, and others. See Policy Coordinating Committee, *U.S. National Strategy for Public Diplomacy and Strategic Communication* (Washington, DC: Government Printing Office, 2007), U.S. Department of State, www.state.gov. See also James K. Glassman, interview by Michael Moran, "State's Glassman Discusses Public Diplomacy for the 21st Century," July 2, 2008, www.america.gov.

5. Policy Coordinating Committee, *U.S. National Strategy*, 3.

6. In Islam, *iftar* refers to evening meals throughout the month of Ramadan that commemorate the end of the daily fasts.

7. Policy Coordinating Committee, *U.S. National Strategy*, 18.

8. This observation holds true on a more general level as well. As noted by former Ambassador Henry Crumpton in a speech on "smart power" at the Center for Strategic and International Studies in January 2008, the State Department is not built for engagement with nonstate actors; it is built to engage foreign ministries. Prior to his assignment as State Department Coordinator for Counterterrorism, Ambassador Crumpton was the CIA operative who orchestrated the overthrow of the Taliban government in Afghanistan following 9/11 (and thus knows firsthand the importance and influence of nonstate actors).

9. Edward Luttwak, "The Missing Dimension," in *Religion, the Missing Dimension of Statecraft*, ed. Douglas Johnston and Cynthia Sampson (New York: Oxford University Press, 1994), 16.

10. Madeleine Albright, *The Mighty & the Almighty: Reflections on America, God, and World Affairs* (New York: Harper Collins, 2006), 76.

11. Douglas M. Johnston, "The Case for a Religion Attaché," *Foreign Service Journal* (February 2002), www.afsa.org.

12. Ibid.

13. Kenton Keith, e-mail message to John W. Kiser, August 27, 2008.

14. "The State Department already faces a chronic shortage of FSOs for field positions; indeed, the Director General of the Foreign Service recently felt compelled to direct overseas posts to identify 10% of their bid-able positions for non-filling. With respect to PD positions specifically, according to official Department analysis, the shortage is particularly acute at the mid-levels, and the vacancy rate has increased in recent years. In other words, there are not enough PD officers, particularly at the mid-levels, to fill the existing job slots." See United States Advisory Commission on Public Diplomacy, *Getting the People Part Right: A Report on the Human Resources Dimension of U.S. Public Diplomacy* (Washington, DC: Government Printing Office, 2008), 28, http://hsgac.senate.gov.

15. Christopher Midura (then Acting Director, Office of Policy, Planning, and Resources, Under Secretary for Public Diplomacy and Public Affairs), interview by ICRD researcher, October 2, 2008.

16. Hugh Wilford, "Labour Diplomacy and Cold War Britain," *Journal of Contemporary History* 37, no. 1 (2002): 45–65.

17. Neil M. Johnson, "Oral History Interview with Philip Kaiser," June 11, 1987, Harry S. Truman Library and Museum, www.trumanlibrary.org.

18. United States Government Accountability Office, *Public Diplomacy: State Department Efforts to Engage Muslim Audiences Lack Certain Communication Elements and Face Significant Challenges,* report to the Chairman, Subcommittee on Science, the Departments of State, Justice, and Commerce, and Related Agencies, Committee on Appropriations, House of Representatives, May 2006, 36–37. http:// gao.gov.

19. Office of the Spokesman, United States Mission to International Organizations in Vienna, *Beginning to Transform the State Department to Meet the Challenges of the 21st Century,* fact sheet, July 29, 2005, http://vienna.usmission.gov.

20. Armen Hareyan, "French Foreign Ministry Establishes Religious Department," *Huliq News,* July 25, 2009, www.huliq.com.

21. Anne O'Leary (former senior recruiter and senior FSO, U.S. Department of State), interview by ICRD researcher, March 18, 2009.

22. Anne O'Leary, interview by ICRD researcher, April 12, 2007.

23. John L. Iskander, e-mail messages to ICRD researcher, August 24, 2009, and September 9, 2009.

24. FSI is currently developing an expanded Human Rights and Democracy course, which, among other things, will help prepare diplomats for promoting religious freedom and engaging more effectively with religious communities. These same themes will constitute the core of a new stand-alone course on religion and foreign policy that is also being developed.

25. Keith e-mail to Kiser.

26. This was a recent recommendation of the U.S. Advisory Commission on Public Diplomacy for mid- to senior-level PD officers. See *Getting the People Part Right,* 28.

27. To understand why this level of inquiry is needed, one has only to imagine how misleading it would be to impose some generic template of Islam as an overlay onto Iraqi Sunnis, Iranian Shiites, Indian Sufis, or Chinese Muslims. The resulting insights would be problematic at best. See John D. Carlson, "Winning Souls and Minds: The Military's Religion Problem and the Global War on Terror," *Journal of Military Ethics* 7, no. 2 (2008): 91–92.

28. Ryan J. Maher, "A Priest Walks Into Qatar and . . . ," *Washington Post,* July 20, 2008, B2. Father Ryan goes on to note that:

a person of Muslim faith and a person of Christian faith engaged in honest conversation about religion are not like two fans pulling for their respective teams. They are more like two men in love with the same woman, each trying to express, safeguard and be faithful to his relationship with his beloved. Love brings with it complexities that football does not.

29. Robert Gates, address to the Association of American Universities, Washington, DC, April 14, 2008.

CHAPTER 8

1. It has reached the point where some Americans fear that the erosion over time of religion's constitutional prerogatives and governmental support in the political sphere is merely a way station en route to religion's eventual extinction.

2. U.S. Constitution, First Amendment.

3. Michael Kessler, "Establishment Clause Doesn't Limit Foreign Policy," *On Faith* (blog), *Washington Post*, February 26, 2010, http://newsweek.washington post.com.

4. Maryann Cusimano Love, *Beyond Sovereignty: Issues for a Global Agenda*, 4th ed. (Belmont, CA: Wadsworth, 2010), 205.

5. Col. Dave West, Command Chaplain SOCCENT, e-mail message to author, June 18, 2008.

6. Mindful of church/state separation in the West, General Petraeus was equally aware of the links between mosque and state in the Middle East more generally and in Iraq in particular. Accordingly, he encouraged engagement with religious authorities in the same way that he directed engagement with other community/national leaders. The senior Multi-National Force chaplain was assigned to oversee this engagement and gave reports on its progress once a week during the daily battle updates. See Col. Steven Boylan (U.S. Army, former Public Affairs Officer for General Petraeus), e-mail message to author, February 27, 2009.

7. Intense discussions between these leaders led to a signed accord on reconciliation and a mutual condemnation of the violence. Lamar Griffin, "Religious Leader Liaison and the Emerging Role for Chaplains in Shaping Full Spectrum Operations," *The Army Chaplaincy* (Winter/Spring 2009), 46–47, www.usachcs.army.mil.

8. Daniel L. Dreisbach, "Letter from Thomas Jefferson to the Danbury Baptist Association, Jan. 1, 1802," *Thomas Jefferson and the Wall of Separation Between Church and State* (New York: New York University Press, 2002), 148.

9. John H. Mansfield, "The Religion Clauses of the First Amendment and Foreign Relations," *DePaul Law Review* 1 (Fall 1986): 1–3, 25–39.

10. Ibid., 36.

11. Jessica Powley Hayden, "Mullahs on a Bus: The Establishment Clause and U.S. Foreign Aid," *Georgetown Law Journal* 95 (2007): 199.

12. *Lamont et al. v. Woods and Santos*, 948 F.2d 825 (2nd Cir. 1991).

13. Alex Luchenitser et al., "Hein, One Year Later: The Future of Church-State Litigation" (panel discussion, Pew Forum, Washington, DC, June 18, 2008), Pew Forum on Religion and Public Life, http://pewforum.org.

14. Ibid.

15. Ibid.

16. U.S. Agency for International Development, *Participation by Religious Organizations in USAID Programs: Final Rule* (Washington, DC: National Archives and Records Administration, 2004).

17. Colum Lynch, "In Fighting Radical Islam, Tricky Cause for U.S. Aid: Separation of Church and State at Issue," *Washington Post*, July 30, 2009, A12.

18. Based on CSIS interviews with Bureau of International Programs officials, February 16, 2007; Liora Danan and Alice Hunt, *Mixed Blessings: U.S. Engagement with Religion in Conflict-Prone Settings* (Washington, DC: CSIS Press, 2007), 44.

19. U.S. Department of State, *U.S. National Strategy for Public Diplomacy and Strategic Communication* (Washington DC: Policy Coordinating Committee, 2007), 25, www.state.gov.

20. Lynch, "In Fighting Radical Islam."

21. *Lamont et al. v. Woods and Santos*, 948 F.2d 825 (2nd Cir. 1991).

22. "1st Amendment: The Opening Phrase," Revolutionary War and Beyond, www.revolutionary-war-and-beyond.com.

CHAPTER 9

1. Georgetown University, *The Foreign Service in 2001* (Washington, DC: Institute for the Study of Diplomacy, School of Foreign Service, 1992), 4–5.

2. Richard L. Armitage and Joseph S. Nye Jr., "Stop Getting Mad, America. Get Smart," *Washington Post,* December 9, 2007, B3.

3. International Commission on Intervention and State Sovereignty, *What's New: The Responsibility to Protect* (Ottawa, ON: International Development Research Centre, 2001), http://www.iciss.ca/menu-en.asp.

4. The NGO World Religions for Peace has established more than 70 such councils around the world and can provide helpful guidance in implementing such initiatives.

5. Andrew Abbott, *Methods of Discovery: Heuristics for the Social Sciences* (New York: W. W. Norton, 2004).

6. John Lofland et al., *Analyzing Social Settings: A Guide to Qualitative Observation and Analysis,* 4th ed. (Belmont, CA: Wadsworth, 2006).

7. HEAT courses are provided in the United Kingdom and United States by former elite military and law enforcement personnel with extensive experience in high-risk, hostile environments.

8. Ibid.

9. Reported in earlier article by the author titled "We Neglect Religion at Our Peril," *U.S. Naval Institute Proceedings,* January 2002, 50 (based on author's conversation with Admiral Owens in 1995).

10. Andrea Kathryn Talentino, "Bosnia," in *The Costs of Conflict: Prevention and Cure in the Global Arena,* ed. Michael Brown and Richard Rosecrance (New York: Rowman & Littlefield, 1999), 27.

11. This refers to the Serbian tactic of sending thugs into villages to incite violence in order to justify occupying the villages and enforcing martial law.

12. Berkeley Center for Religion, Peace, and World Affairs, *Bosnia: Ethno-Religious Nationalisms in Conflict,* Case Study Series (Washington, DC: Georgetown University, 2009), 4.

13. "Muslims" were recognized as a Yugoslav nationality in the 1960s. In 1993 the term "Bosniak" became the national name for Bosnian Muslims. Economics Institute Sarajevo, *Human Development Report: Bosnia and Herzegovina* (United Nations Development Programme, 2002), 112, http://hdr.undp.org.

14. CIA World Factbook: Bosnia and Herzegovina, April 2010, https://www.cia.gov.

15. "Education (Bosnia and Herzegovina)," Europa World Online, Laurence McKinley Gould Library, www.europaworld.com.

16. Steven Woehrel, *Bosnia: Current Issues and U.S. Policy,* Congressional Research Service, August 27, 2009, 11, www.fas.org.

17. Bosnian Serbs have also expressed interest in the possibility of merging with Serbia.

18. Ibid., 5.

19. A view expressed by Valentin Inzko, the Austrian official who currently serves as the High Representative, as reported by Craig Whitlock, "Old Troubles Threaten Again in Bosnia," *Washington Post,* August 23, 2009, www.washingtonpost.com.

20. Patrice McMahon and Jon Western, "The Death of Dayton," *Foreign Affairs* 88, no. 5 (2009), 73.

21. Dan Bilefsky, "Islamic Revival Tests Bosnia's Secular Cast," *New York Times*, December 26, 2008, www.nytimes.com.

22. Ibid.

CHAPTER 10

1. Geneive Abdo, "America's Muslims Aren't as Assimilated as You Think," *Washington Post*, August 27, 2006, B3.

2. Shada Islam, "Muslims and the Tale of Two Continents," *Yale Global Online*, September 14, 2007, http://yaleglobal.yale.edu.

3. Pew Forum on Religion and Public Life, *U.S. Religious Landscape Survey: Religious Affiliation: Diverse and Dynamic* (Washington, DC: Pew Research Center, 2008), 189, www.religions.pewforum.org.

4. Salam al-Marayati, "America's Muslim Ghettos," *Washington Post*, August 15, 2005, A15.

5. Anna Quindlen, "American Forgetting," *Newsweek*, September 17, 2007, 86.

6. Imam Siraj Wahaj, "a charismatic intellectual from the Masjid Al-Taqwa mosque in Brooklyn," in a conversation with Muslim journalist Geneive Abdo, "A More Islamic Islam," *Washington Post*, March 17, 2007, www.washingtonpost.com.

7. It is important to acknowledge the desirability of appointing qualified American Muslims to U.S. ambassadorial posts in Muslim-majority countries where they will command too much respect to be ignored, demonized, or marginalized. By the same token, American Muslim leaders have said their communities will not be able to serve as credible public ambassadors until they feel that the government is giving their views greater weight in the policy process.

8. Imad-ad-Dean Ahmad, ed., *Directory of Policy Experts on Islamic Studies and Muslim Affairs* (Herndon, VA: International Institute for Islamic Thought, 2009).

9. Ed Husain, interview by Krista Tippett, "Reflections of a Former Islamist Extremist," *Speaking of Faith*, NPR, December 7, 2007, http://speakingoffaith.publicradio.org.

10. David Forte, "Islam's Trajectory," *Real Clear Politics*, August 25, 2006, www.realclearpolitics.com.

11. Ibid.

12. Husain, "Reflections."

CHAPTER 11

1. This team, which was led by the International Center for Religion and Diplomacy (ICRD), included Richard Ruffin, then Executive Director of Moral Rearmament USA; Donald Shriver, President Emeritus of Union Theological Seminary; Joseph Montville, then Director of the Preventive Diplomacy Program at the Center for Strategic and International Studies; and Douglas Johnston, President of ICRD.

2. The line community includes those personnel in the military chain of command who are directly responsible for the war-fighting function. Other personnel with responsibilities that are more tangential to the combat mission, such as chaplains, lawyers, physicians, or civil engineers, are considered to be in the staff (as opposed to line) component.

3. Even among those chaplains who are volunteers, it is essential to recognize and accommodate through training the fact that chaplains are not trained negotiators, nor do they typically speak the language or qualify as cultural experts wherever they are stationed. Finally, despite the fact that chaplains have a basic ability to interact with clergy of different faiths, not every volunteer will be temperamentally suited to engage local religious leaders.

4. Douglas M. Johnston, "We Neglect Religion at Our Peril," *U.S. Naval Institute Proceedings* 128 (January 2002): 50–52.

5. Daniel B. Jorgensen, *Air Force Chaplains: Volume 1—The Service of Chaplains to Army Air Units, 1917–1946* (Washington, DC: Superintendent of Documents, U. S. Government Printing Office, 1961), 5.

6. Encyclopedia Britannica Online, s.v. "Adhémar of Monteil," www.britannica.com.

7. Thomas F. Madden, *The New Concise History of the Crusades* (Lanham, MD: Rowman & Littlefield, 2005), 31.

8. David S. Bachrach, "The Medieval Chaplain and His Duties," in *The Sword of the Lord: Military Chaplains from the First to the Twenty-First Century*, ed. Doris L. Bergen (Notre Dame, IN: University of Notre Dame Press, 2004), 69–70.

9. Doris L. Bergen, "Introduction," in *The Sword of the Lord*, 7–8.

10. William Jackson Johnstone, *George Washington, the Christian* (New York: Abingdon Press, 1919), 69.

11. Ibid., 217–18.

12. Derek Davis, *Religion and the Continental Congress, 1774–1789* (New York: Oxford University Press, 2000), 80.

13. John W. Brinsfield, "The Army Chaplaincy and World Religions: From Individual Ministries to Chaplain Corps Doctrine," *Army Chaplaincy* (Winter–Spring 2009): 17.

14. Herbert L. Bergsma, *Chaplains with Marines in Vietnam, 1962–1971* (Washington, DC: History and Museums Division Headquarters, 1985), 151.

15. Based on their position and training, chaplains are better suited to serving as "bridge builders" rather than negotiators.

16. *Military Chaplains as Peace Builders: Embracing Indigenous Religions in Stability Operations*, a report published by the U.S. Army Peacekeeping and Stability Operations Institute, concluded after analyzing competing categories of personnel that chaplains were the staff element best suited for religious leader engagement based on their training, skills, credentials (in the eyes of the local population), and accessibility to the combatant commander. In essence, the multifaith experiences of military chaplains, coupled with their considerable interpersonal skills, are attributes that make them particularly well suited to the complex challenges of religious engagement.

17. Joint Chiefs of Staff, *Religious Affairs in Joint Operations*, JP 1-05 (2009), III-5.

18. A good example cited by Cdr. George Adams was a collaborative effort by Army chaplain Eric Eliason (with the 1st Battalion, 19th Special Forces Group) and Afghan elders and imams to renovate 26 mosques—an initiative that both discredited Taliban and al Qaeda propaganda and won the trust of the local population. USIP, "Chaplains as Liaisons with Religious Leaders," *Peaceworks*, no. 56 (2006): 9.

19. The 2009 International Military Chiefs of Chaplains Conference held in Cape Town, South Africa, February 1–6, 2009.

20. Chaplain (Lt. Col.) Ira C. Houck III, *Strategic Religious Engagement for Peace-building* (USAWC Civilian Research Project, U.S. Army War College, 2009), 15, 20, http://www.dtic.mil.

21. Exacerbating this problem is the fact that the personal religious perspective of the commander often dictates how the chaplain is utilized. Or, taking it even further (and as expressed by one senior Army chaplain), "Personal prejudice against religion among commanders is shameful but real." Chester Lanious, e-mail message to author, June 8, 2009.

22. Paul R. Wrigley, "The Impact of Religious Belief in the Theatre of Operations," *Naval War College Review* (Spring 1996), www.dtic.mil.

23. Maj. Gen. Douglas L. Carver, "From the Chief," *Army Chaplaincy* (Winter/Spring 2009): 1. Ideally, it would also be desirable to develop future chaplain capacity relating to justice, human rights, religious tolerance, ethical engagement, and religious freedom.

24. Indicative of the challenge that awaits is the December 2007 study by Auburn University's Center for the Study of Theological Education in which 2,300 seminary graduates were asked to rank 14 areas of study in order of relevance to their professional life and work. "World religions" was ranked 13. Holly Lebowitz Rossi, "Many Mansions," *Sojourners*, September–October 2008, 34.

25. The Army is currently moving in this direction, having just added a special skill identifier (SSI) for world religion experts based on graduate-level education in the subject.

26. U.S. Navy Chaplain (Cdr.) George Adams, "Chaplains as Liaisons with Religious Leaders: Lessons from Iraq and Afghanistan," *Peaceworks*, no. 56 (2006). This article provides a rich source of anecdotes illustrating a wide range of effective chaplain involvements in Iraq and Afghanistan.

27. Based on an interview with the chaplain involved, who wished to remain anonymous. Also verified independently with other sources by the author.

28. Ibid.

29. John Proctor, "A Short History of Religious Leader Engagement Operations in Operation Iraqi Freedom" (paper presented at the 19th Expeditionary Sustainment Command, Korea, 2008), 3.

30. U.S. Army Chaplain (Lt. Col.) Scottie Lloyd, *USAWC Strategy Research Project, Chaplain Contact with Local Religious Leaders: A Strategic Support* (project submitted to U.S. Army War College, March 2005), 6, www.dtic.mil.

31. Canadian National Defense, *Called to Serve: A Strategy for the Canadian Forces Chaplaincy* (Canada: Canada National Defence, 2008), i, 5.

32. William S. Lee, Christopher Burke, and Zonna Crayne, *Military Chaplains as Peace Builders: Embracing Indigenous Religions in Stability Operations*, Cadre Paper no. 20 (Maxwell Air Force Base, AL: Air University Press, 2004), 21.

33. Ibid., 23.

34. Ibid., 16.

35. John W. Kiser, "An Algerian Microcosm: Monks, Muslims, and the Zeal of Bitterness," *Cisterian Studies Quarterly* 38, no. 3 (2003): 353.

CHAPTER 12

1. Charles Chatfield, "Intergovernmental and Nongovernmental Associations to 1945," in *Transnational Social Movements and World Politics: Solidarity Be-*

yond the State, ed. Jackie Smith, Charles Chatfield, and Ron Pagnucco (Syracuse: Syracuse University Press, 1997), 19–41.

2. Julia Berger, "Religious Non-Governmental Organizations: An Exploratory Analysis" (paper presented at a workshop on religion and international affairs for a Luce Foundation–supported project on Religion and Global Civil Society, Santa Barbara, CA, January 18–19, 2008), 3, www.global.ucsb.edu.

3. Union of International Associations (UIA) Online, 46th ed., 2009–10. "Appendix 3: Table 1a," 1511.

4. Department of the Army, *Stability Operations*, FM 3–07 (Washington D.C.: Army Headquarters, 2008), A-9.

5. "Sins of the Secular Missionaries," *Economist*, January 29, 2000, 25–27.

6. Edward Luttwak, "The Missing Dimension," in *Religion, the Missing Dimension of Statecraft*, ed. Douglas Johnston and Cynthia Sampson (New York: Oxford University Press, 1994), 37–55.

7. Monica Herz and João Pontes Nogueira, *Ecuador vs. Peru: Peacemaking Amid Rivalry* (Boulder, CO: Lynne Rienner, 2002), 47.

8. Dylan Mathews, *War Prevention Works: 50 Stories of People Resolving Conflict* (London: Oxford Research Group, 2001), 76.

9. Ibid., 76–77.

10. Ibid., 77.

11. "Peru, Ecuador Sign Historic Peace Treaty," *CNN.com*, October 26, 1998, www.cnn.com.

12. "Border Dispute Ends with Treaty," *BBC News*, October 24, 1998, http://news.bbc.co.uk.

13. "Peru, Ecuador," *CNN.com*.

14. "Peru and Ecuador Sign Border Treaty," *BBC News*, October 27, 1998, http://news.bbc.co.uk.

15. Ibid.

16. "Peru, Ecuador," *CNN.com*.

17. Mathews, *War Prevention Works*, 77.

18. Ibid.

19. The Global Partnership for the Prevention of Armed Conflict (GPPAC) is an organization dedicated to creating awareness of human rights issues, public safety, and the role of civil society in peace building that seeks to "prevent the escalation of conflict into destructive violence, at national, regional and global levels." Most notably, GPPAC fashioned a network of over 1,030 regional and international civil society organizations, all of which share the same dedication to conflict prevention and peace building. The International American Council for Voluntary International Action, also known as InterAction, is the largest coalition of U.S.-based international NGOs, including more than 175 organizations. The network seeks to (1) improve U.S. development and humanitarian assistance to the world's poor, (2) advance NGO accountability in development and humanitarian activities, and (3) further the alliance of NGOs with common agendas in order to create strategic partnerships.

20. As expressed in the 2008 National Defense Strategy, "The department should also develop . . . the institutional agility and flexibility to plan early and respond effectively alongside interdepartmental, non-governmental and international partners." Robert Gates, *National Defense Strategy* (U.S. Department of Defense, 2008), 5.

21. Andrea Bartoli, *Contributions of NGOs to Conflict Resolution Activities* (Brill Academic Publishers, forthcoming), 70–71.

22. "Afghan Aid Row Flares Ahead of Forum," *Iran Daily Newspaper*, April 4, 2005, www.iran-daily.com.

23. Abdulhaqq Abdullah, "NGOs: Another wing of the U.S. Foreign Policy," *Yemen Times*, July 18, 2006, www.yementimes.com.

24. DOD Directive 30000.05 (November 28, 2005) encourages the military service to work closely with U.S. and foreign nongovernmental organizations in conducting stability operations.

25. Joseph McMahon, *Developments in the Regulations of NGOs via Government Counter-Terrorism Measures and Policies: Policy Briefing Paper 11* (International NGO Training and Research Center, 2007), 5, www.intrac.org.

26. Ibid.

27. Laure Borgomano-Loup, *Forum Paper 2: Improving NATO-NGO Relations in Crisis Response Operations*, ed. Jean Dufourcq (Rome: NATO Defense College Academic Research Branch, 2007), 36, www.ndc.nato.int.

28. Department of the Army, A-10.

29. Caroline Brennan, "Pakistan President Musharraf Bestows Award on CRS In Recognition of Earthquake Recovery Efforts," *InterAction—Media*, July 13, 2006, www.interaction.org.

30. For more information, see BBC World Service Poll, *Evaluations of Global Institutions and Economic Conditions*, at www.worldpublicopinion.org (table on page 6 shows attitudes toward NGOs).

31. Berger, "Religious Non-Governmental Organizations," 2.

32. At one point, posters with Canon White's picture were put up around Baghdad saying "Wanted Dead or Alive." E-mail update from FRRME dated May 7, 2009.

33. "Core Principles," Foundation for Relief and Reconciliation in the Middle East, www.frrme.org.

34. Shawn Teresa Flanigan, *For the Love of God: NGOs and Religious Identity in a Violent World* (Sterling, VA: Kumarian Press, 2009).

35. John D. Carlson and Matt Correa, "How Shall We Study Religion and Conflict? Challenges and Opportunities in the Early Twenty-First Century," *Religion and World Order* 3, no. 2 (2008): 16.

36. Borgomano-Loup, *Forum Paper 2*, 37.

CHAPTER 13

1. As noted in the National Defense Strategy promulgated by the Department of Defense in June 2008, "We must display a mastery of irregular warfare comparable to that which we possess in conventional combat." Robert Gates, *National Defense Strategy* (Department of Defense, 2008), www.defense.gov.

2. Qur'an 2:190.

3. Sohail Hashmi, "Interpreting the Ethics of War and Peace" in *The Ethics of War and Peace: Religious and Secular Perspectives*, ed. Terry Nardin (Princeton: Princeton University Press, 1996), 161.

4. Qur'an 13:11.

5. Gen. 9:25–27 (New International Version). Ham, the ancestor of the Canaanites, was the youngest son of Noah. Upon learning that Ham had seen him

lying naked and drunk and had told his brothers about it, Noah cursed Ham's descendants to become the "the lowest of slaves."

6. Peter Gomes, *The Good Book: Reading the Bible with Mind and Heart* (San Francisco: Harper, 1996), 35.

7. The Awakening Movement in Iraq, a mostly Sunni Muslim force, began in western Anbar Province in 2006 when tribal leaders decided to stop fighting American forces and to cooperate with them in countering al Qaeda in Iraq. Formerly funded by the United States, Awakening members, or Sahwa, as they are called, are now on the payroll of the Iraqi government. Many believe that this movement was the most significant reason for the decline in American casualties since that time. "Awakening Movement in Iraq," *New York Times*, September 22, 2008, http://topics.nytimes.com. Also see Ahmed Ali and Dahr Jamail, "IRAQ: A New Force Called Sahwa Shows Its Muscle," *Inter Press Service*, February 13, 2008, http://ipsnews.net/news.asp.

8. John Kiser, *The Monks of Tibhirine: Faith, Love, and Terror in Algeria* (New York: St. Martin's Press, 2002), 168.

9. As reported by Nadia Aïtzia, an Algerian lawyer who observed the interview twice on local television. Kiser, *Monks of Tibhirine*, 260, 319.

10. Fouad Gouni, Algerian colonel, in conversation with John Kiser, a friend of the author, in April 2008.

11. Ibid.

12. An apostate is one who abandons allegiance to his or her religion, cause, or party.

13. Shaikh Abdul-Malik al-Jazaa'iree, *The Fataawaa of the Major Scholars on the Bloodshed in Algeria* (1999), www.salafibookstore.com.

14. Ibid.

15. The evidence was found in cell phone calls monitored by Algerian counterterror units. Gouni to Kiser, May 2008.

16. Ibid.

17. Ibid.

18. Kiser, *Monks of Tibhirine*, 140–42.

19. Although the initial results of the Yemeni prison dialogue program were highly encouraging, it was later discontinued because of increasing rates of recidivism as prisoners began to "beat the system" by feigning their rehabilitation.

20. Judith Miller, "What I Learned at 'Anti-Jihad U,'" *New York Post*, May 2, 2008, www.nypost.com.

21. Douglas Stone, lecture, U.S. Institute of Peace, Washington, DC, June 11, 2008, www.usip.org.

22. Ibid.

23. Ibid.

24. Ibid.

25. Ibid.

26. Walter Pincus, "U.S. Working to Reshape Iraqi Detainees: Moderate Muslims Enlisted to Steer Adults and Children Away from Insurgency," *Washington Post*, September 19, 2007, www.washingtonpost.com.

27. Alison St John, "S.D.-Based Commander: Major Improvements at Iraq Detention Facilities," *KPBS*, August 12, 2009, www.kpbs.org.

28. Mindy Belz, "The Long Goodbye," *World*, March 28, 2009, www.world mag.com.

29. Leila Fadel, "U.S. Cedes Last Detention Center to Iraq," *Washington Post*, July 16, 2010, A10.

30. Eric Schmitt, "Pentagon Seeks to Overhaul Prisons in Afghanistan," *New York Times*, July 19, 2009, www.nytimes.com.

31. Magdi Abdlehadi, "Saudis to Retrain 40,000 Clerics," *BBC News*, March 20, 2008, http://news.bbc.co.uk.

32. E. Glass and Y. Yehoshua, "Saudi Arabia's Anti-Terror Campaign," *BBC News*, March 20, 2008, http://www.memri.org.

33. Andrew McGregor, "Yemen and the US: Different Approaches to the War on Terrorism," *Terrorism Monitor* 5, no. 9 (2007), www.jamestown.org.

34. The Amman Message, "Summary," www.ammanmessage.com.

35. Muhammad Sayyid Tantawi served as the Grand Mufti of Egypt from 1986 to 1996 and of Al-Azhar University until his death in 2010. Grand Ayatollah Sayyid Ali al-Husayni al-Sistani is the preeminent Twelver Shia cleric in Iraq and around the world and is a notable political figure in post-invasion Iraq. Yusuf al-Qaradawi is an Egyptian Muslim scholar and lecturer best known for his television program *Shariah and Life*, which is broadcast weekly on Al Jazeera and has an estimated audience of 40 million viewers worldwide.

36. Ibid.

37. Sana Abed-Kotob, "The Accommodationists Speak: Goals and Strategies of the Muslim Brotherhood of Egypt," *International Journal of Middle East Studies* 27, no. 3 (1995): 334.

38. Sanjoy Majumder, "Muslim Scholars Decry Terrorism," *BBC News* (Delhi), February 25, 2008. http://news.bbc.co.uk.

39. David Ignatius, "A Saudi Fatwa For Moderation," *Washington Post*, June 13, 2010, www.washingtonpost.com.

40. Nic Robertson and Paul Cruickshank, "New Jihad Code Threatens al Qaeda," *CNN.com*, November 10, 2009, www.cnn.com.

41. Mark LeVine, "University Blasts in Pakistan and the Future of Islam," *Christian Science Monitor*, October 23, 2009, www.csmonitor.com.

42. Jamal Khashoggi, *Al-Watan*, December 23, 2007, quoted in E. Glass and Y. Yehoshua, "Saudi Arabia's Anti-Terror Campaign," *Middle East Media Research Institute*, February 28, 2008, www.memri.org.

43. The mortar boards and tassels one wears at graduation came out of the madrasas as have other traditions of academia, such as funding a chair in a given discipline. See "Inside the Madrasas," *New York Review of Books* 52, no. 19 (2005).

44. The ICRD does not deal with the religious core of the madrasa curriculums but assumes that doing an effective job in addressing human rights and religious tolerance will smooth some of the rough edges. Attitudinal surveys conducted by independent third-party evaluators confirm the validity of this assumption. See Douglas Johnston, Azhar Hussain, and Rebecca Cataldi, *Madrasa Enhancement and Global Security: A Model for Faith–Based Engagement* (Washington, DC: International Center for Religion and Diplomacy, 2008).

45. Craig Davis, "'A' Is for Allah, 'J' Is for Jihad," *World Policy Journal* (Spring 2002): 92–93.

46. See R. Alan King, *Twice Armed: An American Soldier's Battle for Hearts and Minds in Iraq* (St. Paul: Zenith Press, 2006) and Annia Ciezadlo, "A Scholarly Soldier Steps inside the World of Iraq's Potent Tribes," *Christian Science Monitor*, December 30, 2003. www.csmonitor.com.

47. As President Obama pointed out in his January 2009 inauguration speech, these groups will be judged on what they have built, not what they have destroyed.

CHAPTER 14

1. Guy Dinmore, "Washington Hardliners Wary of Engaging with Iran," *Financial Times,* March 16, 2004, 7; see also Meir Javedanfar, "The Grand Bargain with Iran," *Guardian* (Manchester), March 3, 2009, www.guardian.co.uk; Nicholas D. Kristof, "Diplomacy at Its Worst," *New York Times,* April 29, 2007, http://select. nytimes.com; Nicholas D. Kristof, "Iran's Proposal for a 'Grand Bargain,'" *On the Ground* (blog), *New York Times,* April 28, 2007, http://kristof.blogs.nytimes.com; Trita Parsi, "Iran the Key in US Change on Iraq," *Asia Times Online,* November 11, 2006, www.atimes.com; "Washington 'Snubbed Iran Offer,'" *BBC News,* January 18, 2007, http://news.bbc.co.uk.

2. James F. Dobbins, *After the Taliban: Nation-Building in Afghanistan* (Dulles, VA: Potomac Books, 2008), 121. U.S. Treasury Secretary Paul O' Neill, who also attended the conference, was indirectly approached by the Iranians with this same offer through Madam Ogata, head of the Japanese aid agency, who was also in attendance.

3. Ibid., 83. Ironically, in official discussions relating to the proposed Constitution for Afghanistan, it was the Iranians who took the lead in ensuring that the new Afghan government would be required to (1) hold democratic elections and (2) cooperate with the international community in combating terrorism. In addition to an offer in March 2002 to work under the United States in raising and training an Afghan national army, Iran also pledged almost twice as much financial assistance to Afghan reconstruction as the United States.

4. Ibid., 149.

5. Glenn Kessler, "In 2003, U.S. Spurned Iran's Offer of Dialogue," *Washington Post,* June 18, 2006, www.washingtonpost.com.

6. Since January 2007, former Secretaries of State George Shultz and Henry Kissinger, former Secretary of Defense William Perry, and former Senator (and Chairman of the Armed Services Committee) Sam Nunn have collectively lobbied for a world free of nuclear weapons. In doing so, they've outlined several steps toward achieving this goal, which include securing and reducing the current size of nuclear arsenals, eliminating short-range nuclear weapons, ratifying the Comprehensive Test Ban Treaty, monitoring more closely compliance with the Non-Proliferation Treaty, reducing uranium enrichment, eliminating fissile material production for weapons, and renewing efforts toward reducing regional conflicts that could breed new nuclear powers. George P. Schultz et al., "A World Free of Nuclear Weapons," Opinion, *Wall Street Journal,* January 4, 2007, and "Toward a Nuclear-Free World," Opinion, *Wall Street Journal,* January 15, 2008.

7. Theodore Roosevelt, *The Roosevelt Policy: Speeches, Letters and State Papers Relating to Corporate Wealth and Closely Allied Topics,* ed. William Griffith (Harvard University: Current Literature, 1919).

8. John Winthrop, "A Model of Christian Charity" (sermon on board the *Arbella* en route to America, 1630).

9. Robert K. Greenleaf was a "lifelong student of organization" and served in the field of management research at AT&T for 38 years. See Robert K. Greenleaf,

Servant-Leadership: A Journey into the Nature of Legitimate Power and Greatness (Ramsey, NJ: Paulist Press: 1977), 13–14.

10. For entire text, see "Address to the Cherokee Nation, August 19, 1796" in *George Washington: Writings* (New York: Library of America, 1997).

11. The term *smart power* refers to a strategy that "balances our hard (coercive) power with our soft (attractive) power." Richard L. Armitage and Joseph S. Nye Jr., "Stop Getting Mad, America. Get Smart," *Washington Post,* December 9, 2007, B3.

12. See UN Charter, Article 1; International Covenant on Economic, Social, and Cultural Rights, Article 1; International Covenant on Civil and Political Rights, Article 1.

13. James J. Summers, "The Right of Self-Determination and Nationalism in International Law," *International Journal on Minority and Group Rights* 12 (2005): 325–54.

14. See list of secessionist movements at www.constitution.org/cs_separ.htm.

15. Eyal Benvenisti, *The International Law of Occupation* (Princeton: Princeton University Press, 2004), 5.

16. Ibid., 9.

17. Ibid., 14.

18. Melissa Patterson, writing in the *Harvard International Law Journal,* defines *debellatio* as "the ancient doctrine by which a military victor takes title to territory in which the defeated government has ceased to function." Melissa Patterson, "Who's Got the Title? Or, the Remnants of *Debellatio* in Post-Invasion Iraq," *Harvard International Law Journal* 47, no. 2 (2006): 1.

19. Benvenisti, *International Law of Occupation,* xi.

20. Ibid.

21. Douglas M. Johnston, ed., *Foreign Policy into the 21st Century: The U.S. Leadership Challenge* (Washington, DC: CSIS, 1996), 37–40.

22. U.S. Treasury, "OFAC Sanctions Programs," Office of Foreign Assets Control, 2010, www.ustreas.gov.

23. Thomas Jefferson, "First Inaugural Address," in *The Jeffersonian Encyclopedia,* ed. John P. Foley (New York: Funk & Wagnalls, 1900), 326.

24. John Quincy Adams, address to a numerous and "very respectable assemblage of ladies and citizens" (speech presented in Washington, DC, July 4, 1821, on the occasion of the 45th anniversary of independence). See Jerald L. Banninga, "John Quincy Adams' Address of July 4, 1821," *Quarterly Journal of Speech,* no. 1 (1967): 44.

25. George Kennan, *Around the Cragged Hill: A Personal and Political Philosophy* (New York: W. W. Norton, 1993), 64–65, 201, 223–24.

CHAPTER 15

1. Mark Juergensmeyer, *Global Rebellion: Religious Challenges to the Secular State, from Christian Militias to Al Qaeda* (Berkeley and Los Angeles: University of California Press, 2008), 4. Also see 17–20.

2. Ibid.,17.

3. ICRD researcher, personal communication with Groton School administrator, November 5, 2009.

4. Judy Valente, "Trappist Monk's Mass Appeal: Thomas Merton's Influence Continues to Grow 40 Years after His Death," *Washington Post*, December 20, 2008, www.washingtonpost.com.

5. Thomas Merton, *Choosing to Love the World: On Contemplation* (Boulder, CO: Sounds True, 2008), 36.

6. Ibid., 37.

7. Thomas Merton, *Echoing Silence: On the Vocation of Writing* (Boston: New Seeds Books, 2007), 35.

8. Merton, *Choosing to Love the World*, 20.

9. Robert Inchausti, interview by Rob Moll, "The Orthodox Avant-Garde," *Christianity Today*, July 26, 2005, www.christianitytoday.com.

10. Alexander Solzhenitsyn, "A World Split Apart" (commencement speech, Harvard University, June 8, 1978), www.americanrhetoric.com.

11. The view that by "treating the soul as man's only necessary treasure, wrapped for a time in a negligible napkin," helped prompt Thomas Aquinas to argue for embracing the "pagan" Aristotelian heritage that ushered in the Renaissance (thanks to Latin translations from the Arabic). See G. K. Chesterton, *Saint Thomas Aquinas: The Dumb Ox* (New York: Random House, 2001), 17.

12. Solzhenitsyn, "A World Split Apart."

13. Ibid.

14. Ibid.

15. Ibid.

16. Joel Salatin, *Holy Cows and Hog Heaven: The Food Buyer's Guide to Farm Friendly Food* (Swoop, VA: Polyface, 2004), 45.

17. Salatin cites the example of electrified poultry netting. It has polyethylene webbing with stainless steel threads woven through it. By using sophisticated, low-impedance energizers that shorten the pulse to microseconds, a high voltage shock can be delivered through the threads without melting the plastic. It is also very lightweight: 150 feet of fencing weighs only 12 pounds and is easily used by poultry producers or sheep herders to keep predators out while keeping chickens in. Salatin, *Holy Cows*, 42–45.

18. *Taylorism* is a term used to describe the theory of management outlined by Frederick Winslow Taylor in his monographs *Shop Management* and *The Principles of Scientific Management* in which traditional practices were replaced by precise procedures based on careful studies of individuals at work. This method has been seen by some as a driving contributor to dehumanization in the workplace.

19. Salatin, *Holy Cows*, 47.

20. James W. Jones, *Blood That Cries Out from the Earth: The Psychology of Religious Terrorism* (Oxford: Oxford University Press, 2008), 29–32.

21. Sayyid Qutb, *Milestones* (Beirut: Dar al-Ilm, 2003), 7.

22. Basil Mathews, *Young Islam on Trek: A Study in the Clash of Civilizations* (Whitefish, MT: Kessinger, 2008), 216–18. Also cited in Richard W. Bulliet, *The Case for Islamo-Christian Civilization* (New York: Columbia University Press, 2004), 3.

23. Craig Whitlock, "Flow of Terrorist Recruits Increasing; Westerners Attending Camps in Pakistan and Afghanistan Despite Successful U.S. Strikes," *Washington Post*, October 19, 2009, A1.

24. Robert Coram, *Boyd: The Fighter Pilot Who Changed the Art of War* (New York: Back Bay Books, 2002), 391.

25. E. B. Potter and Adm. Chester W. Nimitz, U.S. Navy, *Sea Power: A Naval History* (Englewood Cliffs: Prentice-Hall, 1960), 132.

26. Ibid., 134.

27. The term *g-force* refers to the measurement of acceleration that an object experiences in relation to the pull of gravity. For fighter pilots, failure to anticipate the change in g-forces due to sudden acceleration or turns can result in decreased blood flow and even unconsciousness.

28. The mathematical definition of impossible is one chance in 10^{50}. The odds of a universe existing that can support life are estimated to be 10^{300}. To put that number in context, there are only 10^{80} atoms in the entire universe. These conclusions have withstood the scrutiny of some of the world's most able scientific critics. See Dean Overman, *A Case Against Accident and Self-Organization* (Lanham, MD: Rowman & Littlefield, 1997), 55, 195.

29. Most prophets share in common the fact that they are generally ignored by their contemporaries. It is only with the passage of time that the wisdom of their predictions becomes fully recognized.

30. John Boyd, "Patterns of Conflict," Defense and the National Interest, www.d-n-i.net/boyd/pdf/poc.pdf., slides 118–25. See also, Coram, *Boyd*, 337.

31. Robert M. Gates, "A Balanced Strategy," *Foreign Affairs* (January–February 2009): 29.

CHAPTER 16

1. 1 John 4:16b (New International Version).

2. John W. Kiser, *The Monks of Tibhirine: Faith, Love and Terror in Algeria* (New York: St. Martin's Press, 2002), 14.

3. Robert S. McNamara, *In Retrospect: The Tragedy and Lessons of Vietnam* (New York: Vintage Books, 1996), 322.

4. Condoleezza Rice, "Promoting the National Interest," *Foreign Affairs* 79, no. 1 (2000): 49.

5. Larry I. Bland, "Marshall and the 'Plan,'" George C. Marshall Foundation, www.marshallfoundation.org.

6. Jim Frederick, "General Douglas MacArthur," *Time*, November 13, 2006, www.time.com.

7. David Kilcullen, *The Accidental Guerrilla: Fighting Small Wars in the Midst of a Big One* (New York: Oxford University Press, 2009), 24.

8. Ibid.

9. John Bradshaw, *Reclaiming Virtue: How We Can Develop the Moral Intelligence to Do the Right Thing at the Right Time for the Right Reason* (New York: Random House, 2009), 183–84.

10. Albert Habib Hourani, *Islam in European Thought* (Cambridge, MA: Cambridge University Press, 1991), 37.

11. Ibid., 40.

12. James W. Skillen, "Three Zionisms in the Shaping of American Foreign Policy," in *God and Global Order: Religion and American Foreign Policy*, ed. Jonathan Chaplin and Robert Joustra (Waco, TX: Baylor University Press, 2010) 108.

13. Marc Aronson, *John Winthrop, Oliver Cromwell and the Land of Promise* (New York: Clarion Press, 2004), 40.

14. Skillen, "Three Zionisms," 91–92.

15. Ibid.

16. Michael Oren, *Power, Faith, and Fantasy: America in the Middle East* (New York: W. W. Norton, 2007), 89.

17. Barbara Tuchman, *Bible and Sword: England and Palestine from the Bronze Age to Balfour* (New York: Random House Ballantine, 1956), 178.

18. A variation of "A land without a people for a people without a land" used by Stephen Spector in *Evangelicals and Israel: The Story of American Christian Zionism* (New York: Oxford University Press, 2009), 338.

19. Yehezkel Landau, "Healing the Holy Land: Interreligious Peacebuilding in Israel/Palestine," *Peaceworks*, no. 51 (2003): 13, http://www.usip.org.

20. For English transcript, see Reuters, "Ahmadinejad's Letter to Bush," *Washington Post*, May 9, 2006, www.washingtonpost.com.

21. Thanks are due Imam Feisal Abdul Rauf, Chairman of the Cordoba Initiative, who assisted in crafting this proposed response.

22. Douglas Johnston, "Introduction: Beyond Power Politics," in *Religion, the Missing Dimension of Statecraft*, ed. Douglas Johnston and Cynthia Sampson (New York: Oxford University Press, 1994), 4.

23. Stephen Kinzer, *Reset: Iran, Turkey, and America's Future* (New York: Times Books, 2010), 212.

24. Marshall Breger, based on personal interview with the author, August 11, 2009.

25. Based on the author's observation of the exchange.

26. Personal communication between the parties and the author.

27. Bureau of Democracy, Human Rights, and Labor, *Annual Report on International Religious Freedom* (Washington, DC: Government Printing Office, 2009), U.S. Department of State, www.state.gov.

28. Trita Parsi, "Why the Pro-Israel Crowd is Hyping the Iran Threat," *Salon.com*, August 13, 2010.

29. James Slattery, former U.S. Congressman from Kansas and a frequent participant in the Track Two encounters, played the instrumental role in formulating these insights.

30. Alvin Richman, David B. Nolle, and Elaine El Assal, *Iranian Public Is Not Monolithic: Iranians Divide over Their Government but Unite on Forgoing Nuclear Weapons* (Washington, DC: World Public Opinion, 2009), www.worldpublicopinion.org.

31. Robert Fisk, "The Age of the Warrior" (lecture, World Affairs Council, Washington, DC, September 30, 2008), http://fora.tv. See also Reza Kahlili, *A Time to Betray: The Astonishing Double Life of a CIA Agent Inside the Revolutionary Guards of Iran* (New York: Simon and Schuster, 2010), 227.

32. Hossein Mousavian, "Transcript: Interview with Hossein Mousavian," by Gareth Smyth and Moshen Asgan, *Financial Times*, September 2004, www.ft.com.

33. Javad Zarif, "We Do Not Have a Nuclear Weapons Program," op-ed, *New York Times*, April 6, 2006.

34. HRH Prince Turki al-Faisal, conversation with the author over lunch in his palace, October 9, 2009.

35. President Ahmadinejad, response to the author's question.

36. President of the United States, *National Security Strategy*, May 2010, 26. With specific reference to Iran, the strategy includes the following observation:

In addition to its illicit nuclear program, it continues to support terrorism, undermine peace between Israelis and Palestinians, and deny its people their universal rights. Many years of refusing to engage Iran failed to reverse these trends; on the contrary, Iran's behavior became more threatening. Engagement is something we pursue without illusion.

37. Niccolo di Bernardo dei Machiavelli, *The Prince*, trans. W. K. Marriott (Charleston, SC: Forgotten Books, 2008), 30, www.forgottenbooks.org.

38. Leslie J. Sacks, "Converting America," *Strength and Tolerance* (blog), December 16, 2009, http://strengthandtolerance.com.

39. Although by no means an exact parallel, the Byzantine Empire lasted over twice as long as the Roman Empire because its rulers were able to adapt strategically to diminished circumstances. See Edward Luttwak, *The Grand Strategy of the Byzantine Empire* (Cambridge, MA: Harvard University Press, 2009).

40. Abraham Joshua Heschel, *A Passion for Truth* (Woodstock, VT: Jewish Lights, 2004), 19.

41. See Thomas S. Kuhn, *The Structure of Scientific Revolutions,* 3rd ed. (Chicago: University of Chicago Press, 1996).

APPENDIX B

1. The State Department has recognized the lack of coordination in public diplomacy and attempted to circumvent the problem by beginning to appoint "'dual-hatted' Deputy Assistant Secretaries for Public Diplomacy in each of the six regional bureaus . . . [who] report directly to both their Regional Assistant Secretary and to the Under Secretary for Public Diplomacy and Public Affairs." See United States Government Accountability Office, *U.S. Public Diplomacy: State Department Efforts to Engage Muslim Audiences Lack Certain Communication Elements and Face Significant Challenges,* report to the Chairman, Subcommittee on Science, the Departments of State, Justice, and Commerce, and Related Agencies, Committee on Appropriations, House of Representatives (Washington, DC: GAO, 2006), 6, 9, www.gao.gov.

According to Christopher Midura (then Acting Director, Office of Policy, Planning and Resources, Under Secretary for Public Diplomacy and Public Affairs), every regional bureau has a deputy assistant secretary responsible for public diplomacy. Except for the Bureau of European and Eurasian Affairs, each of these deputy assistant secretaries wears multiple hats and is responsible for other functions in addition to PD.

2. Ibid., 9.

3. In most cases, this is the Ambassador.

4. U.S. Government Accountability Office, *U.S. Public Diplomacy: State Department Efforts to Engage Muslim Audiences Lack Certain Communication Elements and Face Significant Challenges,* 2006, GAO-06-535, 6, www.gao.gov.

5. Ms. Ronna A. Freiberg, former Director of Congressional and Intergovernmental Affairs, USIA, indicated in Congressional testimony that "it would be more efficient, and serve the unique needs of public diplomacy, to have the regional public diplomacy offices report directly to the Under Secretary for Public Diplomacy. One way to accomplish this would be to create a bureau that would

house public diplomacy regional offices and connect to the corresponding field staff." See Senate Committee on Homeland Security and Governmental Affairs, *A Reliance on Smart Power: Reforming the Public Diplomacy Bureaucracy,* 110th Cong., 2nd sess., September 23, 2008, http://hsgac.senate.gov.

6. The Advisory Group on Public Diplomacy for the Arab and Muslim World was formed in June 2003 as a subcommittee of the U.S. Advisory Commission on Public Diplomacy, a bipartisan panel created by Congress and appointed by the President to provide oversight of U.S. Government activities intended to understand, inform, and influence foreign publics.

7. House Committee on Appropriations: Advisory Group on Public Diplomacy for the Arab and Muslim World, *Changing Minds, Winning Peace: A New Strategic Direction for U.S. Public Diplomacy in the Arab and Muslim World,* 108th Cong., 1st sess., 2003, 64, http://www.state.gov.

8. Ibid., 63.

9. Christopher Midura, interview by ICRD researcher, October 2, 2008.

10. Ibid.

11. Joseph Witters (Special Assistant, Office of the Under Secretary for Public Diplomacy and Public Affairs), interview by ICRD researcher, September 9, 2008.

12. Ibid.

13. According to the Advisory Group, "Many proposals to deal with this structural issue have been put forward, including some that, in essence, would recreate USIA within the department." See House Committee on Appropriations, 62–63.

14. Not every embassy has a Public Diplomacy Officer or Cultural Affairs Officer (CAO). If there is a CAO, he or she is usually accompanied by an Information Officer who handles the press. Most Public Diplomacy Officers don't handle culture 100 percent of the time. Sometimes an embassy will employ local staff to do cultural work. It is not completely clear who does what in different locations. Since October 1, 1999, when USIA merged with the Department of State, the Department has been "winging it," owing in large part to the frequent turnover in personnel assigned to serve as Under Secretary of State for Public Diplomacy since then. Anne O'Leary (senior recruiter and senior FSO, U.S. Department of State), interview by ICRD researcher, April 12, 2007.

APPENDIX C

1. Nicholas D. Kristof, "Iran's Proposal for a 'Grand Bargain,'" *On the Ground* (blog), *New York Times,* April 28, 2007, http://kristof.blogs.nytimes.com/2007/04/28/irans-proposal-for-a-grand-bargain/ (accessed December 22, 2009). Documents are available at http://www.washingtonpost.com/wp-srv/world/documents/us_iran_1roadmap.pdf. Also see Glenn Kessler, "2003 Memo Says Iranian Leaders Backed Talks," *Washington Post,* February 14, 2007, www.washingtonpost.com and Trita Parsi, *Treacherous Alliance: The Secret Dealings of Israel, Iran, and the U.S.* (New Haven, CT: Yale University Press, 2007), 345–46.

Glossary

Ahle Hadith—the Islamic school of thought that emphasizes the original principles of Islam and rejects the four traditional schools of Islamic law.

aql—a term used to describe the quality necessary for understanding spiritual truths.

fatwa—a judicial decision or learned opinion concerning Islamic law issued by an Islamic scholar or institution. In Sunni Islam any fatwa is nonbinding, whereas in Shia Islam it could be considered by an individual as binding, depending on his or her relation to the scholar.

gharbzadegi—"occidentosis," "westoxification," or "westernitis." The term was coined by the Iranian writer Jalal Al-e-Ahmad in reference to the intrusion of western influence in his society.

Hadith—narrations concerning the words and deeds of Prophet Muhammad. It includes reports of statements or actions of the Prophet or of his tacit approval of something said or done in his presence.

haram—unlawful.

hudna—a temporary truce or armistice.

ijma—religious and political consensus of the community, a source of Islamic law.

ijtihad—the process of reexamining how religious values should inform daily life in light of major changes in the external environment.

irhab—terrorism.

irhabi—terrorist.

Islamism—"political Islam," synonymous with those political movements seeking to implement social Islamic norms.

Islamist—one who advocates Islamism and, accordingly, the reordering of government and society in accordance with Islamic law.

jahiliyyah—the Islamic concept of ignorance that describes the condition of those living in Arabia before the revelation of the Qur'an to Prophet Muhammad.

jihad—"struggle" or "effort." In the context of the Qur'an, the term jihad is used to denote striving in the path of God. It is a struggle every Muslim goes through in order to truly submit to God. Jihad can be observed through many different means such as working on perfecting one's own spirituality or doing good works in accordance with the will of God.

jirga—a council of respected elders with decision-making authority.

jizyah—poll tax levied on *dhimmi* (non-Muslims) in lieu of having to perform military service for the state.

kafir—"unbeliever" or infidel; one who is "ungrateful" and who rejects Islam.

madrasa—school; used in some countries to connote a religious school.

majlis—literally "a place of sitting" and used to describe various types of special gatherings among common interest groups be they administrative, social, or religious.

mufsiduun—sinners.

mujahideen—plural of mujihad, soldier of God.

musalahah—ceremony of reconciliation.

Nowruz—the traditional celebration of the ancient Iranian New Year, which marks the first day of spring. Observed in Iran as well as in parts of Central and South Asia; also known as Navroz.

Qur'an—the holy book of Islam.

salaf—"those who precede" or "ancestors"; refers to the first three generations of the Muslim community.

Salafi—those Sunni Muslims who follow the path of the first three generations of Muslims, known as "salaf."

Shari'ah—"path"; Islamic law.

shirk—idolatry, polytheism; to associate another deity, person, or thing with God.

Shura—consultation.

sulh—reconciliation.

sulhah—a public method for dispute resolution native to the Bedouin tribes in the Sinai and Negev deserts.

Sunna—normative Islamic practices derived from the behavior of the Prophet Muhammad as recorded in the Hadith.

takfir—apostasy in Islam; the process of declaring oneself or others to no longer be believers.

takfiri—one who practices *takfir*.

ulama—a body of recognized religious scholars.

umma—the global community of Muslim believers.

urf—tribal or traditional norms or values.

Wahhabi—those who follow the 18th-century Muslim scholar Sheikh Muhammad ibn Abdul Wahhab, whose conservative teachings advocated purging Islam of what he considered to be innovations.

zakat—one of the five pillars of Islam, zakat is the annual alms tax of 2½ percent of annual savings, which is used to help the poor.

Index

About the Author

DOUGLAS M. JOHNSTON, JR., is President and founder of the International Center for Religion and Diplomacy. He is a distinguished graduate of the U.S. Naval Academy and holds a Masters Degree in Public Administration and a PhD in Political Science from Harvard University. He has served in senior positions in government, the military, and the private sector, including six years at Harvard where he taught international affairs and was founder and director of the University's Executive Program in National and International Security. Dr. Johnston's most recent assignment was as Executive Vice President and COO of the Center for Strategic and International Studies. He is the principal author and editor of *Religion, the Missing Dimension of Statecraft* (1994), *Foreign Policy into the 21st Century: The U.S. Leadership Challenge* (1996), and *Faith-Based Diplomacy: Trumping Realpolitik* (2003).